MUSIC & MEDICINE

MUSIC

&

MEDICINE

Medical profiles of great composers

John O'Shea

J. M. Dent
London

To the memory of my father, Dr James Patrick O'Shea,
a dedicated, patient and caring physician

© Text, John O'Shea 1990
First published 1990
First paperback edition 1993

Printed in Great Britain by The Bath Press, Avon

for
J. M. Dent
The Orion Publishing Group
Orion House
5 Upper St Martin's Lane
London WC2H 9EA

British Library Cataloguing-in-Publication Data
A catalogue record for this book is available
from The British Library

ISBN: 0 460 86106 9

Contents

CONTENTS

List of illustrations

Acknowledgments and Sources

Much of the research for this book was undertaken in 1985–6 in Europe and the USA. I also visited Europe in the winter of 1987 to collect further material. The final revision of the work was undertaken in 1988 in the United Kingdom and Australia.

To write a book of this nature one must tap diverse sources. Many institutions gave me access to documentary material. The Wellcome Institute provided me with many details of nineteenth-century medication as well as documents pertaining to the medical histories of Grieg, Weber and Paganini. I should like to thank Mr Robin Price and Miss Caroline Peck for their help in providing these rare historical documents.

Information on Chopin's illnesses was provided by the Chopin Society of Warsaw. I wish to thank Mr Antoni Pierschala and Mrs Hanna Wróblewska Strauss for their help. Dr Czesław Sieluzycki, the author of several articles on Chopin's illnesses, offered me useful criticism of my recent paper on the composer which appeared in the *Medical Journal of Australia*.

Information on Liszt's illnesses was gathered from eminent Liszt scholars. Professor Alan Walker and Mr Adrian Williams provided me with much detail about Liszt's last years. Mr Williams is the editor of the British *Liszt Society Journal* and the author of a major forthcoming Liszt biography. His journal, which provides English translations of rare biographical material relating to Liszt, was an important source of information, as was *Liszt Saeculum*, the journal of the International Liszt Centre, Stockholm. Mr Lennart Rabes, the editor, has published many of my early articles on Liszt and the romantic composers in his journal.

The Grainger Museum of the University of Melbourne gave me access to Grainger's medical records. It was decided not to allow me to publish this material directly as Grainger died relatively recently (1961) and some of it is quite alarming. Aspects of Grainger's sadomasochistic behaviour are well documented in John Bird's fine biography and in *The Farthest North of Humanness*, a collection of Grainger's letters edited by Kay Dreyfus, the curator of the Grainger Museum.

The staff of the *Medical Journal of Australia* provided much help with the editing and publication of my papers on Liszt, Chopin and Grainger. I acknowledge the help of the editor, Dr Kathleen King, and of Miss Katrina Ganin.

The most comprehensive source book for information on Beethoven's illnesses is Forster's *Beethovens Krankheiten*, which contains almost all of the medical material relating to the composer. Mr Gerald J. Little, the Melbourne otolaryngologist, provided me with much information about the likely aetiology of Beethoven's deafness. For Mozart, I used the standard reference texts. The books by Carl Bär and Otto Erich Deutsch are the most informative. Dr Peter Davies of Melbourne is a world authority on Mozart's illnesses and I learnt much about the composer through my conversations with him.

Schumann's mysterious mental illness has been well covered by English-language authors. Dr Peter Ostwald has produced a comprehensive biography of the composer which graphically describes the composer's mental decline. It credibly challenges the widely accepted view (an almost unanimous one in the older medical biographies) that the composer suffered from neurosyphilis.

Medical information regarding the more recent composers is freely available and its interpretation is less subjective. Gustav Mahler died of endocarditis in 1911. Dr D. Levy recently published the results of his blood cultures in the *British Medical Journal*. Extensive details of Mahler's final illness are available in the more comprehensive biographies of the composer and in Alma Mahler's memoirs. Most physicians who have an interest in the composers' medical histories will be familiar with Professor Théophile Alajouanine's famous paper on Ravel which appeared in *Brain* in 1948.

I should like to thank the following medical practitioners for their criticism of my work: Professor Peter Phelan and Professor Harold Attwood of Melbourne University, Dr Derek Rodrigues, Dr Christopher Kelsey, Dr Peter Bull, Mr Hugh Tighe, Mr Richard Newing, Mr Peter Ryan, Dr Michael McDonough, Dr Brian McMillan, Dr Paul Egan,

Dr Stephen Cattanach, Mr Z. Y. Miscony, Dr Jocelyn Ellis, Dr Guy Hibbins, Dr Simon Horgan and Dr Leslie Dunn.

My thanks are also due to Mrs Patricia Wilsmore and my sister Miss Moya O'Shea for their help and criticism of my work and their careful preparation of the manuscript.

The following also gave me considerable help: Mrs Mavis Solum, Mrs Marian Berlyn, Mr Paul O'Connor, Dr Maria Eckhardt, Mrs Margaret O'Shea, Ms Julie Brown, Mrs Rosemary Florrimell, Mrs J. Audrey Ellison, Mr Peter Wells, Mr David Hood, Rev Fr Thomas O'Shea, Mrs Gerda Holt, Professor Oliver McDonagh, Rev Daniel Lyons, Miss Anne Donahue, Mr A. S. Cattanach, Mr Stephen Lloyd, Mr David Cahill, Mrs Susan Amigo, Miss Jane Newing, Mrs Mary Goodwin, Mrs May Smith-Price, Miss Rozsi Lados, Captain William Horgan, Mr Simon Fetherston and Mrs S. De Leeuw.

Introduction

The great composers of the eighteenth and nineteenth centuries are surrounded with legend and mythology. In this book I have endeavoured to separate legend from fact and to provide a coherent and factual account of the composers and the illnesses which beset them. Such a book is at times fraught with difficulty. Nineteenth-century medical testimony is often annoyingly inaccurate and unreliable. Accounts of the composers' physical appearances, their mannerisms and their musicianship are often highly subjective and, of course, influenced by the politics and myth-making of the musical establishment of the day.

Paganini is a case in point. There is considerable inaccuracy in the medical testimony relating to him, and often downright charlatanism is involved. The notorious faked photograph which appeared at the turn of the century certainly influenced our perception of his bodily habitus. Much spurious Paganiniana was produced by entrepreneurs. Many plaster casts supposedly of composers' hands were made. More recently a photograph purporting to be of the death mask of Mozart appeared; the claims that the photograph was genuine have been dropped. Plaster casts and portraits are often unreliable representations of the composer's appearance but, if authenticated, they can be of crucial importance in telling us what a musician looked like, and they sometimes hint at the presence of physical disease or deformity. Auguste Clessinger altered the death mask of Chopin to give an impression of serene repose. The first cast, recently discovered in Paris, is a grotesque affair which vividly shows the extent of the composer's suffering.

The notion that Paganini had a physical deformity which was responsible for his virtuosity has persisted in the medical literature. Recent

1

articles have proposed that the composer had Marfan's syndrome. Closer examination of the medical literature shows that contemporary reports were exaggerated by doctors eager to support their theories that physiognomy is indicative of or responsible for genius. Franz Liszt had his hands examined closely by palmists, and the bumps on his head examined by phrenologists, without conclusive results. Scientific explanation of the intangible quality of 'genius' remains elusive today.

Chopin was a mysterious and reclusive figure. Most biographers label him hypochondriacal, but examination of his correspondence does not favour this conclusion. His letters contain scant reference to his illnesses at times when he was known to be seriously ill. Clearly, he made a determined effort not to worry his friends with his medical problems. Liszt wrote in his book on Chopin: 'Chopin's frail and feeble organisation did not permit him any energetic explanation of his passions and friends saw only the gentle and affectionate side of his nature. ... Chopin was afflicted by a hopeless disease which each year became more envenomed and at length laid him in a silent grave.' He also tells us that Chopin's illness severely incapacitated him during the last ten years of his life. The strong possibility that Chopin's illness was a disease other than tuberculosis – either cystic fibrosis or bronchiectasis – supports the conclusion that he was invalided at an early age by respiratory disease, and this dramatically alters our perception of his character and life. He was a determined man who soldiered on despite a serious and debilitating disease with embarrassingly obvious stigmata. Chopin's illness may also explain why he shunned a lucrative career as a concert pianist and concentrated on composition.

Few individuals have been subjected to more severe criticism and burlesque than Franz Liszt. In his own day the powerful anti-Liszt clique included Clara Schumann, Eduard Hanslick, Joseph Joachim and Ferdinand Hiller – a formidable group indeed. Liszt seldom used his considerable influence to silence their criticism of his musicianship and compositions, feeling that posterity would decide the issue. One story is that Liszt, when told of an unfavourable review of his concert by Hanslick, merely quipped that he was glad that Hanslick could earn a living and support his family at the minor expense of Liszt's own reputation. In more recent years Ernest Newman in his controversial book *The Man Liszt* shows Liszt as a man with a weak, divided nature, dependent on drugs and alcohol to perform concerts and propped up by the powerful Princess Sayn-Wittgenstein. The anti-Liszt faction reached the nadir of taste with Ken Russell's film *Lisztomania*.

Examination of Liszt's biography, and particularly of his medical history, shows that these critics were unjust; in leaving the concert stage in his late thirties to concentrate on composition, Liszt was wisely conserving his health. He did not use drugs of addiction; he was prescribed morphine during the terminal stages of his last illness and the profound side effects prove that he had no acquired tolerance to it. There is no evidence that he was an alcoholic, although he did consume alcohol and there were occasional episodes of heavy drinking during his long career. In his last years he was beset with severe cardiac failure and eye disease. He was frail and his health was precarious. Despite this he kept up his hard work in the form of teaching, attending concerts of his works and making occasional appearances as a pianist. His illnesses were usually overlooked because of his fine public bearing.

Beethoven is yet another example of how the essential facts of a musician's life have been altered by another party. During Beethoven's life Anton Schindler served him as a secretary, factotum and companion; the composer, however, had a low opinion of Schindler. When Beethoven died, Schindler became the self-appointed heir to his documents and a protector of his reputation. He destroyed the majority of Beethoven's conversation books, for reasons which remain unclear, and used his new-found power to influence the musical establishment. Often he would unfairly criticize musicians performing at Beethoven concerts, and such was his prestige that his criticisms were influential. It seems clear that Beethoven's consistently high alcohol intake was responsible for his final illness, a fact that was deliberately disguised by Schindler.

The primary aim of my book is to evaluate not only the symptomatology of the illnesses that afflicted some of the great composers but also the degree of physical and emotional disability that beset their lives, and to try to determine how these disabilities may have affected their work. With age and with physical and mental disease there is often a progressive decline in intellectual functioning; I have attempted to trace the mental status of each composer as it was influenced by age and illness and to provide a framework for the reader to assess the influence of these factors on a composer's musical output.

I hope that the book will serve to provide a more rounded picture of these composers as beings of flesh and blood and human frailty who, with immense fortitude and in some cases in spite of severe illness, produced great music.

The Composers
and Medical History

Medical science has advanced rapidly in the two centuries covered by this book. The following is a brief review of the progress of medicine.

At the beginning of the nineteenth century Paris was one of the most productive centres of medical research. René Laennec (1781–1826) advanced the field of pathological anatomy by his meticulous dissections at the Necker Hospital in Paris; he was also the inventor of the stethoscope, a simple instrument which has become an unofficial symbol of the medical profession and which made diagnosis of pulmonary disease immeasurably more simple and accurate. Chopin and Paganini were both examined by disciples of Laennec.

Jean Cruveilhier (1791–1874) was Laennec's successor. Like Laennec he was both a physician and a pathologist. He produced a beautiful atlas of pathology. To Cruveilhier we owe the concept of reactive hyperaemia (compensatory dilatation of blood vessels in reaction to prior ischaemia). Hector Berlioz was a medical student in Paris during this era and in his memoirs left an account (see p. 227) of the initial dissections that led to these discoveries.

Thanks to men like Laennec and Cruveilhier it became possible to classify diseases of the chest more accurately. Laennec is credited with early descriptions of emphysema, spontaneous pneumothorax, bronchitis, bronchiectasis and pulmonary abscess. He was often able to equate pathology with symptomatology by listening to his patients' chests with his stethoscope. Laennec used his diagnostic ability to enable therapeutic measures to be undertaken: for example, he was able accurately to diagnose and drain pleural effusions (18).

4

The diagnoses of these early physicians were not as precise as those of their modern counterparts. They were often confused by multiple pathologies. For example, some thought that tuberculosis caused pulmonary oedema because tuberculous scarring was often seen in the lungs of patients suffering from congestive heart failure. Until Pasteur demonstrated that bacteria caused disease, they were unable to suggest a cause for the lesions they described. Northern physicians were inclined to dismiss infection as a cause of disease. In Paris during the 1840s 18% of deaths were ascribed to tuberculosis (12).

René Laennec's Scottish pupil Sir James Clark (1788–1870) brought many of Laennec's ideas across the Channel to Britain. He himself was a medical pioneer. Clark realized that statistics were necessary to prognosticate disease accurately and to evaluate the results of therapy correctly. It was an important idea and in his treatise on tuberculosis (2) Clark summarized mathematically the results of his work with the sufferers of pulmonary disease. Clark was involved with Chopin's illness in an advisory capacity and he treated the poet John Keats for tuberculosis (7).

Since Clark's time, the mathematical evaluation of statistics has become immeasurably more precise, as has the accuracy of diagnosis; nevertheless, Clark's statistics offered important information to his colleagues and clearly demonstrated the importance of statistical science to medicine. The more scrupulous application of the scientific method to medicine meant that treatment could be more precisely evaluated. (For example, blood letting was stopped when it was realized that patients who underwent venesection actually fared worse than those who were left alone.)

It took the medical profession many years to do away with mercury as a chemotherapeutic agent. (The satirical poet Ulrich von Hutten (1488–1523) was its first critic.) The use of mercury in the treatment of syphilis continued until the 1940s when penicillin, a safer and far more effective antiluetic agent, made its use obsolete. It was difficult to assess the effects of mercury. The lesions of secondary syphilis are very labile and often clear spontaneously. Mercury could elicit a Herxheimer reaction (17) and was undoubtedly of some help in clearing up skin lesions. (The lesions of late benign syphilis, tumour-like lesions called 'gummas', responded very well to bismuth and presumably also to mercury chemotherapy (16).) While the nineteenth century did not see the abandonment of mercury chemotherapy, it did see an increased recognition of the side effects of this dangerous metal. Smaller and more rational doses were used in treatment. Proksch's compilation of 1895 lists 1,121 articles dealing with the use of mercury for syphilis published between 1800 and 1889; 400 of these were related to mercury intoxication, and as a consequence doses of mercury were reduced to a less toxic level as the century progressed. In the nineteenth century, prior to the development of the Wassermann complement fixation test (1907), the diagnosis of syphilis was difficult and at times impossible. Mercury was not without its critics, and 128 articles questioning this therapy or suggesting alternative treatments were published; it was realized that mercury's action did not depend on 'salivation' (5). The famous Oslo Study of Untreated Syphilis (9), conducted from 1910 to 1951 initially by L. P. Boek (1845–1917) and after his death by other practitioners, showed that mercury did nothing to alter the long-term prognosis of syphilis. Of those infected by the disease, 60–70% experienced little or no physical discomfort. At the turn of this century the incidence of syphilis in the general population as estimated by serology (blood testing) was over 10% (9). The disease was represented with far greater frequency in the lower socio-economic classes.

Opium is another drug which is frequently mentioned in nineteenth-century formulas. It has an ancient history. It was grown in the Middle East and transported to Europe and China by the East India Company. Its use was not restricted, and 'laudanum' – a combination of opium and alcohol – was a popular hypnotic and tranquillizer. (Lenin was thinking of this compound when he formulated his famous epigram about religion.) In the eighteenth and early nineteenth centuries the drug was also used to treat syphilis. George Sand's famous 'poetic cigars' were said to contain opium, which was certainly in vogue during the 1840s. Chopin used opium to treat his intractable cough and belladonna to treat his abdominal symptoms.

The Viennese medical school became the most important centre for medical research during the second half of the century. Karl Freiherr von Rokitansky (1804–78) held the chair of pathology. He was not only a brilliant scientist but also a skilful administrator. He centralized the pathology faculty so that he was able personally to oversee the results of 25,000 autopsies during his tenure as professor. The subject of his first autopsy was Ludwig van Beethoven. Rokitansky's systematization enhanced the progress of medical science and probably removed some of the virtuoso element from medicine (in the French school each professor had been his own pathologist). Rudolph Virchow (1821–1902) succeeded Rokitansky as Europe's pre-eminent pathologist. His important work included the concepts of embolus, studies of blood clotting and an early description of leukaemia. He later became professor of pathology in Berlin where he served in parliament in opposition to Bismarck.

Several of Beethoven's physicians have interesting backgrounds. Giovanni Malfatti (1775–1859) was one of the most respected physicians in Vienna. He was the founder of the Viennese Society of Physicians and the author of the influential book *Entwurf einer Pathologie*, which proposed that disease was due to an intricate interplay between physiology and pathology. He was an advocate of healing by magnetism and is said to have recommended the procedure to treat the composer's deafness. Malfatti's account of Beethoven's illness, however, is far less perceptive and reliable than that of Andreas Wawruch.

Andreas Ignaz Wawruch trained in Prague as a surgeon but practised medicine in Vienna. He co-ordinated the treatment of Beethoven's last illness and wrote a remarkably logical, balanced and forthright summary of it a few months after the composer's death. Beethoven disliked Wawruch intensely, and the posthumous reputation of this fine physician (who was also an excellent cellist) has suffered as a result.

Johann Wagner (1800–32) succeeded Lorenz Biermayer as prosector of anatomy and conservator of the anatomy museum in Vienna. He performed Beethoven's autopsy with his student apprentice Karl von Rokitansky. Wagner was a man of considerable manual dexterity and a master of the art of dissection. William Worn was amazed at his skill in 'opening the spinal canal from its lowest end, the sacrum, up to the second vertebra of the neck, within seven minutes' (15).

Rokitansky, however, was somewhat critical of his old chief because he felt that Wagner did not make sufficient effort to correlate pathology with what was known of the evolution of the disease process based on the clinical history. He wrote that 'notwithstanding the daily contradiction between the results of dissection and the records on diseases and diagnoses [he] was not able to grasp the lesson beyond casuistry or to form a clear idea of the reforming impact his subject was to make ...'.

Another of the Viennese medical school who had close musical connections was the great surgeon Theodor Billroth (1829–94). Billroth was one of the world's leading surgeons and performed the first successful gastrectomy in 1881 for carcinoma of the pylorus (the opening from the stomach to the intestines). The operation still bears Billroth's name and was carried out only after years of careful animal experimentation. Billroth was a fine pianist; he was a close friend of Johannes Brahms (who dedicated many works to him) and of the conservative music critic Eduard Hanslick, who edited Billroth's *Wer ist musikalisch?*, on the physiology and psychology of music, for posthumous publication. Billroth wrote to Brahms in 1886, 'I have never met a great scientist who was not basically an artist with a rich imagination and unaffected mentality ... science and art draw upon the same source.'

Billroth did not fully accept Joseph Lister's pioneering work on antisepsis. He used his own method of open wound closure and only in 1875 did he try out the antiseptic method. After numerous experiments he used iodine in preference to carbolic acid. Billroth was the first scientist to observe streptococci and staphylococci in relation to wound infection.

The nineteenth century, then, saw the medical sciences welded into an effective vehicle for prolonging human life and alleviating suffering. Among the most important discoveries was the definitive scientific proof of the infectious nature of many diseases.

European cities were often subject to devastating epidemics. Asiatic cholera reached London and Paris between 1831 and 1832. In Britain there were over 15,000 cases and 5,500 deaths. There were altogether eight global outbreaks of the disease in the nineteenth century. Cholera originated in India and was brought to Europe when the trade routes to the subcontinent were plied by ships carrying cargoes and the troops who maintained control of the 'Jewel in the Crown' of the British Empire. The Romantics were deeply affected by the epidemic. Fontaney chronicled in his journal the three months when cholera ravaged Paris: he described the empty streets where hearses stood in ranks like cabs, cemeteries where huge communal trenches were dug to receive the dead, where old coffins, their contents only half-rotted, were broken up to make way for the new, the bright skies and spring sunshine seeming to mock the suffering of the stricken city. After visiting the Hôtel-Dieu, where the dead were laid out like mummies, he attended a gathering at Victor Hugo's flat. Liszt was seated at the piano. He played a funeral march by Beethoven. 'It was magnificent,' wrote Fontaney, 'What a wonderful scene you could set to it. The dead from cholera marching to Notre Dame in their shrouds.'

Contemporary medical thinking dictated that cholera arose through inhalation of a miasma, the bad air that emanated from a corpse to infect those with susceptible, weakened constitutions – hence the hasty disposal of the bodies.

In Britain during the cholera epidemic of 1831–2 a young physician, John Snow (1813–58), came to the conclusion that 'bad air' had nothing to do with the spread of cholera. He believed that diarrhoea, unwashed hands and shared food and, especially, the water supply were instrumental in the spread of the disease. In 1849 during a later cholera epidemic when he was practising as an anaesthetist in London, he proved his theory with scientific thoroughness. He looked at eighty-three cholera deaths within a three-day period. The common denominator was that the vast majority of people who died had used water from a pump in Broad Street. He also noted that deaths occurred when cracks in pipes created cesspools. When the handle was taken off the Broad Street pump, and the cracks in pipes in the area were repaired, the number of deaths dropped precipitously, proving that the disease was water-borne. Snow's work led to engineering advances in water distribution and processing which saved hundreds of lives. Robert Koch's isolation of the causative bacillus in 1882 discredited the 'miasmic' theory for ever. In addition to distinguishing himself as an epidemiologist, Snow invented a practical chloroform inhaler which gave a mixture of 4% chloroform in air and was a marked improvement over its predecessors.

Franz Liszt (1811–86) perhaps deserves a brief mention in the history of music and medicine. Liszt attended Marie Duplessis, later immortalized by Alexandre Dumas and Giuseppe Verdi, in her last illness, and played the piano to comfort the dying girl. In Paris in the 1830s he would occasionally attend the insane asylum and play to the inmates. He could thus perhaps be reckoned a pioneer of music therapy.

Ignaz Philipp Semmelweis (1818–65) was a pioneer in antisepsis and a profound believer in 'contact infection'. When he was an assistant in the General Hospital in Vienna, the death rate among mothers in the puerperium (the period after childbirth) ranged between 10% and 30%. The cause of the mortality was puerperal sepsis due to the transmission of pyogenic organisms by the medical staff. Semmelweis demonstrated that infective material which conveyed the fever was brought from dead bodies in the dissecting room and from other patients with the condition. By the simple expedient of insisting that medical staff wash their hands in chlorinated water between seeing patients, Semmelweis succeeded in reducing the puerperal mortality rate to about 1% (11).

Franz Liszt's daughter Blandine, who was married to Émile Ollivier, the prime minister of France, died of septic disease at the age of 27

9

during her puerperium in 1862. A breast abscess was lanced with an unsterile instrument, producing a fatal wound infection. It was a too common occurrence.

In his old age Liszt consulted the famous German ophthalmic surgeon Alfred Karl Gräfe (1830–99). He was the cousin of Albrecht von Gräfe (1828–70), who pioneered cataract surgery and who was instrumental in the development of the ophthalmoscope. Alfred Gräfe was both an innovator and a proponent of his cousin's revolutionary methods and assisted him in his practice in Berlin. His most notable achievement was his handbook of ophthalmology *Handbuch der gesamten Augenheilkunde* which he wrote with Theodor Sämisch. The seven-volume lexicon is considered by many to be the greatest single academic contribution to the subject. Liszt was nearly blind when he consulted Gräfe because of bilateral cataracts.

Operations of the 1880s were conducted under anaesthesia and in antiseptic conditions. Inhalation anaesthesia came into use after 1845 when an American, Horace Wells (1815–48), demonstrated that it was possible to extract teeth under a nitrous oxide anaesthetic. A Boston dentist, William Morton (1819–68), was an early advocate of ether; a London dentist named Robinson and the surgeon Robert Liston were the first to use the substance in Europe, in 1846. Sir James Young Simpson used chloroform for obstetrical procedures in 1847 and it became the most popular anaesthetic agent used during the nineteenth century. Sigmund Freud introduced cocaine as a local anaesthetic. Karl Koller used cocaine for ophthalmic operations in 1884.

The idea of 'contagion' was proposed by Fracastoro as early as 1546. Bacteria were observed by Anthony van Leeuwenhoek as early as 1683. However, it was not until the nineteenth century that the doctrine of the 'germ theory' and the role of bacteria in transmitting disease were established by the brilliant French chemist Louis Pasteur (1822–95).

In his youth Pasteur pioneered stereochemistry and from 1859 to 1861 he carried out a series of experiments which conclusively disproved 'spontaneous generation' – the theory that life was generated de novo under appropriate environmental stimuli. Pasteur firstly looked at the role of bacteria in fermentation and then in 1877 demonstrated the role of the anthrax bacillus in producing disease in both animals and humans.

Joseph Lister's paper on antiseptic method appeared in the *Lancet* in 1867. His work on antisepsis was partly based on that of Pasteur. Lister used carbolic acid as an antiseptic to reduce surgical wound infection and, more importantly, he cleaned surgical instruments scrupulously, with the result that surgery became inconceivably more safe and effective. So began the modern era of clinical surgery.

Robert Koch, a general practitioner who became a medical scientist, worked independently of Pasteur and confirmed the former's results. Koch also developed methods of growing bacteria on nutrient media. In 1882 he isolated mycobacterium tuberculosis, the causative organism of tuberculosis. Pasteur demonstrated the development of immunity to the rabies virus in 1881 and by the turn of the century the sciences of bacteriology and immunology had advanced rapidly to become the basis of much of clinical medical practice. The diffusion of medical knowledge to the general public had important consequences for both public health and urban planning.

The most famous clinician after the turn of the century was Sir William Osler (1849–1919), a Canadian who took his medical degree at McGill University in Montreal in 1872 and did postgraduate training in London and Vienna. He became professor of medicine at Johns Hopkins Medical School, Baltimore, and finally at Oxford. His *Principles and Practice of Medicine* was the most widely read and acclaimed textbook of the day and the forerunner of modern scientific textbooks of medicine. Much of Osler's original work was to concern the disease which claimed the life of Gustav Mahler – infective endocarditis. Osler published his original description of endocarditis in the *British Medical Journal* in 1885.

It was Osler's colleague Emanuel Libman (1872–1946) who diagnosed Mahler's illness by taking a blood culture. Libman demonstrated the value of blood cultures in the diagnosis of endocarditis and further substantiated the view that the condition was of microbial origin. He coined the term 'subacute bacterial endocarditis' and noted that the disease was caused by many different bacteria but that streptococcus viridans was most often associated with it. An effective treatment was not found until the discovery of penicillin. Furthermore, heavily damaged heart valves often require prosthetic valve replacement. The first operation on a damaged heart valve, commisurotomy of mitral valve, took place prior to the Second World War. The operation succeeded in repairing damage caused by rheumatic fever.

Effective chemotherapy for bacterial disease dates from the beginning of the twentieth century, although quinine had been used with success in the treatment of malaria since about 1630. Paul Ehrlich (1854–1915) began his work with aniline dyes but switched to arsenicals in search of effective treatment for spirochaetal infections. The causative agent of syphilis, treponema pallidum, had been discovered by Fritz Schaudin in 1905. Ehrlich synthesized over 900 arsenical compounds. He was awarded the Nobel Prize in 1908 for the discovery of salvarsan and for his work on immunity.

Sulphonamide antibiotics were discovered in 1935. In 1928 Sir Alexander Fleming found that certain substances produced by the mould penicillium notatum could destroy bacterial colonies. He isolated the active substance, named it penicillin and noted its low toxicity to animals, but was unable to concentrate the compound. This formidable aim was achieved by Sir Howard Florey and Ernst Chain. After the Second World War it became possible to synthesize penicillin chemically, and a wide range of anti-bacterial substances is available to the doctors of today.

The link between organic disease and dementia and insanity has been discussed in the medical literature for many centuries. Giovanni Battista Morgani (1682–1771) studied and taught anatomy at Bologna. He described syphilitic gummas involving the central nervous system (11).

General paralysis of the insane, a form of neurosyphilis, was described in 1798 by John Haslam (1764–1844), and in 1822 Antoine Bayle (1794–1858) held that the disease was due to chronic meningitis. It was later shown that the tissue of the brain itself was affected by the condition. For many years the aetiological agent responsible for the disease was suspected to be treponema pallidum. However, it was not until 1913 that Noguchi and Moore isolated the causative organism of syphilis from the brains of sufferers of this condition. Similarly, tabes dorsalis was first described in 1875 by Fournier and its luetic origin later confirmed by bacteriology. The role of alcohol as a cause of dementing illness was not fully appreciated until the present century (11).

Diseases of the mind heavily occupied nineteenth-century practitioners' thoughts, but it was not until the beginning of the present century that the need for a single, scientifically based description of mental illness began to attract the general attention of the profession. Sigmund Freud (1856–1939) described the 'unconscious', the turbulent emotional sub-structure of the mind. He acknowledged his debt to the Romantic writers such as Jean Paul Richter and Charles Baudelaire, who elaborated the 'unconscious' in a less scientific and secular way in their writings. Freud recognized that anxieties were the basis of a group of mental disorders, the 'neuroses'. He instituted psychotherapy as a treatment for neurotic behaviour. Freud conceded that the explanation of many types of psychotic behaviour awaited more exacting biochemical and anatomical study of the brain. We are living in an era when this task is finally being undertaken, with very promising results.

Psychiatrists of the nineteenth century were a heterogeneous group indeed. There were many schools, each following a particular theory of mental disease and instituting therapy based on these beliefs. Franz Richarz (1812–87), who treated Robert Schumann, was of the 'organicist' school. He had been taught by Frederick Nasse (1773–1851), who believed that mental disease stemmed from disturbance of the heart and circulation. Patients were treated liberally with drugs and herbs, and physical treatment such as therapeutic bathing was also instituted. The drawback of this method is that it tended to play down personal relationships and their importance in mental health. Schumann was isolated from his family and friends at a time of personal crisis. The outcome must have been deleterious. Schumann was also presumably treated with opium which has no efficacy in manic-depressive illness or organic brain disease.

The last two hundred years have seen the progressive application of the scientific method to medicine. Diseases have been more effectively described and prognosticated, and the physiology of the human body in health and disease is more deeply understood and appreciated. Medical therapy is now instituted which has a greater margin of both safety and efficacy. The knowledge of how hygiene and lifestyle affect disease has permeated all levels of Western society and the accumulated treasury of medical literature and knowledge today enriches human life immeasurably.

REFERENCES

1. R. Laennec, *A Treatise on Diseases of the Chest* (London, 1834, trans. J. Forbes)
2. J. Clark, *A Treatise on Pulmonary Consumption: A Comprehensive Enquiry into the Causes, Nature, and Prevention of Tuberculosis and Scrofulous Diseases in General* (London, 1835)
3. R. Koch, *The Cure of Consumption* (London, 1890)
4. J. K. Proksch, *Die Geschichte der venerischen Krankheiten* (Bonn, 1895)
5. M. W. Ireland (ed.), *The Medical Department of the U.S. Army in the World War*, IX, Communicable Diseases (Washington, 1928), pp. 229–310

6. R. H. Major, *Classic Descriptions of Disease* (London, 1932)
7. H. Williams, *The Healing Touch* (biography of Sir James Clark) (London, 1950), pp. 50–88
8. R. Dubos, *The White Plague* (Boston, 1952)
9. T. Gjestland, *The Oslo Study of Untreated Syphilis* (Oslo, 1955)
10. E. Gurlt and A. Wernich (eds), *Biographisches Lexicon der hervorragenden Ärzte* (Munich, 1962)
11. C. Singer and E. Underwood, *A Short History of Medicine* (Oxford, 1962)
12. S. A. Waksman, *The Conquest of Tuberculosis* (Berkeley, 1964)
13. J. Snow, *Snow on Cholera* (New York, 1967)
14. L. J. Goldwater, *Mercury: A History of Quicksilver* (Baltimore, 1972)
15. E. Lesky, *The Vienna Medical School in the 19th Century* (London, 1976)
16. K. K. St John, 'Treatment of Late Benign Syphilis; A Review of the Literature', *Journal of American Venereal Diseases*, 3 (1976), p. 146
17. 'The Jerish Herxheimer Reaction', *Lancet* (1977), p. 34
18. J. G. O'Shea, 'René Laennec', *Scottish Medical Journal*, 34 (1989), pp. 474–8

J. S. Bach
(1685–1750)
&
George Frederick Handel
(1685–1759)

There is an unusual connection between the worlds of music and medicine in J.S.Bach's case. Bach died in Leipzig on 28 July 1750 and was buried near the St Johannes-Kirche. According to legend he was buried six paces in front of the left-side entrance of the church. In 1894, when the church was to be pulled down and a larger one built, a decision was made to locate and rebury the remains of the great composer.

For this task the church elders recruited the services of the famous anatomist Wilhelm His senior (1831–1904) who held the chair of anatomy at Leipzig. (His son Wilhelm junior was also an eminent anatomist. He described a portion of the conducting system of the human heart which still bears the eponymous name 'His Bundle'.) His senior is known for his contribution to embryology. He found from records that Bach had been buried in an oak casket, one of only twelve such among the 1400 (otherwise of pine) interred in the same year. Excavation was begun near the site of Bach's grave.

On 22 October 1894 three oak caskets were found and opened. One contained the skeleton of an elderly man approximately 170 cm tall and powerfully built. The skull was '"strong and of characteristic form", presenting a receding forehead, a strong glabella, ... and strong jawbones with a slightly protruding lower jaw' (6). The anatomist also noted the large size of the impression of the cochlea and the inferior temporal gyrus[1] of the brain – evidence, to him at least, of the subject's unique mental and auditory endowments.

After observing that the features revealed in portraits of Bach were compatible with the form of the skull, His enlisted the help of the sculptor Karl Seffner who, working from portraits and a plaster cast of the skull, succeeded in constructing a highly convincing portrait bust of the composer. (A control experiment in which Seffner attempted to make a bust of Handel over the skull failed to produce an equally plausible result.)

His left a voluminous account of Bach's disinterment and of his post-mortem examination of the skeleton; these are discussed in detail by Baer (6). See p. 20.

Bach remained in good health for most of his sixty-six years. He was an unpretentious, practical man whose only vice was almost incessant pipe-smoking. His motto, applicable equally to his life and his music, was 'To God the glory', and he was seemingly unconcerned about posthumous fame. One year before he died Bach went blind. Always near-sighted, he experienced a sudden decline in his vision associated with pain behind the eyes. Over the next year his sight deteriorated to such a degree that he could not perceive light at all. Temporal arteritis is a possible cause of the indisposition. He was treated by the infamous Englishman 'Chevalier' Taylor (1703–72), the same oculist who treated Handel. Taylor treated Bach's illness with frequent incisions to the eye, by the use of calomel (mercury) ointment and by bleeding. Not surprisingly, this aggressive and scientifically unsound treatment did nothing to restore Bach's vision and resulted in a painful, chronic ophthalmitis to add to the composer's miseries. The frequent bleedings probably hastened Bach's physical decline. He became very frail, and was nursed in a darkened room. Shortly before his death he suffered a stroke followed by a fever, possibly terminal pneumonia.

Handel, Bach's great contemporary, lived a little longer than his then less famous colleague: he was seventy-four years old when he died on 14 April 1759. He was seized with a deadly attack of 'faintness' six days before on attending a performance of his *Messiah*, and was brought home where he died after being confined to bed. He was apparently conscious during his last illness and on 11 April added a codicil

---

[1] Today it is known that the auditory cortex is located in the region of the superior temporal gyrus and transverse temporal gyri (Brodmann's areas 22, 41, 42).

to his will directing that he be buried in Westminster Abbey. He lies in the abbey today.

Handel was a stouter but more mercurial figure than Bach. He had unbounded energy, was temperamental and had a huge appetite for food and drink; he was also a heavy pipe smoker. In his middle years he was a tall, corpulent, fleshy-faced man with an amazing capacity for hard work, though his usual manifest activity was occasionally interspersed with brief periods of profound depression. Handel was once caricatured by Joseph Goupy, his sometime friend, as a pig playing the harpsichord. Goupy called the cartoon 'The Charming Brute'. This was not appreciated by Handel, who promptly struck Goupy from his will. Handel was an imaginative and vigorous businessman whose music (including his religious works) was often motivated by frankly commercial purposes.

His illnesses date from his middle age. In 1737 he experienced an 'impairment of his health and understanding'. His right arm became useless to him. He took himself to the 'healing waters' in Tunbridge Wells, where the paralysis of his shoulder and its accompanying rheumatism disappeared. In 1743 the problem recurred, and his friend Horace Walpole noted that Handel could not compose owing to a 'palsy' affecting his head and speech which was accompanied by a high fever. Again the composer appears to have recovered without any lasting ill-effects. Definitive diagnosis of the condition is not possible now. Blindness was an insidious and irreversible problem. Handel became almost totally blind by 1743 through cataracts; however, he continued to play the organ and the harpsichord until his death. At a public performance of the oratorio *Samson*, when the tenor John Beard sang 'Total eclipse! no sun, no moon, all dark amidst the blaze of noon', the audience, affected by the sight of the blind composer, were moved to tears. It was a telling measure of the public's affection for this humane and earthy man.

The composer's cataracts were treated by surgery. His eyes were needled, the idea being to displace the hardened and opaque lens (and the 'humor' in front of it) from the visual axis; the operation was unsuccessful and Handel remained blind. 'Chevalier' Taylor performed the operation, and fortunately for Handel there was no infection of the eye by the unsterilized cataract needle. (This must have been a commonplace complication indeed.)

The 'Chevalier' John Taylor himself deserves a mention in the footnotes of history books. He was something of a maverick and a charlatan, and he travelled around Europe performing his eye operations – often leaving town before the consequences and side-effects became apparent to his patients! Despite his title of 'Chevalier' he was not a member of the nobility. He was an Englishman, born in Norwich, and as well as writing many 'treatises' on the eye was a man of considerable social and intellectual pretensions. Samuel Johnson wrote that the Chevalier's career was 'an incidence of how far impudence will carry ignorance', and indeed the spurious physician attended some of the most famous and brilliant people of his day. He was an advocate of hefty doses of mercury for eye conditions as well as for prompt operation. Taylor was not a complete charlatan: he invented a more effective type of cataract needle and he was the first man to describe staphylococcal infection of the eye (a condition caused no doubt by his unsterile cataract needles). However, it is not unreasonable to suppose that, despite a few legitimate discoveries, he did considerably more harm than good. He was a brilliant showman and in his memoirs he falsifies the results of Bach's operation and mendaciously declares it to have been a success; he made similar claims in Handel's case.

Cataracts are one of the pre-eminent causes of blindness in the elderly. The term 'cataract' denotes hardening and opacification of the lens. The lens itself refracts light to the retina to enable a visual image to be formed. Because the lens becomes thickened and opaque, no light is transmitted and the patient becomes blind. In some cases this opacification is so severe that a patient is unable to distinguish light and dark. Cataracts are associated with numerous common diseases, including diabetes mellitus, but they also occur in otherwise healthy people.

A BRIEF HISTORY OF CATARACT OPERATIONS

The earliest accounts of cataract operations come from Hindu medicine long before the Christian era. The Indians apparently used some sort of anaesthesia and they also taught that cleanliness was important in securing a good and complication-free operation. The Hindus used a blunt instrument to displace an intact lens from the visual axis, after first penetrating the sclera (the covering of the eye) with a needle to make an incision. The use of a blunt instrument certainly diminished the complications which would have occurred had the lens been ruptured. This operation was called 'couching' because the lens was knocked down below the visual axis; it was the procedure used on Handel and Bach.

18

European medicine remained far behind the Hindu doctors for many centuries. It was not until the early eighteenth century that it was generally realized in Europe that cataracts were caused by an opacification of the lens itself: it had been thought that they resulted from opacification of the humor which lay in front of the lens, and cataract surgery in which the lens itself was removed began in the early eighteenth century. Jacques Daviel was one of the first men to remove cataracts by surgery; his 1748 treatise on the subject created quite a revolution in ophthalmology. This work ended the widely accepted practice of 'couching'. Results from lens extraction were considerably better than those obtained by the earlier technique. Opium and alcohol were the only means of alleviating the considerable pain of operation.

Cataract surgery made steady advances. In 1884 cocaine analgesia was introduced into the procedure. The cocaine drops were absorbed through the cornea and adequate pain relief was obtained although, of course, immobilization of the eye was not brought about by this procedure. By the early 1930s techniques to immobilize the eye were well known. The introduction of topical antibiotics dates from about the 1940s. In more recent times the development of micro-surgical techniques and of prosthetic intraocular lenses have considerably advanced cataract surgery. Cataracts are now operated on at an earlier stage in their development than has previously been possible, with excellent results. Cataract extraction with the implantation of an intraocular lens is one of the most widely practised and effective operations, and the procedure restores vision to many elderly people.

CODA

Both Bach and Handel were pipe smokers, and it is probable that smoking played a part in their deaths and decline by causing atherosclerosis (hardening of the arteries) and possibly hypertension. It is difficult to be precise about the cause of Handel's death, but a myocardial infarction (heart attack) is a strong possibility. He died suddenly in his bed after being brought home from a performance of his music. Both composers lived to considerable ages and it is true to say that illness influenced their lives far less than it did those of many other great composers. Bach wrote a poem about the joys of smoking which appeared in volume two of the *Clavierbüchlein* for Anna Magdalena in 1725. He called it

'Edifying Thoughts of a Tobacco Smoker'; a short quote from it is illuminating:

Like me, this pipe so fragrant burning
Is made of naught but earth and clay.
To Earth I too shall be returning.
It falls and ere I'd think to say
It breaks in two before my eyes.
In store for me a like fate lies.
On land, on sea, at home, abroad
I smoke my pipe and worship God.

REFERENCES

1. J. F. Agricola and C. P. E. Bach, 'Nekrolog', in L. Mizler, *Neu eröffnete musikalische Bibliotek*, 4/1 (Leipzig, 1754)
2. J. Mainwaring, *Memoirs of the Life of the Late George Frederic Handel* (London, 1760)
3. J. Taylor, *The History of the Travels and Adventures of the Chevalier Taylor, Opthalmiater* (London, 1761)
4. W. S. Rockstro, *The Life of George Frederick Handel* (London, 1883)
5. H. T. David and A. Mendel (eds), *The Bach Reader: A Life of Johann Sebastian Bach in Letters and Documents* (New York and London, 1945)
6. K. A. Baer, 'Johann Sebastian Bach (1685–1750) in Medical History', *Bulletin of the Medical Library Association*, 39 (1951), p. 206
7. M. Keynes, 'Handel's Illnesses', *Lancet* (1980), pp. 1354–5

APPENDIX:

Extract from 'Johann Sebastian Bach (1685–1750) in Medical History' by Karl A. Baer.

Bach was buried on 31 July 1750; evidence that his contemporaries, and particularly his Leipziger "Landsleute," did not properly appreciate his greatness is provided by the fact that the location of his grave fell into oblivion. From an incidental remark in the *Nekrolog*[14] it was known that he was buried near the St. Johannes-Kirche; there was also a "poorly founded" oral tradition to the effect that Bach had been buried "six steps in front of the small entrance

---

[14] Nekrolog, p. 172.

on the left side of the church."[15] When in 1894 the old church was to be replaced by a new and larger one, part of the old cemetery surrounding it had to be included, and it was then decided to search for the remains of Bach while the excavation work was going on.[16] Preliminary archival research yielded the valuable information, finally located in the account books of the Johannes Hospital, that Bach had been buried in an oak casket.[17] This discovery was the more important as only 12 out of 1400 bodies buried in the year of Bach's death were resting in oak caskets; three of these were found on October 22, 1894 and opened in the presence of the great anatomist of the University of Leipzig, Prof. Wilhelm His (1831–1904). One contained the complete skeleton of an "elderly man, not very tall but well-built." The skull was "strong and of characteristic form," presenting a receding forehead, a strong glabella, a nasal bone jutting out at a sharp angle, relatively low orbital cavities whose width exceeded their height, and strong jawbones with a slightly protruding lower jaw. It was immediately evident to His that this was not an ordinary skull ("Dutzendkopf") – a comforting conclusion because any indifferent formation would have excluded further investigation.

The first step in the meticulous process of identification undertaken by His was a comparison of the skull with the few authentic portraits of Bach, particularly the two paintings by J.G.Haussmann then available at Leipzig. The comparison showed not only a general agreement as to the basic form, but the portraits also presented the very physiognomic traits described before as characterizing the skull. His, who was as thorough as he was resourceful, felt that this result was "quite interesting" but not at all conclusive and that only the help of a good sculptor offered some hope of solving the problem. If an artist were able to mould a portrait-like bust over a plaster cast of the skull, then there would at least be proof of the possibility that the skull was Bach's. Accordingly, the sculptor C.Seffner was approached and was set to work in a room containing the Haussmann portraits and a few etchings of Bach; within a few days, he created a work "the distinctive quality of which moved all those who had occasion to see it." His now considered it "likely" that the skull was genuine. A control experiment was next performed by Seffner: a bust of Händel cast over the skull proved to be an "impossibility per se"

---

[15] Wustmann, G. Die Auffindung der Gebeine Johann Sebastian Bachs. Grenzboten 54: 415–425, 1895 (p. 415–416). An earlier article by the same author (Bach's Grab, in Grenzboten 53: 117–126, 1894) was not available for examination.

[16] The following report on the finding and identification of Bach's remains is based on (a) His, W. Johann Sebastian Bach; Forschungen über dessen Grabstätte, Gebeine und Antlitz. Leipzig, 1895, and (b) His, W. Anatomische Forschungen über Johann Sebastian Bach's Gebeine und Antlitz ... Abhandl. d. Math.-phys. Cl. d. k. sächs. Gesellsch. d. Wissensch. 22: 379–420, 1895. Also used was Die Auffindung der Grabstätte J.S.Bach's. Musik. Wbl., 26: 339–340, 1895.

[17] "4 Thlr. zahlte der Todtengräber Müller wegen Herrn Johann Sebastian Bach's eichenem Sarg."

("innere Unmöglichkeit"). It was an acceptable likeness, but areas where the soft parts are very thin, like the forehead, had to be filled out with thick layers of clay while in other areas the bone was almost bare where the soft parts are naturally thick, like the chin. Thereupon, His redoubled his efforts; he had the City Council appoint a Committee of six which, interestingly enough, included one librarian, Dr E. Vogel, an expert on the iconography of Bach. The Committee was first to examine skeleton and skull, then to appraise the Bach portraits and, finally, to "ascertain the degree of certainty attainable in reconstructing the soft parts above a skull."

The skeleton presented numerous exostoses in the area of the vertebral column and elsewhere, while the skull showed an advanced stage of closure of the sagittal coronal, and lambdoidal sutures. These indications that the skeleton belonged to an elderly man were confirmed by F. Hesse (1849–1906),[18] American-trained professor of dentistry at the University of Leipzig, who was able to diagnose senile atrophy of the alveolar processes. Another interesting observation was made by Hesse: even though the skull had only nine teeth, it could be seen that the cutting edges of the incisors rather than their labial or lingual surfaces were worn down. This meant that the lower jaw must have protruded to some extent – a feature clearly present in all the known portraits of Bach.

The next step in the Committee's work was to make a critical examination of the portraits; this task was left to Dr Vogel and Seffner, and as it lay mainly in the field of art criticism, we refer the interested reader to the original sources quoted for further information. In contrast, the problem of reconstructing the soft parts over the skull is of the highest anatomical interest. A few years before, H. Welcker[19] had developed a "profile-method" by which a correct profile of the soft parts could be drawn over a skull. He applied this method, based on a limited number of measurements taken from 13 male cadavers, in the heated controversy on the genuineness of the so-called "Schiller-Schädel."[20] This method could be used only because Schiller's death-mask was available for comparison with the profile thus "calculated" by Welcker, but no death-mask of Bach had been taken and all his portraits showed a frontal view. Therefore, His was justified in stating that "our profile constructed over the skull on the basis of the measurements found was likely to be Bach's profile only if it could be incorporated in a bust agreeing with his en-face portraits."

His's thoroughness in taking these measurements is borne out by the fact

---

[18] Hesse, F. Bericht über Kiefer und Zähne des Schädels. In His, W. Johann Sebastian Bach. Leipzig, 1895, p. 20–22.

[19] Welcker, H. Schiller's Schädel und Todtenmaske nebst Mittheilungen über Schädel und Todtenmaske Kant's. Braunschweig, 1883.

[20] cf. Schaaffhausen, H. Hermann Welcker, Schiller's Schädel und Todtenmaske. Arch. Anthrop. 15: Suppl., 170–185, 1885 and H. Welcker's reply, Zur Kritik des Schillerschädels. Arch. Anthrop. 17: 19–60, 1887.

(particularly remarkable in view of the highly argumentative inclination of German scholars) that the positive result announced by him has found general acceptance. He took 19 different facial measurements of 37 cadavers by using a simple method: A sewing needle over which a thin rubber-disc with a hole in the center had been placed was lubricated and inserted vertically into the skin. Then the rubber disc was pushed down to the skin and, after the needle had been pulled out, the distance from the needlepoint to the disc was measured. The measurements yielded the important result that a certain normal thickness of the soft parts over every area of the face can be assumed; this median thickness of any given area varies only very slightly in normal subjects, according to sex and age. Consequently, the most accurate and reliable results can be obtained by using the median values for the appropriate sex and age group, in our case the men between 50 and 72 years of age. According to these measurements, based on the investigation of eight subjects, a system of fixed points was constructed over the skull and Seffner modelled a third bust, strictly adhering to these values. This bust exhibits all the characteristic features known from the portraits and is more lifelike and expressive than any of them. The final Report of the Commission states that "only a coincidence of the most unlikely kind could have made it possible to come upon a different skull of such strongly pronounced and not at all ordinary form which would correspond to the requirements of genuineness to such an extent as is the case with this skull."

A detailed investigation of the temporal bones undertaken by His in co-operation with Adam Politzer (1835–1920), famed Viennese authority in the field of otology, yielded results suggestive of Bach's musical genius. While His states that it would be futile to attempt to describe the talent of a great composer from the structure of his temporal bones he feels sure that a well organized and well developed ear is indispensable in the making of a great composer. In Bach's case an over-all impression of particularly pronounced development of the temporal bones is immediately apparent. It is confirmed by examination of their components: the abnormally large size of the fenestra rotunda (diameter of 2.5 mm. as opposed to a normal of 1.5 mm.);[21] the extraordinary thickness and firmness of the mastoid process, particularly in its cortical part; the remarkable width of the incisura mastoidea; the prominence of the petrous ridge; the unusual hiatus subarcuatus.

Further observations throw an interesting sidelight upon the problems of localization of cerebral function. The impressions of the fusiform and inferior temporal gyri on the skull suggest a particularly strong development of these

---

[21] Cunningham's Textbook of anatomy, ed. by J.C.Brash and E.B.Jamieson. 8th ed. New York, 1943, p. 1145.

areas. The large size of the first coil of the cochlea speaks for an unusual development of the cochlear ganglion and, accordingly, of the higher sensory centers. An attempt to interpret these findings is beyond the scope of this paper.

(*Bulletin of the Medical Library Association*, 39 (1951), pp. 206 ff. Extract reprinted with the permission of the Medical Library Association.)

Wolfgang Amadeus Mozart
(1756–91)

Wolfgang Amadeus Mozart was born on the evening of Sunday, 27 January 1756, in Salzburg. He was one of seven children of whom only two survived beyond infancy. The boy was destined to become the most spectacular child prodigy and one of the greatest musical geniuses of all time. The thematic catalogue of Ludwig von Köchel records a huge output from a man who died at barely thirty-six years of age: 626 works, including twenty-two operas, twenty-seven string quartets, fifty symphonies, twenty-eight piano concertos and seventeen masses. All these were produced during a life of travelling, economic woes, financial frustrations and chronic illness. Mozart's music encompasses the full range of human emotion and reflects the pathos of a unique and awesomely gifted human being adrift in an often harsh and uncomprehending world.

Mozart was a man preoccupied with his music and his work to such a degree that it is not surprising that his contemporaries found his character wanting in some respects and that he seemed to lack elementary graces and skills in communicating. His detractors have selected some of his letters to show that he was childlike and irresponsible, others point to the fact that he left little comment on literature, art and scholarship, showing that he was poorly educated. Others talk of his miraculous natural endowment without mentioning the hard work and dedication with which he cultivated it.

Mozart's musical ability was well in evidence at the age of three. He could pick out chords on the clavier and memorize passages he heard when his father gave lessons to his sister, Nannerl, who was five years older. He was composing by the age of five. The boy's childhood was a time of great success and excitement but simultaneously one of hardship and deprivation. Dressed in a powdered wig and sporting a sword, Wolfgang with Nannerl travelled the length and breadth of Europe in a series of concert tours. Between the ages of six and sixteen years, Mozart spent only six months at home. He travelled everywhere by stage coach; the roads were often poor and passage difficult. He was often ill during his travels, and most of his chief medical biographers have concluded that it was the ramifications of the cumulative stresses of those early years, combined with overwork and poor self-care, that led to his early demise. However, it must also be said that no boy of the eighteenth century enjoyed such a vast array of educational and social experiences, mixing as he did with all levels of society.

As an adult, Mozart was received with less courtesy by his patrons than he had been as a miraculous prodigy. He was physically unprepossessing. There were disagreements with his father, who wished to find a secure provincial position for his son. Mozart detested the patronage system and wanted the freedom to create works of unprecedented stature which would tax his energy and imagination. It was a difficult time. Mozart was ostensibly arrogant, and was frustrated by those around him who did not share his vision. Despite all the problems came a consistent output of works of an ever increasing standard and maturity.

A well-known and much discussed aspect of Mozart's character was his cruel tendency to criticize: he was, of course, the supreme musician of his day and many of these criticisms were probably well founded. To his contemporaries, however, they were hurtful, tactless and spiteful and did little to advance the young man's career. In Mozart's defence it must be observed that his life was often profoundly frustrating in a world dominated by birth, patronage and privilege, where native ability and talent counted for little. He lived lavishly and often drank heavily, perhaps partly in reaction to his frustrating circumstances. Mozart's worldly lifestyle was not unique to him – many of his friends, including minor members of the aristocracy, lived life to the full: it was, after all, short and precarious, and one had to enjoy it while one could.

Much of the essential information that one would expect to find in a good Mozart biography is either controversial or absent. It is now thought that the composer's financial situation was reasonably secure, and there is much evidence that it was improving in his last year: *The Magic Flute* ran for a hundred consecutive nights in Vienna and Mozart is estimated to have earned twice as much as Haydn. One obvious expense that burdened the Mozarts was the high cost of physicians' fees and medications, and Constanze, his wife, took an expensive trip to the spa in Baden in June 1791. While Mozart's last years were not without their difficulties, the short hiatus between his death and general public acknowledgment of his greatness as a composer, and also the more favourable economic climate which developed for composers and publishers in Vienna shortly after his death, suggest that his material circumstances might have been more comfortable had he lived beyond 1791.

Mozart's life was punctuated by periods of depression and despair, exacerbated by his renal disease. Constanze is said to have sustained him greatly during these times. Several sources state that he was occasionally unfaithful to his wife but that his passions were of only a brief duration. This is at best hearsay written long after the event: the strength of Mozart's love for his wife was apparent to all observers.

Many of the reminiscences that we have of Mozart talk of his superficial affections and capriciousness, but it should be borne in mind that many of these were written by slight or merely professional acquaintances; Mozart had a close circle of devoted friends and family to whom he was in turn deeply devoted. Constanze's sentiments are revealed in the entry she made in Mozart's album on the day of his death:

> What thou once wrote to thy friend on this page, do I now in my affliction write to thee, dearly beloved husband; Mozart – never to be forgotten by me or by the whole of Europe – now thou too art at peace – eternal peace!! ... About one o'clock in the morning of the 5th of December in this year he left in his 36th year – alas! all too soon! – this good – but ungrateful world! – dear God! – For 8 years we were joined together by the most tender bond, never to be broken here below! – O! could I soon be joined with thee for ever,
>
> Thy grievously afflicted wife
> Constanze Mozart née Weber

The composer's early death, though not entirely unexpected by the more observant of his contemporaries, deeply shocked and distressed those close to him. It was almost inconceivable that a talent such as Mozart's could be silenced by death in his thirty-sixth year. And we are still speculating about the cause of his early demise.

PHYSICAL APPEARANCE

Mozart's physical appearance militated against his success in adult life; though by no means ugly he was not particularly striking or attractive.

He was about 1.52 metres tall, with a large head and a prominent aquiline nose. He had large blue eyes and was said to be a little near-sighted. In the words of the Irish tenor Michael Kelly he had a 'profusion of fine fair hair'; he evidently thought this his best feature, and most of the time kept his hair tidy and elegantly powdered. He liked wearing wigs, in keeping with the fashion of the day, and favoured expensive clothes in vivid colours, particularly red.

There is no portrait of Mozart by any first-rate artist. The most flattering, which is also said to be the most accurate, is the unfinished one by Joseph Lange executed probably in 1789 and now in the Mozarteum. The portrait of the composer as a Knight of the Golden Spur is also said to be a good likeness. The numerous cameos indicate an unimpressive profile with a too-large nose and a receding chin. Most of the artists show Mozart as having a sensitive and gentle countenance, which is said to be his characteristic expression.

Mozart's hearing was extraordinarily acute and he could detect the slightest errors of pitch. Remarkably, he had a deformity of the left ear which still bears the appellation 'Mozart ear' and is well described in the medical literature. ('Mozart ears' are not known to be associated with any internal abnormality – in particular there is no connection with renal disease – nor with exceptional musical talent as was once believed.) The first illustration of the composer's ear appeared in a biography of the composer written in 1828 by G.N. von Nissen, the husband of Mozart's widow Constanze (1).

The condition is hereditary and uncommon; according to Alex Paton, it occurs in less than one in a thousand people (16). In 90% of cases it occurs in only one ear. The ear is flat and there is little development of the antihelical curve. Mozart's son inherited his father's facial features and ear deformity (2,15,16,17), and there is evidence that Franz Xavier was the model for the illustration in Nissen's biography. (See plate 1.)

MOZART'S ILLNESSES
AND THEIR AFTERMATH

Mozart's final illness had its origin in a series of childhood infections which struck the young prodigy. In 1762, at the age of six, he was struck with a high fever and a rash. The red blotches that covered his body were painful and said to be the size of a Kreutzer (a coin about 3 cm in diameter). The child was sick for four weeks and was treated with black powder, an antiperspirant. Physicians have diagnosed the rash as erythema nodosum, caused by the first of a number of severe streptococcal infections that were to plague Mozart.

Mozart's childhood was characterized by recurrent bouts of streptococcal tonsillitis. He fell victim to the malady twice in 1762 and again in 1764 and 1765. In December 1762 he had a severe polyarthritis[1] associated with the disease; his knees were affected and he could scarcely stand. It has been speculated that the disease was rheumatic fever, but it may have been an early manifestation of Henoch–Schönlein syndrome which Peter Davies claims eventually took Mozart's life (15). (Both illnesses are an auto-immune reaction to streptococcal throat infection and would have been relatively common in Mozart's day.)

In November 1765 both Mozart and his sister were stricken with a febrile illness while at The Hague. Nannerl became delirious and her throat was inflamed. She received the Last Sacraments but made an unexpected recovery. Wolfgang was ill for a month, emaciated and dehydrated; his lips lost their skin three times and became hard and black. Firm diagnosis of the condition is impossible but endemic typhoid fever is favoured by most medical practitioners who have an interest in Mozart's illnesses.

In November 1766 Mozart had a recurrence of fever and polyarthritis; the knees were again affected and he was unable to walk or move his toes or knees.

In 1767 Mozart contracted smallpox at Olmütz during an epidemic. He was critically ill for three weeks and Nannerl wrote that her brother had been disfigured by the disease. During his recuperation he learned fencing.

In January 1772 Mozart was again ill in Salzburg, seemingly with a recurrence of chronic streptococcal tonsillitis.

In August 1784 Mozart was once more seriously unwell. On the 23rd, while attending a Paisiello opera in Vienna, he sweated so profusely that his clothes were drenched. Mozart also complained of colic and vomiting, and remained unwell until the end of September. Leopold Mozart describes his son's illness as 'rheumatic inflammatory fever'. Mozart's health declined steadily after this illness. He was seriously unwell in 1787 and again in 1790, when he suffered from rheumatic pains, a headache and toothache. Once more there is evidence (cervical

---

[1] arthritis affecting multiple joints

29

adenopathy[2]) for a low-grade tonsillitis as the triggering factor of the illness.

Jean-Baptiste Suard provides first-hand evidence of Mozart's state of health, and lays the blame for his chronic illness squarely on the pressures to which he was subjected as a child: 'It has constantly been observed that too prompt and too rapid a development of the moral faculties in children only operated at the expense of their physique. Mozart provided new proof of this. His body did not sustain normal growth as he grew older. All his life he remained weak and frail in health.' (8)

MOZART'S FINAL YEAR

Many remarked on Mozart's pallor and weakness during the early months of 1791. The composer became prone to depression and paranoid behaviour. Some authors have suggested that his plump hands and swollen face were connected with the development of renal disease. Despite deepening melancholy and worsening illness, Mozart was extraordinarily productive musically; he made few concessions to his illness and would often sleep as little as four hours a night. He is known to have eaten poorly and drunk heavily.

In the latter half of 1791 Mozart's health declined markedly. He became pale and sickly, his depression worsened and he became preoccupied with thoughts of death. He began to faint frequently, and his ankles became swollen. The emotional situation became even more highly charged when a 'stranger' who would not give his name called in August to commission a Requiem Mass from Mozart. The episode is one of the most famous stories in the Mozart literature. The stranger was Anton Leitgeb, the servant of Count Franz Walsegg-Stuppach, who wished to pass Mozart's Mass off as his own. In the composer's depressed and paranoid mind, the visitor became a messenger of death. By October Mozart had lost a great deal of weight, and when Leitgeb came to collect the Requiem he was already dead. His long illness is best explained by chronic renal failure perhaps complicated by hypertensive cerebral disease. He was probably also severely anaemic.

[2] swelling of the lymph glands of the neck

MOZART'S DEATH

Mozart's final illness lasted fifteen days after he took to his bed on 20 November. He had been unwell for a few weeks before doing so. He was beset with a high fever, and there was much sweating as well as abdominal pain and vomiting. Mozart's feet and hands were grossly swollen and he complained of pain on movement. Davies contends that this was due to polyarthritis and oedema (15).

Mozart's attendants included Constanze, Sophie Haibel and her mother, Schack, Hofer and his former pupil Süssmayr. Many friends and professional acquaintances also made calls. Mozart's medical attendant was Nicholas Closset. When he became alarmed by his patient's decline he sought the help of Mathias von Sallaba, Chief of Medicine at the general hospital. Both physicians were deeply pessimistic about the composer's prognosis, but they did not suspect foul play. Mozart in his terminal agony suspected that he had been poisoned by aqua toffana (lead).

Von Sallaba noted a rash and diagnosed a 'heated miliary fever'. Davies concludes that the rash must have been present on the legs and buttocks because it was not noted by his non-medical attendants (15). A venesection was performed and a sedative, probably opium, was administered. Cold compresses were given to keep the fever down. (To attempt to lower bodily temperature is the correct treatment of fever.)

There is no evidence that Mozart was given toxic medications such as mercury purgatives or antimony 'diaphoretics', but it is not impossible that they were administered to treat his febrile illness in accordance with common eighteenth-century medical principles.

Mozart's illness was certainly not iatrogenic[3] in origin, and by applying compresses and sedating the patient his physician gave effective symptomatic treatment and helped to alleviate his sufferings. Some of Mozart's friends were highly critical of his professional care, and the opinion that his illness was iatrogenic has persisted in the medical literature, but the evidence is not there. There were over twenty different mercury preparations available to both physicians and the public in Mozart's day, and they were used to treat many different diseases. If Mozart took any of them they would have exacerbated his condition, but it seems that his kidney condition followed recurrent streptococcal infection. There is no evidence of the tremor, dementia or particularly

[3] caused by his doctors

salivation which accompanies mercurialism and which made Paganini's existence so painful.

Sophie Haibel maintained, in a letter written in 1825, that Mozart was alert until about two hours before he died, but it is more likely that he was delirious for several days beforehand. Her account conflicts with that of Suard, who seems to suggest that the composer was in a debilitated state for some months before he died and that he composed the Requiem with the greatest difficulty. Suard's account fits the established medical facts better. (The accounts of Mozart's last illness were written many years after his death, and the testimony of distressed friends and relatives is of dubious value. Early medical testimony does not attach as much importance to the assessment of the level of consciousness as we do today.)

According to Haibel, Mozart struggled to complete his Requiem fully aware of impending death. On Sunday, 4 December, friends gathered at his bedside. Only seven bars of the 'Lacrimosa' were written down and the composer attempted to sing the alto part, puffing out his cheeks in an attempt to imitate the trumpets and in this manner to dictate it to Süssmayr. He told his friends, 'I already have the taste of death on my tongue'. This is a reference to uraemic waste products which accumulate and foul the breath. That night, a fever came on, possibly due to broncho-pneumonia – those dying of uraemia are susceptible to chest infections – and Mozart became delirious and stuporous. A few hours before his death, Closset was called. He ordered ice compresses to treat the fever. A priest delivered the Last Sacraments, and on attempting to rise to receive the host, Mozart fell back dead, fifty-five minutes after midnight on 5 December 1791.

The registrar of deaths of St Stephen's parish recorded the cause of death as 'heated miliary fever' on 6 December 1791. No autopsy was performed, and the death certificate is now missing.

DIAGNOSTIC POSSIBILITIES

There is nearly 200 years' worth of medical literature pertaining to Mozart's death, and the subject is a study in itself. I do not claim deep familiarity with all the literature; the conclusions of the many medical authors are shown in Table 2. I concur with the diagnosis of chronic renal failure exacerbated by terminal infection, probably broncho-pneumonia with, perhaps, streptococcal throat infection. Hypertensive encephalopathy and certainly uraemic encephalopathy[4] seem to have been present for many months, as was anaemia.

TABLE 1

Symptomatic Diagnosis of Death	Possible Clinical Explanations
'Dropsy of the heart' Obituary (1791)	Oedema due to renal and/or cardiac failure
'Deposit on the brain' Closset (1791)	Hypertensive encephalopathy; delirium or coma; cerebrovascular accident
'Heated miliary fever' Sallaba (1791)	Fever and exanthem (rash); delirium
'Rheumatic inflammatory fever' Guldener von Lobes (1824)	Fever; exanthem; auto-immune disease; myalgia; arthritis/arthralgia
Weight loss, debility, fainting fits, self-neglect, oedema, paranoia, depression Suard (1804)	Chronic uraemia; hypertensive encephalopathy; affective disorder

(source 8)

The origin of Mozart's renal disease was probably in the recurrent streptococcal infections which ailed him during his brief life. Chronic streptococcal infection of the throat and skin causes an auto-immune cross-reaction which produces nephritis (inflammation of the kidney). The antigens (surface proteins) of the bacteria resemble the proteins of the epithelial cells of the kidneys, and in the body's attempt to rid itself of the streptococcus an antibody cross-reaction is produced which damages the kidney. Hypertension, anaemia and chronic infection exacerbate renal failure as do many medications. Death from post-streptococcal glomerulonephritis was a common event at the turn of the century when streptococcal infection was endemic and treatment ineffective. Mozart died of what must have been a common ailment. Richard Bright described oedema relating to nephritis in 1836, many years after Mozart's

---

[4] hypertensive and uraemic encephalopathy: diseases of the brain secondary to raised blood pressure and kidney disease respectively

TABLE 2

Causes of Mozart's illnesses as postulated by modern medical writers

Shapiro (1968)	Septicaemia complicated by acute renal failure
Belza (1953) Kerner (1969)	Heavy metal poisoning mercury lead (aqua toffana)
Barraud (1905) Carp (1970) Fluker (1972)	Post-scarlet fever nephritis
Bokay (1906)	Rheumatic fever
Bär (1966)	Rheumatic fever Haemorrhagic shock, secondary to venesection (bleeding)
Clein (1959)	Infective endocarditis
Davies (1983)	Bipolar affective disorder Henoch–Schönlein syndrome polyarthritis acute on chronic renal failure rash Terminal staphylococcal broncho-pneumonia and cerebral haemorrhage

(sources 7, 11, 12, 15)

death. Davies's recent paper strengthens the case for post-streptococcal nephritis (17).

The presence of possible hypertensive disease and the effects of this and uraemia on Mozart's mentation have been well elaborated by Davies (15). Paranoid delusions and depression are common among sufferers of uraemia and they formed a prominent part of Mozart's symptom complex. Davies argues that Mozart suffered from a bipolar affective disorder (manic–depressive illness); he has little space to justify his conclusions, but the subject is well worth further elaboration, particularly by musicologists and psychiatrists with an interest in medical history.

Mozart's terminal illness may have been staphylococcal bronchopneumonia, which would account for the fever and delirium. Davies also argues plausibly for a cerebral haemorrhage in the terminal phase of Mozart's illness (15). Carl Bär argues that repeated venesections (bleedings) may have been responsible for Mozart's demise (7), citing the records of Sallaba's treatment of other patients where the doctor certainly displayed a heavy hand with the lancet. There is no conclusive evidence that Mozart was bled heavily, though Constanze gives reliable documentation of one venesection. Haibel remained critical of the cold compresses but nowhere suggested that venesection caused a decline in the patient's condition. The issue is too poorly documented for definitive conclusions to be drawn. Bär argues that Mozart's physicians may have taken four pints of blood which is, one hopes, an excessive estimate. Renal failure contraindicates venesection and makes the procedure hazardous.

Davies argues concisely and logically for the Henoch–Schönlein syndrome, a systemic auto-immune disease which causes nephritis and follows streptococcal infection. He points to Mozart's rashes and frequent bouts of polyarthritis and rheumatic pain as evidence for the syndrome; the presence of these additional stigmata strongly support the diagnosis of post-streptococcal nephritis (15). There are of course many other possible causes for chronic renal failure in a man of Mozart's years, but Davies's hypothesis furnishes a single explanation for the many bouts of illness suffered by the composer and fits the established facts well. As Mozart's illnesses are so poorly documented (largely because of the primitive state of eighteenth-century internal medicine) and there was no autopsy, no explanation of Mozart's death can be regarded as definitive. It may well be that his illnesses were due to several concurrent disease processes. To the long list of illnesses proposed by his medical biographers (Table 2) could be added several others, for example renal tuberculosis and erythema nodosum. The diverse extrapulmonary manifestations of tuberculosis could account for many of the features of Mozart's last illness. An infective process is likely as the triggering factor of his death because infection was endemic in the urban environment. Iatrogenic illness, self-medication and alcohol abuse may have exacerbated his illness.

There is little evidence that Mozart had syphilis. Although the disease was endemic in eighteenth-century Europe, it had a marked preponderance for the socio-economically deprived. The principal vector was prostitution. Mozart was familiar with the disease and wrote that he avoided women whose morals were suspect. He did not have gonorrhoea, which was ubiquitous and had no class preponderance (as the autopsies of many famous men attest). He was a less libidinous figure than most biographers insinuate. Speculation by Suard that Mozart suffered from syphilis was based solely on rumour and gossip, but we can neither implicate nor exclude that illness. Mozart's chronic illness and rash may have been equated with syphilis by his contemporaries, but we know now that other diseases were more likely to have been responsible.

WAS MOZART POISONED?

Theories that Mozart was poisoned rely principally on causation; they are superfluous from the medical point of view as there are plenty of possible natural causes for Mozart's death. Mercury poisoning is particularly unlikely as Mozart had none of the stigmata of chronic mercurialism. Aqua toffana (lead) would be more difficult for the biographer to exclude, but Mozart's crowded room would have afforded few possibilities for the would-be poisoner. Mozart's poor relationship with his Masonic brothers was exaggerated by some authors so as to provide a motive for poisoning, as were his achievements in the boudoir with other men's wives!

When Salieri became senile in 1823 he accused himself of poisoning Mozart. There is little evidence that he had the knowledge or connections to carry out Mozart's murder, however. His confession started a public furore and rumours not altogether silenced; he was chivalrously defended in public by Dr Guldener von Lobes (8).

The Mozarteum in Salzburg possesses a skull which may be that of Mozart. Its authenticity is dubious indeed, but it has not yet been evaluated by modern forensic pathology. If it proved to be Mozart's skull the presence of mercury might revive the poisoning theory; but, since mercury was used for medicinal purposes, traces of it would by no means prove that the composer was poisoned. Franz Hofdemel, the husband of one of Mozart's pupils, committed suicide on the day of the composer's funeral, and advocates of the 'poisoning theory' have tried, but without success, to connect his death with Mozart's.

MOZART'S FUNERAL

On 7 December a third-class funeral costing 8 Florints and 56 Kreutzer – a paltry sum – took place. Mozart's body was laid out in the house where he died. It was removed to St Stephen's Cathedral, where it was consecrated in the open Renaissance hall in front of a pulpit marked by a cross and known popularly as the 'Crucifix Chapel'. The extremely simple funeral was the cheapest available, but it was not the funeral of a pauper.

After the consecration the massed bodies were removed to a grave in St Mark's cemetery. Mozart was buried, along with his neighbours from his quarter who had died on that day, in a common grave about 2.25 metres deep. The bodies were buried in two layers, each covered with lime; the graves were later reopened and another layer of bodies was buried. The graves were not marked.

Mozart's mourners included Süssmayr and Salieri. Constanze was not present, probably because of illness (she suffered from painful phlebitis) or grief. The mourners attended the consecration of the body but did not accompany its progress, with the other bodies, through the Landstrasse suburb to St Mark's. It was said that the mourners did not accompany the body because of bad weather, but recent research has shown that although the day began misty, later a light north wind blew away the mist to reveal a clear sky. The story of the mourners being deterred by the weather is an attempt by later authors to dismiss what earlier writers had felt to be a cruel indifference to the composer, but in fact it was not the convention of the day to accompany a body to a mass grave.

Mozart's character continues to elude us. He was a private man, and his biographers must wade through a mass of rumour, contradictory statements, innuendo and scandal to attempt a realistic portrait. His character is probably revealed more clearly in his music than it could ever be in biographical sketches, hampered as they are by insufficient information and poor documentation. The composer's life has been used as an allegory to illustrate many themes of the human condition – including the role of the hand of God in man's affairs. After 200 years it seems that man has still not come to terms with the essential tragedy of Mozart's death.

REFERENCES

1. G. N. von Nissen, *Biographie W. A. Mozart's nach Originalbriefen* (Leipzig, 1828)
2. 'L'oreille de Mozart', *La chronique médicale*, 5 (1898), p. 576
3. H. Mersmann (ed.), *Letters of W. A. Mozart* (London, 1928)

4. R. H. Major, *Classic Descriptions of Disease* (London, 1932)

5. E. Anderson (ed.), *The Letters of Mozart and his Family* (London, 1938, rev. 3rd edn, 1985)

6. A. Einstein, *Mozart: His Character, his Work* (New York, 1945)

7. C. Bär, *Mozart: Krankheit, Tod, Begräbnis* (Kassel, 1966, rev. 2nd edn, 1972)

8. O. E. Deutsch, *Mozart: A Documentary Biography*, 2nd edn (London, 1966) [Ger. original Kassel, 1961]

9. O. Jahn, *Life of Mozart*, 3 vols (London, 1968) [Ger. original Leipzig, 1856–9]

10. C. J. Polson and R. N. Tattershall, *Clinical Toxicology* (London, 1969)

11. L. Carp, 'Mozart: His Tragic Life and Controversial Death', *Bulletin of the New York Academy of Medicine*, 46 (1970), pp. 267–9

12. J. L. Fluker, 'Mozart: His Health and Death', *The Practitioner*, 209 (1972), pp. 841–5

13. L. J. Goldwater, *Mercury: A History of Quicksilver* (Baltimore, 1972)

14. H. Ottaway, *Mozart* (London, 1979)

15. P. J. Davies, 'Mozart's Illnesses and Death', *Journal of the Royal Society of Medicine*, 76 (1983), pp. 776–85

16. A. Paton, A. L. Pahor and G. R. Graham, 'Looking for Mozart Ears', *British Medical Journal*, 293 (1986), p. 1622

17. P. J. Davies, 'Mozart's Left Ear, Nephropathy and Death', *Medical Journal of Australia*, 147 (1987), p. 582

Ludwig van Beethoven
(1770–1827)

Beethoven's music has a rare power to uplift and ennoble the human spirit. Much of it evokes a heroic ideal of mankind and the triumphant struggle of the individual against adversity and oppression – a powerful theme in the Europe of Napoleon Bonaparte, and one of personal significance to Beethoven, invalided at an early age by deafness.

Many people have difficulty reconciling the beauty and the humanitarianism embodied in Beethoven's music with what they know of its creator. The popular picture of Beethoven is that of a dishevelled, misanthropic man with an explosive temper who shunned the company of his fellow men and made all personal matters subservient to the creation of his music. While this picture has some validity, it is by no means a wholly accurate one. Many of the difficulties in Beethoven's social dealings stemmed from two factors, an unfavourable childhood and chronic illness. By the age of twenty-eight he had already experienced profound hearing loss, to the detriment of his self-esteem and the jeopardy of his professional and artistic future. His life was also made miserable by intractable diarrhoea and abdominal pain. The crisis Beethoven underwent at Heiligenstadt in 1802 was to plague his life and make him the isolated being familiar to us.

To appreciate the genesis of Beethoven's problems, we must return to his formative years. He was born in Bonn in 1770, the second son of Johann van Beethoven who was the court tenor and something of a drunkard and a wastrel. (Ludwig's date of birth is unknown; he was baptized on 17 December.) The household was not a happy one and certainly not a fitting one for a child of genius (27, pp. 32, 39–50; 18, vol. 1). Beethoven's idol was his grandfather, a distinguished old man

who had been court Kapellmeister. It was Beethoven's ambition throughout his life to hold the position and emulate his illustrious grandfather,
whose portrait he always carried with him (27, pp. 25–7, 32–3).
Beethoven loved his mother, Maria Magdalena, but she was unrespon-
sive towards his affection. Her life with Johann was difficult and she
devoted little time to the young Ludwig.

Beethoven's early education seems to have been poor and he did
not distinguish himself. At school, he mixed little with the other boys,
his grades were low and his appearance dirty and neglected. He showed
musical precocity but his musical education was precarious and
influenced by the destructive relationship between himself and his father.
Beethoven's father, who was his earliest teacher, recognized the phenomenal aptitude of the child. He was proud of having fathered him yet
angry because the boy underlined his own mediocrity. There may have
been frequent beatings; certainly the father discouraged Beethoven's
improvisations – the first indications of an exceptional talent. Johann
was also something of a charlatan: seeking to make money from the
child prodigy, he passed Ludwig off as being two years younger than
he was (18, 27). Fortunately, Beethoven's later education was attended
to by Christian Gottlob Neefe, the court organist, who encouraged the
boy and taught him much (27, p. 53).

When Beethoven left Bonn for Vienna in 1792, he was already an
accomplished musician and piano player, and was eagerly sought after
in the salons. Czerny talked about Beethoven's 'titanic execution' and
excused Beethoven's frequent breaking of strings at concerts as merely
the result of the composer demanding more from the primitive pianos
of the day than they were capable of. He also spoke of Beethoven's
listeners being moved to tears by his improvisations. Thus the early
Vienna years were years of success and glamour for the young performer.

His first compositions, the piano trios, also received very favourable
reviews. He was, then, a justifiably confident young man with a great
future. At the time of this success, Beethoven took a good deal of care
with his personal appearance. He dressed neatly and strove for more
courtly manners. Although small (about 165 cm) and swarthy, with a
slightly pock-marked face, he was by no means regarded as being unat-
tractive. His natural impulsiveness, temperament and lack of general
education sometimes showed him up socially yet, in the main, he was
a sought-after and by no means ungainly figure (18).

The myth of Beethoven's virginity was popularized by Schindler,
his confidant of the latter years and his first biographer. We know from

Ries and earlier contemporaries, however, that during the earlier days in Vienna Beethoven enjoyed an active social and sexual life. Impulsiveness, ambivalence and a disordered and idiosyncratic lifestyle kept him from longer-term relationships with women, but he was not misogynous: he took pleasure in the company of women and appreciated female beauty. More platonic relationships with his female admirers lasted for many years (9, p. 55; 27, p. 365).

Crises in his health intervened abruptly at a time when Beethoven's success seemed assured. Deafness and abdominal pain made his life pitiable and thwarted social interaction. Within a few years of the onset of these illnesses, Beethoven's physical appearance had changed. Observers now referred to him as an 'original caveman' or 'fantastic gargoyle' or 'simian' in his ugliness. He became so negligent of his appearance and attire that on being lost in town one day he was locked away in jail as a tramp (27, pp. 357–9). Let us trace the evolution of the composer's illnesses and note their effects on his life.

RESPIRATORY ILLNESS

Beethoven suffered from asthma. There are frequent references to respiratory infection throughout his life and many to his 'weak chest'. We need not necessarily conclude that the composer had tuberculosis, as many biographers have done, although Beethoven's mother and infant sister are said to have died of this condition. Tuberculosis was overdiagnosed in the nineteenth century. No autopsy was performed to confirm the diagnosis. His father was rumoured to have syphilis but, again, the evidence is far from conclusive. (The view that Beethoven had congenital syphilis has been discredited. His skull did not show the stigmata of this condition.) Dr Davies contends that Johann Beethoven died of congestive heart failure (35).

CHRONIC PANCREATITIS

The next illness to emerge in Beethoven's medical history is the bowel disease that he referred to as 'colic'. This caused central abdominal pain and was often associated with diarrhoea. In 1812 the illness confined Beethoven to his bed and caused dehydration and prostration. The disease increased in its frequency and severity as Beethoven aged. The first attack occurred in 1801 when the composer was 31. Associated with these attacks was anorexia, and consequently Beethoven ate irregularly and poorly when he experienced 'colic'. Initially he began to drink heavily to ease these abdominal pains, but later in life he found that alcohol exacerbated the condition. There is no mention of bloody diarrhoea or melaena[1] (9, p. 221).

The 'irritable bowel syndrome' has been postulated for these recurrent abdominal pains. This is unlikely as it does not lead to dehydration or prostration. Beethoven's autopsy provides a likely explanation for the disease. It was found that 'the pancreas was ... hard and firm, its excretory duct being as wide as a goose quill'. This is suggestive of chronic pancreatitis. Beethoven did not suffer from gallstones and the bowel was presumably macroscopically normal. The doctors performing the autopsy remarked that the bowel was 'much dilated with air, but provided no evidence for a stricture causing a partial bowel obstruction nor did they note any mucosal abnormalities[2] to suggest inflammatory bowel disease. Indeed, a bowel dilated with air is a common postmortem finding in those suffering from cirrhosis, according to Sherlock (32). The aetiological factor responsible for pancreatitis was probably alcohol. Beethoven died of liver disease, further evidence of possible end organ disease caused by alcohol. Moreover, dilatation of the pancreatic ducts is highly suggestive of alcohol-induced pancreatitis (32).

Beethoven's life was marked by stress from an early age. His colic emerges as a symptom at the period when he was beginning to become deaf. His promising career was under threat and he was, according to his will, written in 1802, beginning to isolate himself from his fellow men to disguise his affliction. It is likely, therefore, that he was drinking heavily at this period; the emerging colic perhaps afforded him a socially acceptable excuse for his drinking.

Thayer, one of Beethoven's early biographers, suspected strongly that Beethoven had a problem with alcohol. Thayer was a Bostonian who travelled to Europe to chronicle the life of his boyhood hero. It is said that he developed psychosomatic headaches when he learned more about Beethoven's erratic lifestyle. The composer did not fit the heroic model proposed by his friend Schindler, his first biographer, who had destroyed many of the 'conversation books'. The real Beethoven existed behind a smokescreen carefully constructed for posterity by his ambitious friend. It is said that Thayer discovered aspects of Beethoven's conduct which were so alarming that in his determination to discourage their further

[1] a sign of bleeding from the upper bowel
[2] changes in the bowel wall

spread he would not print them (27, pp. 10–12).

What is appearing from current Beethoven study is the picture of a man who is an object not of scorn but of pity. Beethoven emerged by hard work from a difficult childhood with little parental love into a world of success and recognition. At the crucial point in his career deafness intervened and threatened to take this success from him. He was demoralized and disillusioned, and underwent a crisis of spiritual belief which threatened to destroy his sanity. He contemplated suicide. Beethoven resolved this crisis by devoting himself completely to composition, making of it the means through which he could express his benevolent and humanitarian impulses. He sublimated all to music, and his private life became one of emotional disarray and increasing isolation (12, pp. 38–9).

BEETHOVEN AND ALCOHOL

Thayer strongly suspected that alcohol was the aetiological agent responsible for both Beethoven's physical problems and his bizarre behaviour. He conscientiously recorded the cost of Beethoven's wine purchases and noted a consistently high alcohol consumption – a pattern of drinking which slowly causes end organ damage over a long period.

Andreas Wawruch,[3] who attended Beethoven in his final illness, wrote a detailed summary of Beethoven's medical history (reproduced below as Appendix 2, Document 2); it is dated 20 May 1827, a few months after the composer's death. He implicated alcohol as the causal agent of Beethoven's illness along with poor nutrition which may have exacerbated the pathological effects of alcohol on his body. The noting of a concomitant nutritional disease shows Wawruch's astuteness as a physician.

Wawruch tells us that Beethoven began to drink ostensibly to control diffuse abdominal symptoms resembling irritable bowel syndrome. He dated Beethoven's alcohol consumption and abdominal pain to the time when his deafness and tinnitus evolved – around his thirtieth year. Beethoven then drank heavily for twenty-six years. He was not necessarily drunk or intemperate: those who consume large doses of alcohol over a twenty-four-hour period can develop cirrhosis without becoming obviously inebriated. Wawruch also tells us that Beethoven had a near-fatal attack of hepatitis seven years before he died. He did not cut down

[3] Wawruch's forenames are given variously as Andreas Ignaz and Anton Johann in the literature.

on his drinking despite the advice of his doctors, denying vigorously that it was a problem. Wawruch's testimony links Beethoven's digestive problems with his deafness.

Beethoven, then, suffered over a seven-year period from recurrent bouts of abdominal pain, exacerbated by alcohol. This suggests chronic pancreatitis, which was confirmed at autopsy. He had recurrent bouts of hepatitis and jaundice but refused to stop drinking. Even Schindler, the staunch defender of the composer's posthumous reputation, admits to alcohol as the cause of Beethoven's illness. He mentions Beethoven's fondness for punch and adulterated wines in his biography of 1840, but tactfully implies that it was the poor quality of the wines which caused Beethoven's demise: 'Among wines he preferred the Hungarian Ofen variety. Unfortunately he liked best the adulterated wine which did damage to his weak intestines. Warnings were of no avail in this case. Our master also liked a good glass of beer in the evening ... Beethoven still often visited the taverns and coffee houses in his last years.'

Beethoven's secretary, Karl Holz, noted that his employer 'drank a great deal of wine at table, but could stand a great deal, and in merry company he sometimes became tipsy.' Later, a paradoxical decline in Beethoven's alcohol tolerance was noted by his friends. He died of cirrhotic liver failure. The disease was of at least five years' duration and for some months before he died he wore a bandage around his abdomen, which was chronically distended by ascites. Beethoven's consumption of alcohol remained high during the last five years of his life. During his last illness one of his physicians ordered an alcoholic iced punch as a palliative treatment for his illness. The palliation had to be withdrawn because it was noted that the patient abused his medication (9, p. 224; 27, pp. 396, 358–9).

DEAFNESS

The most famous of Beethoven's illnesses is his deafness; its cause is still controversial. Psychologically, it devastated Beethoven and he poured out his frustration, misery and paranoia in the Heiligenstadt testament of 1802 (see below, Appendix 1). Despite its obvious exaggerations, this is the most touching and personal of Beethoven's letters; it also highlights some of the strange paradoxes of his character. The will is addressed to his two brothers, for whom Beethoven professes deep affection; however, the name of his brother Johann is not written down in the will: there is a blank space ominously left in the text three times. This omission is tangible evidence of the ambivalence Beethoven felt towards many of those close to him. He did not approve of his brother's marriage – he referred to his sister-in-law as 'the Queen of the Night' – and had found it unbearable to address his brother by his first name since his marriage (18).

The testament is a will which Beethoven made at or shortly after the lowest ebb of his depression. He contemplated suicide but decided that his art justified his existence. He wrote:

> for the last six years I have been afflicted with an incurable complaint which has been made worse by incompetent doctors ... I was soon obliged to seclude myself and live in solitude ... Alas! how could I possibly refer to the impairing *of a sense* which in me should be more perfectly developed than in other people, a sense which at one time I possessed in the greatest perfection ... Joyfully I go to meet Death – should it come before I have had an opportunity of developing all my artistic gifts, then in spite of my hard fate it would still come too soon ... Farewell; and when I am dead, do not wholly forget me. (17).

Despite a slightly exaggerated and histrionic tone, the testament is a succinct appraisal of Beethoven's situation and the direction his life was to take. His sensitivity and his pride would isolate him from society; art and creativity would increasingly become his purpose in life.

In a letter to his friend Franz Gerhard Wegeler in 1801, Beethoven himself provides a very good clinical description of his already severe deafness: 'I have to place myself quite close to the orchestra in order to understand what the actor is saying ... at a distance I cannot hear high notes of instruments or voices ... Sometimes too I can scarcely hear a person who speaks softly; I can hear sounds, it is true, but cannot make out the words. But if anyone shouts, I can't bear it.' (17, vol. 1, p. 60) Beethoven's deafness began in his left ear and soon afterwards the right ear was affected. The deafness grew progressively worse and it was accompanied by tinnitus, a sensation of ringing or, rather, roaring in the ears. Beethoven's illness began shortly before his twenty-eighth year and by his thirty-ninth year the constantly droning tinnitus would drive him to the brink of suicide: 'If I did not know what I must do I would kill myself.' Beethoven's letter to Wegeler indicates that his deafness was profound by 1800. While there may have been a further progressive element to the disease, most of the pathology was established by this time.

By 1815, Beethoven was almost stone deaf. The conversation books start about 1817. Mercifully, when Beethoven became totally deaf, the tinnitus ceased. Beethoven did not experience vertigo or symptoms attributable to vestibular disease, making Menière's disease[4] an unlikely diagnosis (11, 18, 27). The decline in Beethoven's piano playing paralleled the course of his deafness. The violin virtuoso Louis Spohr attended a rehearsal of the Trio in D in Beethoven's house and described the event in his autobiography in terms that show all too vividly the composer's now pathetic condition.

> It was not an enjoyable experience. In the first place, the piano was terribly out of tune – which did not trouble Beethoven in the least, since he could not hear it. In addition, little or nothing remained of the brilliant technique which used to be so much admired. In the loud passages the poor deaf man hammered away at the keys smudging whole groups of notes and unless one followed the score one lost all sense of the melody. I was deeply moved by the tragedy of it all – Beethoven's melancholy was no mystery to me. (9, p. 100)

Medical science has not reached the final verdict on the cause of Beethoven's deafness. The medical world is divided as to whether the deafness was due to direct damage to the auditory nerve, causing sensorineural deafness, or to thickening and fixation of the ossicles, the three bones which conduct sound through the middle ear (otosclerosis). The autopsy report describes the ear and brain in some detail but, surprisingly, the ossicles are not mentioned in the report. Johann Wagner, who performed the autopsy, saved the ossicles and the petrous portions of the temporal bones for later examination, but the bones were lost. Beethoven's body was exhumed twice, in 1863 and 1888: the missing ossicles were not found. Without them, otosclerosis cannot be excluded from the differential diagnosis of Beethoven's disease (14).

The description of the ear and brain at postmortem is as follows:

> The external ear was large and regularly formed; the scaphoid fossa, but more especially the concha, was very spacious and half as large again as usual; the various angles and sinuosities were strongly marked. The external auditory canal was covered with shiny scales, particularly in the vicinity of the tympanum which was concealed by them. The eustachian tube was much thickened, its mucous lining swollen and somewhat contracted about the osseous portion of the tube. In front of its orifice and

---

[4] a common cause of deafness and vertigo

towards the tonsils some dimpled scars were observable. The principal cells of the mastoid process, which was large and not marked by any notch, were lined with a vascular mucous membrane. The whole substance of the petrous temporal bone showed a similar degree of vascularity, being traversed by vessels of considerable size, more particularly in the region of the cochlea, the membranous part of its spiral lamina appearing slightly reddened.

The facial nerves were of unusual thickness; the auditory nerves, on the contrary, were shrivelled and devoid of their sheaths; the accompanying arteries were dilated to more than the size of a crow quill and cartilaginous. The left auditory nerve, much the thinnest, arises by three very thin greyish striae, the right by one strong clear white stria from the substance of the fourth ventricle which was at this point much more consistent and vascular than in other parts. The convolutions of the brain were full of water, and remarkably white; they appeared very much deeper, wider and more numerous than ordinary. The calvarium[5] exhibited throughout great density and a thickness amounting to about half an inch. (14, 25, 33)

DIAGNOSTIC POSSIBILITIES

Otosclerosis is the commonest cause of deafness in a man of twenty-eight years, but the high-frequency hearing loss described by Beethoven is not typical of the condition and makes the diagnosis doubtful. Cochlear otosclerosis[6] is rare in such a young patient. Many cases of deafness still defy medical explanation, and even with modern diagnostic methods it is possible that if Beethoven were alive today no cause for his ailment would be found.

Johann Wagner in the autopsy report identified the auditory nerves;

[5] vault of the skull

[6] This is a form of otosclerosis complicated by secondary degeneration of the cochlea, an organ of the inner ear which converts mechanical sound waves into nervous impulses. It causes profound deafness and the 'hearing' loss also involves high frequencies. Although an early account of uncomplicated otosclerosis exists (Antonio Valsalva described ankylosis of the stapes in 1791), it was not until the late nineteenth century that the pathology and symptomatology of the condition was comprehensively understood: Adam Politzer coined the term 'otosclerosis' in 1894 when he described the microscopic pathology of the condition. Politzer's patient had committed suicide because of the dreadful tinnitus which often accompanies the condition. Beethoven's desperation can only be guessed at: it must be remembered that the pathologists who conducted the postmortem did not undertake a microscopic examination of the inner ear and its tissues, and they could not have been familiar with modern concepts of diseases of the ear. We must therefore be guarded about the validity of their statements and conclusions.

his description of them clearly indicates that he thought they were implicated in the pathological process which caused Beethoven's deafness.
The appearance of the auditory arteries seems more typical of atherosclerosis (hardening of the arteries) than of endarteritis obliterans, which
would have been seen in a chronic inflammatory condition such as
syphilis although only microscopy could confirm this.

Beethoven's hearing loss fluctuated as would be typical of syphilis,
according to Wawruch's testimony. At the outset Beethoven noted a
few remissions of his deafness, but three years later it was evident that
the condition was permanent, progressive and severe. Beethoven's deafness was preceded by a febrile illness called 'typhus' by the composer
and his early biographers – possibly meningitis due to secondary syphilis.
There are at least three cases of similar deafness described in the medical
literature (20, 21) and rapidly progressive sensorineural deafness is a
rare but widely recognized complication of secondary syphilis (30). It
has been well documented that neurosyphilis follows a very unpredictable course, and it is conceivable that Beethoven had had syphilis and
that the disease had 'burnt itself out' at an early stage without causing
more profound neurological damage; but there is no medical historical
evidence that Beethoven had parenchymal neurosyphilis or tabes dorsalis.[7] The report on the postmortem state of the brain is very cursory
indeed and no definitive statement can be made about the presence
of organic disease of the cerebral cortex from the autopsy report. There
is no record of the recurrent rash of secondary syphilis in Beethoven's
medical history. Sufferers of syphilis typically have a recurrent red,
blotchy rash.

The pathology of otosclerosis was not fully elucidated in the early
nineteenth century and there is only anecdotal evidence that the pathologists examined the ossicles; their findings (if any) are not recorded.
Otosclerosis is due to fixation of the ossicles (the bones of the middle
ear) by fibrous tissue and also by alteration in the shape of the stapes
bone. It causes profound deafness and tinnitus.

The description of the external auditory meatus with its 'scales' relates
to membranous otitis externa.[8] Thus Beethoven was correct that 'sense-
less physicians' aggravated his deafness: numerous medicaments and
mechanical devices were placed in his ears, and these caused an otitis
externa which would certainly have contributed about fifteen decibels
to Beethoven's hearing loss. Systemic remedies may also have exacer-

[7] a type of neurosyphilis that affects the spinal cord and the eyes
[8] inflammation of the outer ear – the auditory canal

48

bated Beethoven's deafness and contributed to the sensorineural component of his hearing loss.[9]

THE FINAL ILLNESS

Beethoven died of liver failure caused by cirrhosis of the liver. The mode of death was protracted coma. 'Cirrhosis' is a term used to describe a liver which has been damaged by disease. A liver showing cirrhotic change is characterized by damage to the cells and by nodular areas which represent cell regeneration.

One of the commonest causes of cirrhosis is high alcohol consumption, for which there is considerable evidence in Beethoven's case. The account of his final years was expurgated by his friend, Schindler, who destroyed the majority of the 400 conversation books (records of Beethoven's everyday conversations) on the grounds that they contained either trivia or politically sensitive material. Modern scholars are disinclined to believe this. It is their view that Schindler edited the conversation books to disguise the pitiful emotional disarray of Beethoven's last years; Beethoven's alcohol intake, it is suggested, was in large part a response to ill-health and the sad repercussions of the wranglings over the custody of his nephew Karl. Schindler's 'editing' of the conversation books can be seen as a service to his friend to prevent misunderstanding and to perpetuate the heroic image of the composer. Doctors will be aware of the difficulties of eliciting a history of alcoholism in their present-day patients, let alone tracing this habit in a man who died over 150 years ago. Beethoven's cirrhotic liver disease was of long standing; the liver was grossly shrunken, and splenomegaly[10] due to portal hypertension[11] was seen. Beethoven was plagued by

[9] Although there is no definitive explanation of Beethoven's deafness, the author favours the diagnosis of otosclerosis. Syphilis is still considered the cause by many German otologists, and, indeed, syphilitic deafness was common during the early nineteenth century. However, it is doubtful that syphilis could have produced isolated neurological damage without more profoundly affecting Beethoven's physical well-being. Syphilis is typically a multisystem disease.

The atypical features of Beethoven's otosclerosis are accounted for by iatrogenic illness (i.e. caused by his doctors) and by possible involvement of the cochlea. That Beethoven's physicians exacerbated his hearing loss is evident from the post mortem and from contemporary biographical literature (see pp. 60 ff.).

Rare connective tissue diseases such as polyarteritis nodosa can also cause deafness, as can other auto-immune diseases. Davies has noted this in his recent article on Beethoven's deafness (35).

[10] enlargement of the spleen

[11] increased blood pressure in the veins leading to the liver

pyoderma[12] during his last few years, suggesting that his resistance to infectious disease was lowered by hepatic disease. He was also beset with nose bleeds and haemoptysis[13] suggesting thrombocytopenia due to hypersplenism (enlargement of the spleen, which hinders blood clotting) (9, pp. 168, 221).

In 1821, Beethoven became ill with jaundice which lasted for several months. It had remitted by September of that year. His physicians wisely restricted his intake of wine. The disease progressed slowly over the next five years and was marked by recurrent attacks of jaundice and hepatitis. There were several attacks of jaundice in 1825 and hepatic failure may have emerged slowly and progressively during this year. (9, p. 221).

By November 1826 Beethoven was beset with his mortal illness. It occurred when he left Vienna for the country to work on the quartets Opp. 130 and 135. Even as he left Vienna, Beethoven was suffering from mild symptoms which may be related to decompensated cirrhosis. He felt weak and anorectic, and his abdomen was distended. This distension was presumably due to ascites, fluid which collects in the abdomen as a consequence of liver failure. Beethoven also complained of dependency oedema (swelling of the ankles) for many months before the onset of his final illness (9, p. 221). Beethoven initially ignored the warning signs of illness: he kept composing, often outdoors in inclement weather. His condition continued to deteriorate. He developed the symptoms of cough and fever and, fearing a serious impending illness, made a slow journey back to Vienna in the rain. By the time he reached Vienna, an illness resembling pneumonia declared itself. This infection probably triggered the terminal phase of Beethoven's illness. (Infection is a prominent cause of liver failure in those with established liver disease.)

Beethoven consulted Andreas Wawruch, who noted that he was severely short of breath, coughed blood and complained of a pain in the right side of the chest. He was treated with bed rest and his health gradually improved over the next five days. He recommenced work on an oratorio, *Saul and David* (9, p. 225). On the seventh night of his illness, however, Beethoven suddenly developed severe vomiting and diarrhoea. Jaundice declared itself the next morning, and deepened over the next week; his abdomen continued to distend owing to the accumulation of fluid. Beethoven's ankles began to swell severely, and

---

[12] infection of the skin
[13] expectoration of blood

breathlessness and choking plagued his nights. He became anuric and began to experience paroxysmal nocturnal dyspnoea (a type of breathlessness occurring when the body is overloaded with fluid).

By the third week, Wawruch recommended paracentesis (tapping of the ascitic fluid). This procedure was carried out, and 11 litres of straw-coloured fluid was produced. Beethoven's relief was marred by a severe infection which developed in the wound site, no doubt caused by the non-sterile instruments of the day. Careful dressing of the infected wound halted the progression to gangrene. From the autopsy it is also evident that the procedure produced a low-grade peritonitis. Tapping of the fluid was only a palliative measure and could not alter the progressive course of the disease. Three subsequent operations were performed (the second yielding 22 litres of fluid). Beethoven became increasingly anorectic and emaciated. Loss of plasma proteins in the ascitic fluid would have exacerbated his liver disease. The paracentesis wound did not close and continuously leaked ascitic fluid.

Dr Giovanni Malfatti, a friend of the composer, was asked to attend him and consented. He prescribed an alcoholic iced punch which helped Beethoven to sleep for the first time in weeks. Encouraged by the effects of the punch, Beethoven began to consume large quantities of the beverage. This exacerbated his cirrhotic liver failure and he became semi-comatose and irrational. Thenceforth, alcohol was restricted, although he procured and enjoyed some Rhenish wine (9, p. 225).

It has been suggested that Beethoven's physicians provided inappropriate treatment which hastened the composer's death. This is a rather harsh judgment: the presence of tense ascites and of long-standing hypersplenism and profound portal hypertension point to the inescapable conclusion that the composer was probably terminally ill. Although the leaking paracentesis possibly abrogated all hope of recovery, it also relieved the pain caused by the tense ascites as did the alcohol and sedatives administered by the physicians. (There is a current tendency among French and Spanish physicians to treat similar patients palliatively with paracentesis (31).)

Deterioration continued more slowly over the next three months. Beethoven became an unruly and questioning patient. Depression, no doubt spurred by the realization of impending death, set in. On 24 March 1827 he received Extreme Unction, afterwards writing in his conversation book, 'Plaudite, amici, comedia finita est.' A few hours after receiving the last rites, Beethoven became comatose, his breathing increasingly laboured.

26 March was a stormy day. At 6.00 p.m., at the height of the storm, Beethoven was roused by a loud thunderclap and seemed to shake his fist at the heavens. He collapsed back to his pillow and died (9, pp. 219, 221). The story of Beethoven apparently 'shaking his fist at the heavens' in one final act of defiance before oblivion has been dismissed as a romantic fiction by most Beethoven biographers. Surprisingly, it is an accurate clinical observation: people who die of hepatic failure often act in an exaggerated way to sudden stimuli such as bright light. This is due to the accumulation of toxic waste products normally excreted by the liver. Beethoven's gesture may be seen as having been due to the cerebral irritation which accompanies hepatic failure, not as a conscious act.

The cause of Beethoven's death – liver failure due to cirrhosis – was confirmed by the autopsy performed by Johann Wagner and Karl von Rokitansky. In cirrhosis, the liver responds to damage with regenerative nodules. These were clearly seen in the postmortem examination. The description of the thorax and abdomen is worth quoting in its entirety.

> The cavity of the chest, together with the organs within it, was in the normal condition. In the cavity of the abdomen, 8 litres of greyish-brown turbid fluid was effused. The liver appeared shrunk up to half its proper volume, of a leathery consistency and greenish-blue colour, and was beset with knots, the size of a bean, on its tuberculated surface, as well as in its substance; all its vessels were very much narrowed, and bloodless. The gallbladder contained a dark-brown fluid, besides an abundance of gravelly sediments. The spleen was found to be more than double its proper size, dark coloured and firm. The pancreas was equally hard and firm, its excretory duct being as wide as a goose quill. The stomach, together with the bowels, was greatly distended with air. Both kidneys were invested by a parenchymal [cellular] membrane an inch thick, and infiltrated with a brown turbid fluid; their tissue was pale red when cut. Every one of their calyces was occupied by a calcified concretion of wart-like shape and as large as a split pea.[14] The body was much emaciated and was covered with black petechiae.[15] (14)

The essential feature of the autopsy was thus macronodular cirrhosis of long standing with concomitant portal hypertension. Macronodular cirrhosis is less common than micronodular cirrhosis in alcoholic liver

---

[14] i.e. kidney stones
[15] black spots

disease but certainly occurs frequently. The brown turbid fluid represented infected ascites. The changes in the kidneys were probably due to renal stones, parenchymal oedema and chronic pyelonephritis. By modern standards the autopsy is incomplete, but it provides us with much information about Beethoven's illness. The strong likelihood of concomitant pancreatitis combined with a history of high alcohol intake makes alcohol by far the most likely agent responsible for Beethoven's disease. The green colouring of the liver was due to bile stasis[16] caused by infection.

The evidence for tertiary syphilis causing Beethoven's liver disease is far from convincing. Syphilis usually causes enlargement of the liver due to infiltration of tumour-like 'gummata'; Beethoven's liver was small and contracted. Syphilitic cirrhosis is a rare entity and usually occurs in combination with alcohol abuse. Chronic active hepatitis due to viral or auto-immune disease is a possibility, but it is not necessary to invoke this as an explanation in a patient known to have been drinking heavily over a thirty-year period (28).

Beethoven's funeral, like that of Chopin, was a major public event; a crowd of ten thousand is said to have attended the ceremony. The Viennese regarded Beethoven highly and, knowing him to be a genius and an eccentric, were intimately curious about his habits and lifestyle. Many musicians and other public figures were present at Beethoven's death bed and lying in state, and have left accounts that show an attitude to death in the nineteenth century which differs markedly from that of the present day. They were curious and matter-of-fact and not over-sentimental about death, for early death was then a frequent occurrence. Franz von Hartmann's account of his visit to Beethoven's death bed is typical:

On the 29th March, 1827, I contemplated the body of the divine Beethoven who died the day before yesterday at 6.00 in the evening. Already entering his room, which is large and somewhat neglected, I was moved by its desolate look ... No monument had as yet been erected but he still lay on the mattress of his bed. A cover was spread over him and a venerable old man ... uncovered him for me. There I saw his splendid face which, unhappily, I had never been able to see in life. Such a heavenly dignity lay spread over him despite the disfigurement he was said to have suffered that I could scarcely look my fill. I departed full of emotion and only

---

[16] obstruction of the bile flow

when I was down stairs could I have wept for not having begged the old man to cut me off a few of his hairs.

Ferdinand Sauter, whom I had arranged to meet but whom I had missed, ran across me and I turned back with him telling him of my plan. The old man showed him to us once more and he uncovered the chest for us which, like the grossly swollen abdomen, was already quite blue. The smell of corruption was very strong already. We passed a gratuity into the old man's hand and asked him for the hair from Beethoven's head. He shook his head and motioned us to be silent. So we sadly trundled down the stairs when suddenly the old man softly called us from the banisters upstairs asking us to wait at the gate until the three fops had departed who were viewing the dead hero ... issuing from the door and putting his fingertips to his lips, he gave us the hair in a piece of paper and vanished. (18, vol. 1, p. 227)

Franz Schubert was one of the thirty-six torch bearers at the funeral. Beethoven's body now rests in the central cemetery in Vienna next to Schubert's and a monument to Mozart, whose burial site is unknown.

At the time of his death, Beethoven was still at the height of his powers as a composer, and his new oratorio was to have been as powerful a work as the Ninth Symphony or the Mass in D. Beethoven's illnesses were far more intense than many of his biographers have indicated. Many of the 'character disparities' noted in Solomon's 'psychological' biography of Beethoven were actually occasioned by severe, organic illness (27). Isolated, physically frail, often sick and in pain, Beethoven's life and creativity are witness to the struggle which is a part of the human condition. He wrote of the often difficult genesis of his works: 'The true artist has no pride; unhappily he realises that art has no limitations. He feels darkly how far he is from the goal and, while perhaps he is admired by others, he has not yet reached the point where the better genius will shine before him like the distant sun.'

TABLE 1

Cause of Beethoven's deafness as postulated by his medical biographers
(1816–1988)

POST TYPHUS/MENINGITIS	Weissenbach	(1816) [cited in (18)]
POST TRAUMATIC SENSORINEURAL	Von Frimmel	(1880)
SYPHILIS:		
(a) Meningiovascular	Jacobsohn	(1910)
(b) Congenital	Kloz-Forest	(1905)
(c) Early	McCabe	(1958)
OTOSCLEROSIS	Sorsby	(1930)
VASCULAR INSUFFICIENCY	Stevens, Hemenway	(1970)
COCHLEAR OTOSCLEROSIS	Stevens, Hemenway	(1970)
PAGET'S DISEASE OF BONE	Naiken	(1971)
IATROGENIC	Gutt	(1970)
AUTO-IMMUNE SENSORINEURAL	Davies	(1988)

(The favoured diagnosis is cochlear otosclerosis.)

TABLE 2

Causes of Beethoven's liver disease as postulated by his medical biographers

ALCOHOL-INDUCED CIRRHOSIS (exacerbated by malnutrition)
A. Wawruch (1827)
S. J. London (1964)
G. Böhme (1981)
F. H. Franken (1986)
A. Newmayr (1987)

AUTO-IMMUNE – Chronic Active Hepatitis
E. Larkin (1971)
Aterman et al. (1982)
(This is the principal differential diagnosis)

POST VIRAL INFECTION (Endemic Hepatitis B)
M. Piroth (1960)
P. C. Adams (1987)

SYPHILITIC CIRRHOSIS (unlikely)
L. Jacobsohn (1910)
E. Newman (1927)

REFERENCES

1. *Actenmäßige Darstellung der Ausgrabung und Wiederbeisetzung der irdischen Reste von Beethoven und Schubert* (Vienna, 1863)
2. R. Wallace, *Beethoven's Letters* (New York, 1867)
3. J. Paget, 'On a Form of Chronic Inflammation of Bones (Osteitis deformans)', *Medico-chirurgical Transactions*, 60 (1877), p. 37
4. T. von Frimmel, *Beethovens Leiden und Ende* (Vienna, 1880)
5. J. Paget, 'Additional Cases of Osteitis deformans', *Medico-chirurgical Transactions*, 65 (1882), p. 225
6. C. Langer von Edenberg, 'Die Cranien dreier musikalischer Koryphäen', *Mitteilungen der Antropologischen Gesellschaft Wein*, 17: *Sitzungsbericht vom 19.4.1887*
7. Kloz-Forest, 'La Surdité de Beethoven', *La Chronique Médicale*, 12 (1905), pp. 321–31
8. Kloz-Forest, 'Les Infirmités du génie', *La Chronique Médicale*, 13 (1906), p. 209
9. O. G. Sonneck (ed.), *Beethoven: Impressions by his Contemporaries* (New York, 1926, reprinted 1972; London, 1927)
10. L. Jacobsohn, *Deutsche medizinische Wochenschrift*, 53 (1927), pp. 1610–12
11. E. Newman, *The Unconscious Beethoven* (London and New York, 1927)
12. M. Sorsby, 'Beethoven's Deafness', *Journal of Laryngology and Otology*, 45 (1930), p. 529
13. W. Schweisheimer, 'Beethoven's Physicians', *The Musical Quarterly*, 30 (1944), pp. 289–90
14. W. Forster, *Beethovens Krankheiten und ihre Beurteilung* (Wiesbaden, 1955)
15. B. F. McCabe, 'Beethoven's Deafness', *Annals of Otology, Rhinology and Laryngology*, 67 (1958), pp. 192–206
16. M. Piroth, *Beethoven Jahrbuch* (1959–60), pp. 7–35
17. E. Anderson (trans. and ed.), *The Letters of Beethoven* (London, 1961)
18. E. Forbes (ed.), *Thayer's Life of Beethoven* (Princeton, 1964, 2nd edn 1967)
19. S. J. London, *Archives of Internal Medicine*, 113 (1964), pp. 442–5
20. R. R. Wilcox, 'Nerve Deafness in Early Syphilis', *British Journal of Venereal Diseases*, 41 (1965), p. 300
21. T. J. Balkany and P. E. Dans, 'Reversible Sudden Deafness in Early Syphilis', *Archives of Otolaryngology*, 10 (1968), p. 466
22. R. W. Gutt, 'Beethoven's Deafness an Iatrogenic Disease', *Medizinische Klinik*, 65 (1970), pp. 2294–5
23. K. M. Stevens and W. G. Hemenway, 'Beethoven's Deafness', *Journal of the American Medical Association*, 213 (1970), pp. 434–7
24. E. Larkin, 'Beethoven's Illness: A Likely Diagnosis', *Proceedings of the Royal Society of Medicine*, 64 (1971), pp. 493–6

25. V. S. Naiken, 'Did Beethoven have Paget's Disease of Bone?', *Annals of Internal Medicine*, 74 (1971), pp. 995–9
26. A. Czeizel, *Lancet* (1977), p. 1127
27. M. Solomon, *Beethoven* (New York and London, 1977), pp. 10, 12, 23–51, 53, 93–106, 225–407
28. S. L. Robbins and R. S. Cotran, *Pathologic Basis of Disease*, 2nd edn (Philadelphia, 1981), pp. 406–10, 1021, 1041–56
29 Aterman et al., *Canadian Medical Association Journal*, 126 (1982), pp. 623–8
30. K. K. Holmes (ed.), *Sexually Transmitted Diseases* (New York, 1984), pp. 288–380
31. Qunitero et al., *Lancet* (1985), pp. 611–12
32. S. Sherlock, *Diseases of the Liver and Biliary System*, 7th edn (London, 1985), pp. 78–177, 250–73, 334–62
33. W. Jesserer and H. Bankl, 'Ertaubte Beethoven an einer Pagetschen Krankheit?', *Laryngologie, Rhinologie, Otologie* [Stuttgart], 65 (1986), pp. 592–7
34. P. C. Adams, 'Historical Hepatology: Ludwig van Beethoven', *Journal of Gastroenterology and Hepatology* (1987), no. 2, pp. 375–9
35. P. J. Davies, 'Beethoven's Deafness: A New Theory', *Medical Journal of Australia*, 149 (1988), pp. 644–9
36. P. Harrison, 'The Effects of Deafness on Musical Composition', *Journal of the Royal Society of Medicine*, 81 (1988), p. 598

APPENDIX 1

The Heiligenstadt Testament

To Caspar Anton Carl and [Nikolaus Johann]
van Beethoven

Heiligenstadt, *October 6*, 1802

For my Brothers Carl and [Johann] Beethoven

O my fellow men, who consider me or describe me as unfriendly, peevish or even misanthropic, how greatly do you wrong me. For you do not know the secret reason why I appear to you to be so. Ever since my childhood my heart and soul have been imbued with the tender feeling of goodwill; and I have always been ready to perform even great actions. But just think, for the last six years I have been afflicted with an incurable complaint which has been made worse by incompetent doctors. From year to year my hopes of being cured have gradually been shattered and finally I have been forced to accept the prospect of a *permanent infirmity* (the curing of which may perhaps take years or may even prove to be impossible). Though endowed with a passionate and lively temperament and even fond of the distractions offered by society I was soon obliged to seclude myself and live in solitude. If at times I decided

57

just to ignore my infirmity, alas! how cruelly was I then driven back by the intensified sad experience of my poor hearing. Yet I could not bring myself to say to people: 'Speak up, shout, for I am deaf'. Alas! how could I possibly refer to the impairing *of a sense* which in me should be more perfectly developed than in other people, a sense which at one time I possessed in the greatest perfection, even to a degree of perfection such as assuredly few in my profession possess or have ever possessed – Oh, I cannot do it; so forgive me, if you ever see me withdrawing from your company which I used to enjoy. Moreover my misfortune pains me doubly, in as much as it leads to my being misjudged. For me there can be no relaxation in human society, no refined conversations, no mutual confidences. I must live quite alone and may creep into society only as often as sheer necessity demands; I must live like an outcast. If I appear in company, I am overcome by a burning anxiety, a fear that I am running the risk of letting people notice my condition – And that has been my experience during the last six months which I have spent in the country. My sensible doctor by suggesting that I should spare my hearing as much as possible has more or less encouraged my present natural inclination, though indeed when carried away now and then by my instinctive desire for human society, I have let myself be tempted to seek it. But how humiliated I have felt if somebody standing beside me heard the sound of a flute in the distance and *I heard nothing,* or if somebody heard *a shepherd sing* and again I heard nothing – Such experiences almost made me despair, and I was on the point of putting an end to my life – The only thing that held me back was *my art.* For indeed it seemed to me impossible to leave this world before I had produced all the works that I felt the urge to compose; and thus I have dragged on this miserable existence – a truly miserable existence, seeing that I have such a sensitive body that any fairly sudden change can plunge me from the best spirits into the worst of humours – *Patience* – that is the virtue, I am told, which I must now choose for my guide; and I now possess it – I hope that I shall persist in my resolve to endure to the end, until it pleases the inexorable Parcae to cut the thread; perhaps my condition will improve, perhaps not; at any rate I am now resigned – At the early age of 28 I was obliged to become a philosopher, though this was not easy; for indeed this is more difficult for an artist than for anyone else – Almighty God, who look down into my innermost soul, you see into my heart and you know that it is filled with love of humanity and a desire to do good. Oh my fellow men, when some day you read this statement, remember that you have done me wrong; and let some unfortunate man derive comfort from the thought that he has found another equally unfortunate who, notwithstanding all the obstacles imposed by nature, yet did everything in his power to be raised to the rank of noble artists and human beings. – And you, my brothers Carl and [Johann], when I am dead, request on my behalf Professor Schmidt, if he is still living, to describe my disease, and attach this written document to his record, so that after my death at any rate the world and I may be reconciled as far as possible – At the same time I herewith nominate you both heirs to my small property (if I may so describe it) – Divide it honestly, live in harmony and help one another. You know that you have long ago been forgiven for the harm you did me. I again thank you, my brother Carl, in particular, for the affection you have shown me of late years. My wish is that you should have a better and more carefree existence than I have had. Urge your children to be *virtuous*, for virtue alone can make a man happy. Money cannot do this. I speak from experience. It was virtue that sustained me in my misery. It was thanks to virtue and also to my art that I did not put an end to my life by suicide – Farewell and love one another – I thank all my friends, and especially *Prince Lichnowsky* and *Professor Schmidt*. I would like Prince L[ichnowsky]'s instruments to be preserved by one of you, provided this does not lead to a quarrel between you. But as soon as they can serve a more useful purpose, just sell them; and how glad I shall be if in my grave I can still be of some use to you both – Well, that is all – Joyfully I go to meet Death – should it come before I have had an opportunity of developing all my artistic gifts, then in spite of my hard fate it would still come too soon, and no doubt I would like it to postpone its coming – Yet even so I should be content, for would it not free me from a condition of continual suffering? Come then, Death, *whenever* you like, and with courage I will go to meet you – Farewell; and when I am dead, do not wholly forget me. I deserve to be remembered by you, since during my lifetime I have often thought of you and tried to make you happy – Be happy –

Ludwig van Beethoven

For my brothers Carl and [Johann]
To be read and executed after my death –
Heiligenstadt, October 10, 1802 –Thus I take leave of you – and, what is more, rather sadly – yes, the hope I cherished – the hope I brought with me here of being cured to a certain extent at any rate – that hope I must now abandon completely. As the autumn leaves fall and wither, likewise – that hope has faded for me. I am leaving here – almost in the same condition as I arrived – Even that high courage – which has often inspired me on fine summer days – has vanished – Oh Providence – do but grant me one day *of pure joy* – For so long now the inner echo of real joy has been unknown to me – Oh when – oh when, Almighty God – shall I be able to hear and feel this echo again in the temple of Nature and in contact with humanity – Never? – No! – Oh, that would be too hard.

(*The Letters of Beethoven*, trans. and ed. Emily Anderson, Macmillan, 1961)

APPENDIX 2
Documents Relating to Beethoven's Health

1. *Extracts from Two Letters to Franz Gerhard Wegeler*

Beethoven describes the abrupt decline in his hearing and the attempts by various physicians to cure his deafness. Wegeler was one of his closest friends during the early years at Bonn.

Vienna, 29 June 1801

... You want to know something about my present state; well, at the present moment it's not so bad. My compositions are bringing in a goodly sum and, I may add, it is scarcely possible for me to execute the orders given. Also, for every work I have six, seven publishers, and if I choose, even more. They do not bargain with me; I demand and they pay. You see how pleasant it is ...

Only my envious demon, my bad health, has thrown obstacles in my way. For instance, my hearing has become weaker during the last three years. Frank wished to restore me to health by means of strengthening medicines, and to cure my deafness by means of oil of almonds, but, *prosit!* nothing came of these remedies; my hearing became worse and worse. This continued until the autumn of last year, and ofttimes I was in despair. Then an Asinus of a doctor advised cold baths, a more skilful one, the usual tepid Danube baths. These worked wonders; but my deafness remained or became worse. This winter I was truly miserable; I had terrible attacks of colic, and I fell quite back into my former state. So I remained for about four weeks, and then went to Vering. He ordered tepid Danube baths, and whenever I took one, I had to pour into it a little bottle full of strengthening stuff. He gave me no medicine until about four days ago, when he ordered pills for the stomach, and an application of herbs for the ear. And through these I can say I feel stronger and better; only the humming in my ears continues day and night without ceasing. I may truly say that my life is a wretched one. For the last two years I have avoided all society, for it is impossible for me to say to people, 'I am deaf.' Were my profession any other, it would not so much matter, but in my profession it is a terrible thing; and my enemies, of whom there are not a few, what would they say to this? To give you an idea of this extraordinary deafness, I tell you that when at the theatre, I am obliged to lean forward close to the orchestra, in order to understand what is being said on the stage. When somewhat at a distance I cannot hear the high tones of instruments, voices. In speaking it is not surprising that there are people who have never noticed it, for as a rule I am absent-minded, and they account for it in that way. Often I can scarcely hear any one speaking to me; the tones yes, but not the actual words; yet as soon as any one shouts, it is unbearable. What will come of all this, heaven only knows! Vering says that there will *certainly be improvement, though perhaps not a perfect cure.*

16 November [1801]

My Good Wegeler!

I thank you for the fresh proof of your anxiety concerning myself, and all the more as I am so little deserving of it. You want to know how I am, what I am taking; and however unwillingly I may discuss the matter, I certainly like best to do it with you. For the last few months Vering has ordered blistering plasters to be constantly placed on both arms; and these, as you will know, are composed of a certain bark. This is a most unpleasant cure, as, until the bark has sufficiently drawn, I am deprived for a day or so of the free use of my arms, to say nothing of the pain. I cannot, it is true, deny that the humming, with which my deafness actually began, has become somewhat weaker, especially in the left ear. My hearing, however, has not in the least improved; I really am not quite sure whether it has not become worse. Especially after I have taken lukewarm baths a few times, I am fairly well for 8 or 10 days. I seldom take anything strengthening for the stomach; I am now applying herbs according to your advice. Vering won't hear of shower-baths, but I am really very dissatisfied with him; he shows so little care and forbearance for such a malady; if I did not actually go to him, and that costs me a great effort, I should never see him. What is your opinion of Schmidt? I do not like making a change, yet it seems to me that Vering is too much of a practitioner to be able to take in new ideas through books. Schmidt appears to me a very different kind of man, and perhaps would not be so remiss. Wonders are told about galvanism; what do you say about it? A doctor told me he had seen a deaf and dumb child in Berlin who had recovered his hearing, also a man who had been deaf for seven years. I have just heard that your Schmidt is making experiments with it . . .

(*Beethoven's Letters*, ed. A.C. Kalischer. English trans. 1909)

2. Andreas Wawruch's Summary of Beethoven's Medical History

Ludwig van Beethoven declared that from earliest youth he had possessed a rugged, permanently good constitution, hardened by many privations, which even the most strenuous toil at his favorite occupation and continual profound study had been unable in the slightest degree to impair. The lonely nocturnal quiet always had shown itself most friendly to his glowing imagination. Hence he usually wrote after midnight until about three o'clock. A short sleep of from four to five hours was all he needed to refresh him. His breakfast eaten, he sat down at his writing-desk again until two o'clock in the afternoon.

When he entered his thirtieth year, however, he began to suffer from haemorrhoidal complaints and an annoying roaring and buzzing in both ears. Soon his hearing began to fail and, for all he often would enjoy untroubled intervals lasting for months at a time, his disability finally ended in complete deafness. All the resources of the physician's art were useless. At about the same time Beethoven noticed that his digestion began to suffer; loss of appetite was followed by indigestion, an annoying belching, and alternate obstinate constipation and frequent diarrhoea.

At no time accustomed to taking medical advice seriously, he began to develop a liking for spirituous beverages, in order to stimulate his decreasing [sic] loss of appetite and to aid his stomachic weakness by excessive use of strong punch and iced drinks and long, tiring excursions on foot. It was this very alteration of his mode of life which, some seven years earlier, had led him to the brink of the grave. He contracted a severe inflammation of the intestines which, though it yielded to treatment, later on often gave rise to intestinal pains and aching colics and which, in part, must have favored the eventual development of his mortal illness.

In the late fall of the year just passed (1826) Beethoven felt an irresistible urge, in view of the uncertain state of his health, to go to the country to recuperate. Since owing to his incurable deafness he sedulously avoided all society, he was thrown entirely upon his own resources under the most unfavorable circumstances for days and even weeks at a time. Often, with rare endurance, he worked at his compositions on a wooded hillside and his work done, still aglow with reflection, he would not infrequently run about for hours in the most inhospitable surroundings, defying every change of temperature, and often daring the heaviest snowfalls. His feet, always from time to time oedematous, would begin to swell and since (as he insisted) he had to do without every comfort of life, every solacing refreshment, his illness soon got the upper hand of him.

Intimidated by the sad prospect, in the gloomy future, of finding himself helpless in the country should he fall sick, he longed to be back in Vienna, and, as he himself jovially said, used the devil's own most wretched conveyance, a milk-wagon, to carry him home.

December was raw, wet, cold and frosty. Beethoven's clothing was anything but suited to the unkind season of the year, and yet he was driven on and away by an inner restlessness, a sinister presentiment of misfortune. He was obliged to stop overnight in a village inn, where in addition to the shelter afforded by its wretched roof he found only an unheated room without winter windows. Toward midnight he was seized with his first convulsive chills and fever, accompanied by violent thirst and pains in the side. When the fever heat began to break, he drank a couple of quarts of ice-cold water, and, in his helpless state, yearned for the first ray of dawn. Weak and ill, he had himself loaded on the open van and, finally, arrived in Vienna enervated and exhausted.

I was not sent for until the third day. I found Beethoven with grave symptoms of inflammation of the lungs; his face glowed, he spat blood, when he breathed he threatened to choke, and the shooting pain in his side only allowed him to lie in a tormenting posture flat on his back. A strict anti-inflammatory mode of treatment soon brought the desired amelioration; nature conquered and a happy crisis freed him of the seemingly imminent danger of death, so that on the fifth day he was able to sit up and relate to me with deep emotion the story of the adversities he had suffered. On the seventh day he felt so passably well that he could rise, move about, read and write.

Yet on the eighth day I was not a little alarmed. On my morning visit I found him quite upset; his entire body jaundiced; while a terrible fit of vomiting and diarrhoea during the preceding night had threatened to kill him. Violent anger, profound suffering because of ingratitude and an undeserved insult had motived the tremendous explosion. Shaking and trembling, he writhed with the pain which raged in his liver and intestines; and his feet, hitherto only moderately puffed up, were now greatly swollen.

From this time on his dropsy developed; his secretions decreased in quantity, his liver gave convincing evidence of the presence of hard knots, his jaundice grew worse. The affectionate remonstrances of his friends soon appeased the threatening excitement and Beethoven, easily conciliated, soon forgot every insult offered him. His illness, however, progressed with giant strides. Already, during the third week, nocturnal choking attacks set in; the tremendous volume of the water accumulated called for immediate relief; and I found myself compelled to advocate the abdominal puncture in order to preclude the danger of sudden bursting. After a few moments of serious reflection Beethoven agreed to submit to the operation, the more so since the Ritter von Staudenheim, who had been called in as consulting physician, urgently recommended it as being imperatively necessary. The premier chirurgeon of the General Hospital, the Mag. Chir. Hr. Seibert, made the puncture with his habitual skill, so that Beethoven when he saw the stream of water cried out happily that the operation made him think of Moses, who struck the rock with his staff and made the water gush forth. The relief was almost immediate. The liquid amounted to 25 pounds in weight, yet the afterflow must have been five times that.

Carelessness in undoing the bandage of the wound at night, probably in order quickly to remove all the water which had gathered, well-nigh put an end to all rejoicing anent the improvement in Beethoven's condition. A violent erysipelatic inflammation set in and showed incipient signs of gangrene, but the greatest care exercised in keeping the inflamed surfaces dry soon checked the evil. Fortunately the three succeeding operations were carried out without the slightest difficulty.

Beethoven knew but too well that the tappings were only palliatives and hence resigned himself to a further accumulation of water, the more so since the cold, rainy winter season favored the return of his dropsy, and could not help but strengthen the original cause of his ill, which had its existence in his chronic liver trouble as well as in organic deficiencies of the abdominal intestines.

It is a curious fact that Beethoven, even after operations successfully performed, could not stand taking any medicine, if we except gentle laxatives. His appetite diminished from day to day, and his strength could not help but decrease noticeably in consequence of the repeated large loss of vital juices. Dr Malfatti, who henceforth aided me with his advice, a friend of Beethoven's for many years and aware of the latter's inclination for spirituous beverages, therefore hit upon the idea of recommending iced punch. I must admit that this recipe worked admirably, for a few days at any rate. Beethoven felt so greatly refreshed by the iced spirits of wine that he slept through the whole of the first night, and began to sweat tremendously. He grew lively; often all sorts of witty ideas occurred to him; and he even dreamt of being able to complete the oratorio *Saul and David* which he had commenced.

Yet, as was to have been foreseen, his joy was of short duration. He began to abuse his prescription, and partook freely of the punch. Soon the alcoholic beverage called forth a powerful rush of blood to the head; he grew soporose and there was a rattle when he breathed like that of a person deeply intoxicated; he wandered in his talk and to this, at various times, was added an inflammatory pain in the neck with consequent hoarseness and even total speechlessness. He grew more violent and now, since colic and diarrhoea had resulted from the chilling of the intestines, it was high time to deprive him of this valuable stimulant.

It was under such conditions, together with a rapidly increasing loss of flesh and a noticeable falling off of his vital powers that January, February and March went by. Beethoven in gloomy hours of presentiment, foretold his approaching dissolution after his fourth tapping, nor was he mistaken. No consolation was able longer to revive him; and when I promised him that with the approaching Spring weather his sufferings would decrease, he answered with a smile: 'My day's work is done; if a physician still can be of use in my case (and then he lapsed into English) his name shall be called wonderful.' This saddening reference to Handel's *Messiah* so profoundly moved me that in my inmost soul and with the deepest emotion I was obliged to confirm the truth of what he had said.

And now the ill-fated day drew ever nearer. My noble and often burdensome professional duty as a physician bade me call my suffering friend's attention to the momentous day, so that he might comply with his civic and religious duties. With the most delicate consideration I set down the admonitory lines on a sheet of paper (for it was thus that we always had made ourselves mutually understood). Beethoven, slowly, meditatively and with incomparable self-control read what I had written, his face like that of one transfigured. Next

64

he gave me his hand in a hearty, serious manner and said: 'Have them send for his reverence the pastor.' Then he grew quiet and reflective, and nodded me his: 'I shall soon see you again', in friendly wise. Soon after Beethoven attended to his devotions with the pious resignation which looks forward with confidence to eternity.

When a few hours had passed, he lost consciousness, began to grow comatose, and breathed with a rattle. The following morning all symptoms pointed to the approaching end. The 26th of March was stormy, and clouded. Toward six in the afternoon came a flurry of snow, with thunder and lightning. – Beethoven died. – Would not a Roman augur, in view of the accidental commotion of the elements, have taken his apotheosis for granted?

Nicolò Paganini
(1782–1840)

INTRODUCTION:
THE LEGEND OF NICOLÒ PAGANINI

Nicolò Paganini was a figure of scandal in the musical world. No musician had ever created such a furore and his amazing virtuosity was considered evidence of conspiracy with the devil. One usually staid Viennese critic actually wrote that he had seen the devil guiding the violinist's bow. The educated musical establishment of the day, while being aware that Paganini's dazzling technique was due to a precocious technical gift, were no less mesmerized by the Italian virtuoso. The young Franz Liszt was directly inspired by Paganini's playing and began feverishly practising at the piano in order to emulate the impact which Paganini made. Under Paganini's hands the violin acquired every technical device known to the modern violinist.

Paganini encouraged the hysteria which accompanied his performances. He shrouded himself in secrecy and would disappear from the stage for many years only to appear more hauntingly and technically perfect. He kept his greatest technical discoveries a secret and would perform the cadenzas of his compositions only during the performance, never rehearsing them in the company of potential rival violinists. Often during a performance, the strings of the violin would break; unperturbed, he would continue on only one string.

Paganini's physical appearance was another factor which allowed him to stun the audience. It is said that no artist could capture his features, and what we know of his physique and face indicates that he was indeed an extraordinary individual. Emaciated by chronic illness, he was so gaunt that he actually looked very tall. He had a cadaverous white face with a prominent aquiline nose; his hair was black, long and straggly. When he performed, Paganini would wear dark blue eyeglasses to shield his delicate eyes from the footlights. His dark eyes were sunk in hollows, and looked like holes burnt into his head. He wore a frayed black frock coat that sagged from his shoulders. He played the violin with extravagant gestures and would sweep the bow towards the audience. The kinetic, angular figure and gaunt face, the reputation enhanced by wild legends and, above all, the uncanny technique were proof positive to much of the public that the creature was not of this world.

It was in Genoa, on 27 October 1782, that Paganini was born. His mother told of an angel visiting her before the child's birth and offering to fulfil any wish. She asked that her son become the greatest violinist in the world. When Nicolò was six years old, he was abandoned for dead after an attack of measles. He was placed in his shroud and the funeral service commenced. Fortunately, a slight movement was noticed and he escaped premature burial. It is said that Paganini's father recognized the child's musical genius and locked him in his room for periods of up to twelve hours in order that he practise. The young Nicolò made astonishing progress despite his father's harshness. He gave his first concert at the age of nine and was appointed court virtuoso at Lucca at twenty.

When Paganini was freed from his father's domination he entered into a life of unashamed debauchery: 'When at last I was my own master I drew in the pleasures of life in deep draughts.' His conquests included Élise Bonaparte, whom he deserted in his reckless search for new lovers. Ugly and profane, he was nevertheless passionately pursued by many women. Paganini loved gambling. His entourage included sycophants, gamblers and wastrels. He would gamble immense fortunes in the pursuit of pleasure. The infirmities of his later years may relate to some extent to his early life of dissipation and abandonment but there is no clear evidence that he actually contracted syphilis. Paganini's European fame was secure after a triumph in Vienna when he was forty-two. (Dalliance had kept him from earlier concert tours.) The English, who strongly disapproved of his excesses, showed coldness and hostility when he toured in 1831. Unflattering captions and verses appeared in the newspapers, but the professional musicians in the audience continued to be astounded by his playing.

The last years of Paganini's life were horrendous. He was plagued by laryngeal disease and racked with severe abdominal pain. He struggled to keep afloat financially amid a sea of debts occasioned by the failure of his casino. An incompetent dentist had removed all the teeth from his lower jaw and the violinist subsisted on a monotonous semi-liquid diet supplemented by numerous medicaments.

Paganini spent his last days in Nice and died in 1840. Such was the animosity of the Church hierarchy to his amoral lifestyle that they refused to allow his body to be buried in consecrated ground. Father Caffarelli, who visited him shortly before his death, said that the violinist had refused the Last Sacraments. Furthermore, the priest was horrified to see obscene pictures on the wall which obviously indicated that the man was licentious. He also mentioned a picture of Leda and the swan in his report. Paganini was declared an atheist by the Catholic Church, and his body began a series of posthumous journeys and public exhibitions unparalleled in musical history. The cadaver was embalmed and, dressed in the virtuoso's livery, was put in a coffin with a glass pane above the face. A dealer in secondhand objects offered the Comte de Cessole, who had been appointed trustee to Paganini's son, Achille, the sum of 30,000 francs to exhibit the corpse in England.

The coffin was deposited at the Villa Franca, a local quarantine house used to store fish. By day curious sightseers filed by the body. Local fishermen reported hearing ghostly sounds and music in the middle of the night and seeing satanic figures around the coffin. The coffin was hastily buried near an olive oil factory, which fouled the grave. Paganini had written shortly before he died: 'One hope remains to me. It is that after my death the calumny will have spent itself and those who criticized me so cruelly for my success will let my ashes repose in peace.' At various stages over the next eighty-six years the body was to be exhumed, re-embalmed and reburied. In 1893 the Czech violinist František Ondříček prevailed upon Achille to open the coffin in order that he might see the body. It is said that although putrefaction was well advanced, the features of Paganini were still recognizable. His black coat was in tatters, his legs 'a heap of bones'. In 1926 the body was again moved, to its final resting-place in the Camposanto of Genoa. The inscription on the tomb somewhat ironically reads: 'Nicolò Paganini, who drew from his instrument divine sounds'.

Modern medical science can perhaps provide a rational explanation both for Paganini's virtuosity and for his rather bizarre behaviour. Czerny is said to have exclaimed 'nature herself has produced a pianist' when he first met the young Liszt, and a parallel claim could be made for Paganini. Several natural gifts, luckily combined, produced a musician of unique stature.

The first factor is an innate musical talent: Paganini was a musical genius, with a perfect ear and an infallible sense of pitch. Liszt, Schubert, Chopin and Mendelssohn all attest that he always tuned his violin with an exquisite degree of precision. He seems not to have suffered from intonation problems, and also had a phenomenal memory. Like Franz Liszt, he was a brilliant sight reader and enjoyed publicly exhibiting this facility.

Paganini's unique bodily habitus also helped his playing; Francesco Benati, an eminent physician who attended Paganini for a number of years, stated:

> Without the peculiar conformation of his body, of his shoulders, arms and legs, he could never have become the incomparable virtuoso we admire today. His left shoulder is higher than the other – a circumstance that makes his right side appear longer than it is when he stands erect with his arms hanging by his sides. The elasticity of the shoulder tendons, the relaxation of the muscles which connect the wrist with his forearms, the base of the hands with the phalanges can easily be observed.
>
> His hand is no longer than normal but thanks to the elasticity peculiar to all parts of his body his span is doubled. By these means, for example, he can – without altering the position of his hand – bend the upper joints of the fingers of the left hand in a lateral direction, and with the greatest ease and rapidity. Nature must have bestowed an organic disposition on Paganini which practice perfected.

Paganini's left hand had an unusual flexibility and the violinist fully exploited this advantage. It enabled him to stretch three octaves – four Cs with one bow. The shoulder joint was also abnormally flexible, and it was noted that as Paganini played he crossed his 'elbows practically on the top of one another'. Certain passages of the twenty-four Caprices remain unplayable by anyone else. Paganini's speed and co-ordination were of an amazing order; he is known to have played some of his showpieces far faster than do modern violinists. Louis Spohr, Paganini's German contemporary and rival, stated both admiringly and laconically, 'He even played in tune in the fastest passages'. Even at a rapid tempo no nuance of intonation and expression was lost. Liszt himself said that the Italian's virtuosity at the violin was 'unsurpassable' and Chopin described the virtuoso's playing as 'perfection'.

While Paganini's technique so transcended that of his contemporaries it was beyond reproach by critics of the day; they offered, however, interesting discussion of his musicianship. If Paganini had a flaw, it was his inability to produce a large tone or volume. This was probably related to lack of physical strength – he was never a well man. If Paganini's flexibility was related to ligamentous laxity, then it would also explain his lack of physical strength. The majority thought Paganini combined technique with considerable musicianship. It was commonly said that he demonstrated his genius as a musician most profoundly in the slow movements of his violin concertos. His expression was remarkable, and Schubert stated after attending a Viennese concert, 'I have heard an angel sing'. A report by the critic Ludwig Rellstab bears eloquent testimony to the musicianship of Paganini:

> The adagio of the concert was so straight-forward that any student could have played it without difficulty ... but never in my life have I heard such weeping. It was as if the lacerated heart of this suffering mortal was bursting with sorrow. I never knew that music contained such sounds. When he produced the melody at the end of the harmonies it was as if he stood alone in the vast auditorium, all who sat there held their breath as if afraid to rob the player of air. When the concluding piece came, a burst of jubilation broke loose and it seemed as if the earlier applause had not existed.

Paganini's personality calls for comment. He held ordinary morality in contempt and could act harshly. When the critics antagonized him he would quadruple the prices of theatre tickets to show defiantly his hold over the audience. His obsessive gambling and his promiscuity have been commented on. He became a recluse from society in later years. On a more tender note, he had a close and touching relationship with his illegitimate son, Achille; his love and regard for the boy were deep. He had difficulty forming anything more than a superficial relationship with a woman. Paganini, with his often strange and self-destructive behaviour, is more a figure of pity than of scorn. He had a most unhappy childhood, driven by a ruthless and ambitious father, and this probably contributed to some of the more bizarre aspects of his later life. Both Beethoven and Mozart, who were also musical child prodigies, showed difficulty in coming to terms with the conventions of adult life.

One of the great myths surrounding the virtuoso is that of Paganini's 'secret'. This was a legendary violin method which could turn the mediocre player into a phenomenal virtuoso almost overnight, but no trace of it has ever been uncovered. Paganini invented new techniques of bowing, of tuning the violin and of double stopping. He expanded the range of sounds the violin could make so dramatically that audiences, critics and professional musicians alike were both amazed and bewildered. Paganini worked and practised very hard to attain this unique level of proficiency. He was said to practise seven hours a day. Liszt wrote, 'Heavens, what sufferings, misery and tortures are in those four strings.'

The last factor in Paganini's impact was his demonic appearance, which never escaped the critics' attention:

> On the stage of the Hamburg Komödienhaus there appeared a sombre figure that seemed as if arisen from the nether regions. It was Paganini, in his black dress suit; the black coat and black vest of a barbarous cut ... the black pantaloons draped flabbily around the wasted legs. The long arms looked still longer as he came on holding in one hand his violin, and in the other his bow, hanging down almost to the floor, and bowed to the audience with unheard-of elaborations. In the angular bendings of his body there lay a ghastly suggestion of woodenness, together with a clownish animality, that made this entrance scene strangely provocative of laughter; but his face, still more lividly corpse-like in the glaring illumination of the orchestra, took on such an imploring, meekly idiotic expression that a shuddering sympathy repressed the impulse to laugh. Is this the imploring look of one sickened to death, or does it mask the mockery of a shrewd miser? ... But all such questioning was incontinently silenced when the marvellous master set the violin beneath his chin and began to play. (6, vol. 2, p.6)

By 1832 Paganini had reached the pinnacle of his success. The public mania surrounding the virtuoso had reached a veritable frenzy. His career came to an abrupt close shortly after a series of brilliant concerts in Paris.

PAGANINI'S LEFT HAND

Paganini's impact on the musical world was so great that contemporary musicians and scientists competed to explain his astonishing virtuosity. More rational musicians attempted to account for the phenomenon by analysing Paganini's tuning, his general method of playing the violin and, where possible, his fingerings. There was considerable debate among the scientific community. Paganini's physician, Francesco Benati, produced a long report of his observations of both the violinist's hands and his bodily habitus. The report was published in the *Revue de Paris* in 1831 (2). Benati believed that the violinist's unique physiognomy was inherited and was responsible for his virtuosity and, indeed, his musical genius.

Goethe was deeply impressed by Benati's theory. He wrote to his friend Carl Friedrich Zelter:

> He sets out in a very clever way how the musical talent of this extraordinary man, through the conformation of his body, through the proportions of his members, was predetermined, favoured, in fact compelled, to bring forth the incredible, the impossible. He leads us back to the conviction that the organism in its determinations produces the most singular manifestations in the living creature. Since I have still a little space, I will jot down one of the most profound sayings left us by our forefathers: animals are taught by their organs. Now if we consider how much of the animal still remains in man and that the latter has the faculty of teaching his organs, one returns again and again to this intriguing train of thought.

The belief that physiognomy dictated talent and intellectual ability was widely held in the early nineteenth century. Benati's observations are mainly tenable and accurate but the testimony of his colleague Sirus Pirondi shows obvious scientific 'fudging'. Pirondi became acquainted with Paganini in 1839. He wrote: 'The fingers of the left hand are more than a centimetre longer than those of the right hand and, as a result, no doubt, of a particular disposition of the right shoulder muscles, he does not place the bow on the violin till he has described a wide circle with his extended arm.' It is highly doubtful that Paganini's left hand was indeed larger than his right hand. Pirondi tells us that he heard Paganini play often, but these stories are an obvious fabrication: we know that Paganini seldom played in his last years and by 1839 was extremely ill.

The distinguished writer François-Joseph Fétis believed that Paganini's unusual flexibility was acquired and due to years of practice. He published this description of Paganini's hands in his short biographical essay on the composer (4): 'Paganini's hands were large and nervous. His fingers by dint of excessive practice had acquired suppleness and aptitude difficult to conceive. The thumb of the left hand fell easily on the palm of his hand when necessary for the execution of certain shifting passages.'

The issue of whether Paganini's unusual flexibility was congenital or acquired is raised in the letters of Matthaus de Ghetaldi, a magistrate who made Paganini's acquaintance in Venice. The letters are worth quoting in full for they contain some interesting anecdotes:

21 September 1824.

Yesterday I made the acquaintance of Signor Nicolo Paganini of Genoa at Messer Naldi's. He looks unwell. Of moderate height, he carries himself badly. He is also very thin, pale, and dark complexioned. He laughs a lot, and enjoys it. His head is too large for his body, and he has a hooked nose. His hair is black and long, and never dressed. His left shoulder is higher than the right, probably owing to his playing. When he walks he swings his arms. We spent a very jolly afternoon. In the beginning I was under the impression that he was an uncanny, taciturn, and morose man – he was so described to me. But he is very lively and talks almost incessantly. When he laughs he slaps his shoulders with his thin hands. He is really very homely.

2 October 1824.

After the concert we chatted for a long time with Paganini, who was very exhausted, probably because when he plays he uses his whole body; and he is physically very weak. While playing he gave the beat continually with his left foot, which was very disturbing. Then he would bend the upper part of his body, and straighten up again. Twice he waved his bow in the air and made fearful grimaces. I think he's a charlatan, even though he's very accomplished. His style of playing pleases the people enormously. In the evening he showed his left hand to Dr Martecchini (who had just arrived from Trieste). It's astounding what he can do with it; he can move the joints laterally and can bend the thumb back till it touches the little finger. He moves his hand as flexibly as though it were without muscles or bones. When Dr Martecchini remarked that this must be the result of his mad passion for practice, he flatly contradicted him. Yet every child knows that he still practises seven hours a day, only his vanity won't let him admit it. However, Dr Martecchini stuck to his guns, whereupon Paganini began to rage and shout, calling the doctor a thief and a robber. It was very unpleasant but we had to laugh ... How he can have such a demonic effect in the concert hall is beyond me. When he tore round the room swearing, he looked very ridiculous. Later he quieted down when Mme Bianchi arrived around ten o'clock. He then showed us some astounding tricks on his violin. For instance, he plays a melody with two fingers while he plucks an accompaniment with the three first fingers. It often sounded as though three people were playing. His passages in double stops are dazzling, and I've never heard anyone run over the strings so fast[1] ... Then he imitated a donkey, a parrot, and a thrush – all wonderfully natural. This annoyed Messer Naldi, who whispered to me that that was something for the village fair

[1] J.Eskenhasy relates Paganini's facility in pizzicato playing and in playing on the G string to lefthandedness and to unusual independence of the fourth finger (23).

but not for the concert hall. Later, Dr Martecchini tried to play on his violin and found, to his astonishment, that it was completely out of tune. Whereupon Paganini simply doubled up with laughter, and said that he always played on a mistuned violin.

Sivori, Paganini's only pupil, confirms that Paganini practised regularly and demanded that scales be played each day. Thus the virtuoso practised feverishly, despite denying it, and this no doubt heightened his flexibility. Unfortunately, none of the observers took the trouble to see whether unusual movements could be executed with the right hand, a simple observation which would have neatly decided the issue as to whether the virtuoso's flexibility was congenital or acquired.

More recently it has been suggested, by M.R.Schoenfeld (27), that Paganini suffered from Marfan's syndrome, a congenital connective tissue abnormality. People with the Marfanoid bodily habitus are often abnormally thin and tall and often have very large, hyperflexible hands with exceptionally long fingers (arachnodactyly). Many have abnormalities of the eyes and cardiovascular system. The evidence of Paganini possessing the features of the syndrome is, however, far from compelling. We know that his hands were of normal size and that their flexibility was apparent only when he stretched his fingers. Pirondi states that:

> The shape and suppleness of his left hand are really unique: for instance, he can bend his thumb back to an extraordinary degree, and without the slightest effort. It was once thought that his fingers were unusually long, but this is a great mistake. They are of normal length in repose, but very thin and slender. In playing he can extend his reach in a manner that only the savants can explain.

Pirondi's statements are confirmed by Benati's observations (2). Benati also confirmed that Paganini could laterally flex the distal phalanges. (He could probably execute this movement passively, using arm or wrist movement, when his left hand was fixed to the violin. The muscles and tendons of the forearm are not so arranged as to make active lateral flexion of the fingertips possible.) Repeated mechanical trauma to the ligaments leads to ligamentous laxity. Lateral flexion of the fingertips could have been due to laxity of the collateral ligaments of the fingers induced by repeated movement. Before puberty damaged ligaments repair themselves and after repeated movements they may actually lengthen. Paganini's incessant practising may have induced a chronic Grade II sprain to the ligaments of the left hand, which could account for his unusual flexibility. We know that Paganini in his youth resembled his son, Achille, in his bodily habitus, but photographs of Achille do not show a man of the Marfanoid bodily habitus. Paganini was noted to be of 'middle height', again not consistent with Marfan's syndrome.

Claims that Paganini's other illnesses were due to internal abnormalities of Marfan's syndrome seem unfounded. If an explanation of Paganini's hyperflexibility is to be made which involves a connective tissue disease, he may have had a mild variant of the Ehlers–Danlos syndrome. In such variants the only stigmata are those of 'double-jointedness'. (The presence of this syndrome can now be neither proven nor disproven but it seems superfluous to invoke the explanation of a connective tissue disease.)

The important features of Paganini's hand structure and body habitus are as follows:

1. Although thin and gaunt, Paganini was not abnormally tall and probably did not have Marfan's syndrome.
2. Paganini's left shoulder was higher than his right – a postural deformity caused by playing the violin.
3. Paganini's left hand was of normal proportions.
4. Paganini could rapidly initiate unusual movements of the left hand (hyperextension of the thumb, possibly passive lateral flexion of the distal phalanges, long stretches).
5. Paganini could stretch his left hand to cover three octaves on the violin.

PAGANINI'S LAST ILLNESS

Paganini's correspondence first mentions serious health problems in 1820. In that year he was beset with a chronic cough and began to lose weight. He consulted a Palermo physician, who prescribed the 'Roob cure'. Roob was a laxative made from concentrated fruit essences. Later, the virtuoso would abuse laxatives and develop a serious disease as a consequence. The laxatives were prescribed to remove the 'hidden poisons' from his system. Paganini's cough persisted. He consulted Dr Sira Borda in 1823. Borda noted the patient's hacking cough and hoarse voice and evidently knew something about his long history of casual sexual relations. He diagnosed Paganini's affliction as being due to 'a hidden syphilitic infection of long standing'. Borda prescribed mercury for Paganini's disease and opium as a cough suppressant.

Paganini wrote to his friend Luigi Germi of the 'murderous doses' of mercury. The mercury was administered both orally and as an ointment. The immediate consequence of the treatment was stomatitis, gastro-intestinal complaints and loosening of the teeth. By 1828, Paganini's eyesight began to fail and his handwriting started to deteriorate. He consulted other physicians. Their diagnoses were even more pessimistic. The violinist was told that he was consumptive and that he would be dead within a year. Paganini was naturally deeply alarmed by this. He persisted in taking mercury. He wrote to Germi, 'My cough is still fierce but the sputum isn't bad.' Paganini was bled by his doctors and horse riding was prescribed, evidently to relieve the chronic constipation and abdominal pain which was due to his medication.

Paganini consulted Francesco Benati during his concert tour of Austria in 1828. Benati correctly surmised that the virtuoso was suffering, inter alia, from chronic mercury poisoning. His summary of the virtuoso's medical history is worth quoting at length and serves as a starting-point for a more comprehensive discussion of Paganini's illnesses, which were well established by 1831:

> I have been on an intimate footing with him for more than ten years, first in Italy and then in Vienna, where I had occasion to treat him for several months so that no part of his physical constitution is unknown to me. I am inclined to believe that no one but a friend could obtain the details necessary for judging his physical organism both in respect to his present state of health and to his previous maladies. It would have been impossible to make a thorough physical examination (his organs, the conformation of his body, etc.), so that one would have had no data upon which to base an opinion ...
>
> In early childhood, as well as in maturity, his nervous system was hypersensitive and all the maladies from which he has suffered have been complicated by a number of extraordinary phenomena stemming from this source. First of all, I would mention the two eruptive fevers during childhood and the role played by the nervous system at this time. In my opinion nearly all his later ailments can be traced to the extreme sensitivity of his skin. It is remarkably fine in texture and is very sensitive all over his body. His pores open easily. During the summer, perspiration is copious; even in winter the slightest thing will make him perspire. There is such a close relation between his nervous reactions and his skin that the pleasure of listening to music or the emotional excitement of playing are sufficient to dilate his pores and make his body break out in a soft, agreeable perspiration. The skin is therefore extremely

alive and sensitive, and to this is due his addiction to colds and the catarrhal affections that follow in their train.

Although he has taken the precaution from an early age to wear flannel underwear, he has been by no means immune from the maladies to which the vicissitudes of the seasons have exposed him. All the mucous membranes have been affected in turn. Those of the larynx, the bronchial tubes, and the bladder have been the seat of an acute irritation from which he still suffers at times. The parenchyma of the lungs has frequently been inflamed ... When he first went to Lucca, he began to suffer from hemorrhoids, which have given him much trouble, but they have disappeared as a result of a special regimen and baths ... For several years he enjoyed good health till at Naples he had a severe catarrhal fever accompanied by suffocation and a convulsive cough which only antispasmodics were able to alleviate. He continued to improve when after a time his voice underwent an alteration, accompanied by a pain in the larynx that worried him. The physician who was treating him considered this affection (which was perhaps only nervous in origin) as the beginning of laryngeal phthisis and, attributing it (rightly or wrongly) to syphilis, prescribed mercury for internal and external use. This medicament has had the most disastrous effect upon his health. It attacked his stomach and his gums. His teeth decayed and fell out, and he did not even have the satisfaction of being cured of the malady for which the treatment was prescribed. The evil was great, but it was increased through the use of another ill-advised and less violent remedy that he took on his own responsibility for two years, namely, Leroy's purgative and emetic. Tired of having vain recourse to the physicians of Italy and Germany, weary of hearing that his days were numbered, he turned to medical quackery for the aid that medicine admittedly was unable to offer him. Certainly, this panacea had worked no wonders for him when I met him in Vienna in 1828. On the contrary, it had produced its usual effect, for it was hard for anyone to be in a more debilitated condition than he was when, on my advice, he interrupted its use ... The affection of the larynx also ceded to treatment little by little; but I admit that with respect to his emaciation and persistent hacking cough, I was very inclined to share the opinion of the Italian and German doctors who diagnosed the case as tuberculosis. However, since he had not yet been examined by Laennec's stethoscope, my diagnosis, like that of my colleagues, could have no positive basis. In fact, our fears of an already tuberculous condition were groundless, as I assured myself the moment he arrived in Paris. Nevertheless, since one might not have perfect confidence in my judgment, I wanted a colleague long versed in the use of the stethoscope and the diagnosis of maladies of the chest (Dr Miguel) to examine him with me. Now we are happy to assure Paganini's numerous friends that his lungs up to now are perfectly sound. His chest is narrow and arched, the left side is a little smaller than the right and a little depressed in the upper part. His respiration is regular and easy; but the right side dilates more than the left ... He is therefore not consumptive, as was hitherto believed. I have mentioned his emaciation but this is not due to the presence of tubercles in the lungs nor to any lesion of other vital organs. He is thin because it is his nature to be thin. I would even say that it is necessary for him to be so, for without this he would not be Paganini (2).[2]

One illness that undoubtedly affected Paganini is an iatrogenic[3] illness, chronic mercury poisoning. Its most obvious manifestation was the mouth and gum disease which led to the extraction of his lower teeth.

Mercury was the mainstay of treatment for syphilis for four hundred years until the introduction of arsenicals in the early twentieth century. The effects of mercury on the mouth and gums had been known from the Middle Ages. Ulrich von Hutten, a German monk and a colleague of Erasmus, had lost his teeth to mercury chemotherapy. Another side effect of mercury was 'ptyalism' (increased salivation). Contemporary textbooks detailed that three pints of saliva needed to be produced for mercury to be effective (11). The more subtle of the protean manifestations of mercury poisoning were not described until the turn of the present century. It is likely that many of Paganini's ills resulted from mercury poisoning.

In 1828, Paganini sought treatment from A.M. de Vergani, an Italian dentist, because of a dental abscess. Vergani found that, because of the mercury treatment, Paganini's teeth were 'hanging by a thread'. In order to masticate, Paganini had threaded his teeth together with twine. (6, vol. 1, p. 282) Vergani opened the abscess and removed the offending molar. Soon after this the infection spread to the lower jaw as an osteomyelitis. Vergani and a team of three other dentists treated this by extracting all of Paganini's lower teeth. Paganini was forcibly held down during the painful procedure. The infection of the tissues, probably considerably damaged by mercury, took a long time to resolve and Paganini wore a white bandage to support his painful jaw (13, p. 264). He also began to smoke opium cigars, ostensibly to control the chronic pain.

Another consequence of mercury poisoning, as mentioned earlier,

[2] translated by De Courcy (6, vol. 2 pp. 37–9)
[3] caused by his doctors

was ptyalism. Paganini was constantly expectorating the foul mucus produced by his salivary glands and the glands of the upper respiratory tract. This symptom was disguised by or was the cause of his original one – a productive cough.

Paganini's eyesight began to deteriorate. He found that blue glasses protected his eyes and aided his vision. The deterioration in his eyesight clearly dates from the five-year period when he was taking heavy doses of mercurials (1823–8).

Perhaps the effects on the composer's psyche were more subtle. From being a rather rash, aggressive, ambitious and self-confident man, he became reclusive and apathetic. This is probably due to 'erethism', the psychological changes due to chronic mercurial poisoning (10, p. 233). The virtuoso began to become nervous about appearing in public, depressed and somewhat 'shy'. He also seems to have lost his considerable interest in the opposite sex. Benati tells us that the composer became easily startled by sudden noises and nervous if he could not actually see the person he was talking to. Benati also says that one had to stand in front of Paganini to talk to him – possible evidence of 'tunnel vision'. All observers remark on the change in Paganini's appearance between 1823 and 1828, his 'deathly pallor' and 'greyish complexion'. Paganini himself wrote that he had become 'very ugly' (6, vol. 2, pp. 37–46).

Another feature of chronic mercury poisoning is the tremor, the so-called 'hatter's shakes'. This may occur late in the illness. Paganini's handwriting deteriorates rapidly after 1828 and although there are no mentions of an actual tremor at this stage, observers frequently describe the composer's 'jerky movements' and 'comical animality'. Tremor can occur late in the illness and it is possible that it caused Paganini's disappearance from the concert stage after 1834. Certainly Paganini could no longer support his casino project by public concerts, as he intended, by 1836. We hear reports of Paganini's 'shaking hands that could scarcely hold a pen' in letters written by observers at his deathbed (6, vol. 2, p. 320).

Paganini became almost completely obsessed by his bowel habits. His 'red books' (diaries) for 1836 contain nothing but references to them. The following is a sample:

Mai	1. Purgitavo	5. Vomitivo
	2. Riposo	6. Figlio presso
	3. Purgitavo	7. Purgitavo
	4. Riposo	8. Figlio Purga

Paganini's obsession with laxatives was initiated by the gastro-intestinal side effects of the combined treatment with mercury and opium. His favoured laxative was 'Elixir Leroy'. The makers of 'Leroy' appended this explanation of their medical philosophies to the packet of 'Leroy'. Its vivid style and unbridled advocacy of purging must have had an obvious appeal to the dedicated bowel hypochondriacs who purchased it in great quantities:

> Bleeding is an abominable practice. The use of leeches is the most pernicious of all human inventions. Mercury is one of the worst enemies of the human race. Quinine is the cause of an endless number of incidents, almost all irremediable. Diet is unnatural. There is only one effective medicine: the purge – loosen, remove, refine, rarefy, expel, clean, purify, eject the material that irritates and aggravates.

Archange Leroy wrote a famous treatise on the use of purgatives. It was published in Paris in 1767 under the title 'Essay sur l'Usage et les Effets de l'Ecorce du Garou'. He was not medically qualified. He advocated the use of purgatives, all made from vegetable matter, for many ailments. One of his claims which had an obvious appeal to Paganini was that a purgative made from the bark which covered the root of the mezereon (Daphne) could cure not only the cutaneous lesions of syphilis but also the side effects of mercury poisoning, particularly ulceration of the mucous membranes (1, p. 215). Leroy eventually stopped using this medication because of its toxic effects. The purgative which Paganini purchased was manufactured in four 'grades'. The content of the Grade 2 purgative is as follows (3, p. 366): Scammonee, 64 grams; Turbith Vegetal, 32 grams; Jalap, 250 grams.[4] Paganini took five spoonfuls of the purgative twice a day, usually Grade 4, the strongest available. (The drastic purgatives were deleted from the British Pharmacopoeia around 1920 because of their toxicity. They have an action similar to podophyllin, which is used for removing superficial skin tumours and is barred from internal use.) 'Leroy' and mercury were not the only dangerous medications that Paganini used. Another was 'calomel', a compound containing mercurous chloride which Paganini made into a tea. This compound is known to cause both a rash and pharyngitis as well as mercury poisoning. Again Paganini used

---

[4] scammony = root of *Convolvulus scammonia* (Syria); turbith = Indian purgative plant *Ipomea turpethum*; jalap = root of *Exogonium purga* (Mexico)

this substance as a purgative (5, pp.119–30). He also tried rosewater to cure his now chronic constipation.

The direct consequence of all this corrosive medication is that Paganini developed a stricture of the oesophagus. All the maestro's food was minced for him and by his own testimony he had to 'spend two hours at table'. He tells Germi that 'this allows the cook to prepare all the courses of my meal thoroughly' (April 1840). Paganini continued to become sicker and to lose weight. In 1837 he developed acute urinary retention; he was taught to treat this by introducing tin catheters. He developed chronic cystitis and orchitis in consequence.

Paganini to Germi, 31 January 1837:

> Like you, I am most distressed at not having been able to do as I had so greatly hoped, that is, give the desired concert in Turin on 3 February. But who would ever have thought ... I would fall ill with nervous fever and be menaced with an inflammation of the bladder, for which I am now under treatment by the famous Dr Spitzer, who, when I was being treated by Borda and Aglietti in Milan and was condemned by them to die of consumption, came to see me and felt they were wrong: on the contrary, he thought that by abandoning all medicine for a time and keeping perfectly quiet I could set out on my journey to astound Europe – which I did! This doctor promises me complete recovery, but it will take a little patience and a little time. For the moment I'm taking certain powders that tend to diminish the tenesmus and I'm introducing graduated tin catheters into the bladder to draw off the urine. I'm now at no. 3. As soon as I reach no. 6, he will introduce a medicament at the neck of the bladder so as to enable me to draw off the urine without an instrument, that is, so that I can void urine naturally and freely.

Paganini to Germi, Nice, 6 March 1837:

> I left Marseilles on Saturday, accompanied by a horrible wind on Sunday all the way to Nice. I was obliged to go to bed after dinner on account of a rheumatic fever. Thursday, I felt better as soon as I managed to perspire and I thanked the Almighty for having freed me from such suffering. But in the final stage of my prayer what was my surprise to discover that the left testicle had swollen to the size of a large pear, or a little pumpkin – and you can well imagine the rest! This malady is called orchitis and comes from using a catheter and jolting about in the carriage. Now I'm weaker than ever because of the diet – nothing but pap day and night. Confined to my bed, the semi-baths and weakness will prevent my getting up for another five or six days, and then of course only with a truss. May God give me patience! As soon as I regain my

strength, I'm planning to go to Genoa by steamer since my surgeon advises me not to go by carriage unless the swelling has gone down at least four-fifths, which may take a month yet. So with such a great affliction, I can't say if I suffer more on account of not being able to go to Turin, as I so long to do, or from my bodily ills.

16 March:

I've been confined to my bed since 26 February, first with rheumatism, then with orchitis, and in addition, fever, haemorrhage, tenesmus, and finally grippe with catarrhal cough. Today I'm a little less depressed on noting an improvement in the testicle. The swelling seems to be going down, so tomorrow I can get up for several hours, with the truss, and in this way gradually regain my strength ... I've answered Watson's letter, which you sent me, telling him that it will be impossible for me to keep our agreement in view of my present state of health; but if he advises it, I shall be able to undertake such a voyage the end of June. I've only notified the people at Havre so that the two reservations that he made on the packet won't be charged to him.

By March 1840, it was evident to all that Paganini was dying. His letters mention new symptoms – dependency oedema and haemoptysis (coughing blood):

4 April:

My head won't work any more. The weakness has made my legs swell back of the knees so that I can't walk about in my room, to which I have been confined for five months – in other words, since the day of my arrival.

18 April:

I stopped taking the Guasconi drink because I easily expectorate the mucus and pus; but what frightens me is the enormous discharge day and night and also at table – three or four saucerfuls. My food does me no good. I'm losing my appetite and my weakness is increasing. The swelling in my legs has risen to behind the knees so that I walk like a snail and if I bend down it's hard to straighten up again. (6, vol. 2)

Contemporary accounts tell of Paganini's 'trembling hands' – perhaps a carping reference to the fact that Paganini was deemed an atheist by the Church and was going to meet his maker fearful and unrepentant.

It is probably actually indicative of a tremor induced by chronic mercurial poisoning. He also complained of a severe headache. Paganini wrote that he now coughed blood from the respiratory canal frequently. His cough became more frequent and at night it stifled him. It is possible to attribute both the cough and gross dependent oedema to mercury poisoning. Mercury poisoning causes nephrotic syndrome, chronic renal failure, as well as upper airways disease.

Paganini died on 27 May 1840, at 5.00 p.m. He was fifty-eight years old. The cause of death was given as 'tuberculosis of the lungs and larynx'. The body was embalmed but no autopsy was performed (13, pp. 446–8). An article appeared in a French paper to the effect that the improvisation that the virtuoso performed on the night he died was the greatest feat of his life. Given the severity and chronicity of his final illness, the story is undoubtedly a fabrication.

The question remains, did the composer actually have syphilis or tuberculosis of the larynx? The diagnosis of tuberculosis of the larynx is perhaps easy to refute. Tuberculosis of the larynx is usually secondary to cavitating pulmonary tuberculosis. It has a poor prognosis and it is doubtful that Paganini would have survived almost twenty years with the condition. Moreover, Miguel's examination with a stethoscope failed to diagnose lung pathology. Paganini's cough was a productive cough and the 'catarrh' and froth in the upper airways is consistent with the diagnosis of mercury poisoning. Moreover, after long periods of mercury ingestion, sputum becomes 'fouled'. It is likely that this symptom was due to mercurial poisoning. The initial symptoms of cough may have been due to a relatively trivial illness or, more probably, to calomel abuse by the virtuoso. Lithographs of the violinist on his deathbed do not show clubbing of the fingers.

Paganini himself describes his symptoms thus:

My malady of the oesophagus is the result or consequence of the horrible shocks that I have suffered for a period of fifteen years, the most horrible every third day. My so-called nervous cough is due to a tickling sensation (more or less as though tickled lightly with a straw) in the air passages at the back of the throat. This makes me cough and interferes with my breathing. I have to make such violent efforts (to inhale) that I can be heard from here to the Bois de Boulogne, with the result that my voice is sometimes weak and hoarse for a whole day. This tires my lungs and I have to lie down for several hours. Not being able to get rid of the tickling sensation that forces me to make such diabolic efforts, my oesophagus, which has become relaxed through this long affliction, cannot

83

get well. It is also weak, since I am no longer young. This tickling takes place inside the now diseased oesophagus and no one has been able to give me any remedy for it (6, vol. 2).

(Paganini is obviously confusing the oesophagus with the trachea.)

Benati, who trained as a laryngologist, did not think that Paganini's symptoms were due to syphilis: he felt that they were 'nervous in origin'. Indirect laryngoscopy was not available to the physician. This technique made its appearance in the 1850s,[5] one of its early proponents being Sir William Wilde, the father of Oscar Wilde. None the less, the statement of an obviously very competent physician experienced in the diagnosis of laryngeal tuberculosis and syphilis must carry some weight. The initial symptom of chronic cough would not be equated with 'hidden syphilis' by modern physicians. One must be very careful about a diagnosis of syphilis made during this era. Syphilis was differentiated from gonorrhoea as late as 1838 by Philippe Ricord. (Dr Bell, an English physician, had actually proved that the two diseases were different entities slightly earlier, but his work was not known on the Continent.)

Paganini began to experience laryngeal pain and voice change after taking mercury. He mistakenly thought that his condition was a progressive one due to an occult disease. His voice became weaker and after 1838 he became aphonic (unable to speak) and used conversation cards to communicate. The weak voice coincided with general debility and worsening respiratory symptoms.

Given that Paganini suffered from mercury poisoning, there is no need to attribute this or any other pathology to the encroaching effects of neurosyphilis. Although he was unsteady on his feet, he was able to walk and had no signs of general paralysis (13, pp. 446-7):

The celebrated maestro eats only with the greatest difficulty. At table his meat is minced for him either by one of his neighbours or his servant. His days are passed entirely in playing billiards or walking with a friend. He is much amused by reading the 'Charivari' but his gaiety soon passes off and he then sinks into a state of depression, the result, no doubt, of his illness. With his cap on his head he retires to the environs of the bath and remains plunged in deep meditation interrupted by sudden movements as if he wished to shake off reflection. He then strikes the ground repeatedly with his feet like a man who, on rising from his seat, is afraid that his legs will give way under the weight of his body.

[5] The laryngoscope, an angled mirror used in visual examination of the larynx, was invented by the singer Manuel García in 1855.

1. Mozart. Silverpoint drawing (1789) by Doris Stock. The hair obscures the deformity of Mozart's left ear.

2. Mozart's left ear. P.H. Gerber's drawing, from the *Deutsche Medizinische Wochenschrift* (2 June 1898), is based on an earlier illustration in G.N.von Nissen's biography of 1828. The polygonally shaped ear has no lobe and shows fusion of the antihelix (A) and helix (c). There is slit-like narrowing of the orifice of the external auditory canal and filling out of the concha (d).

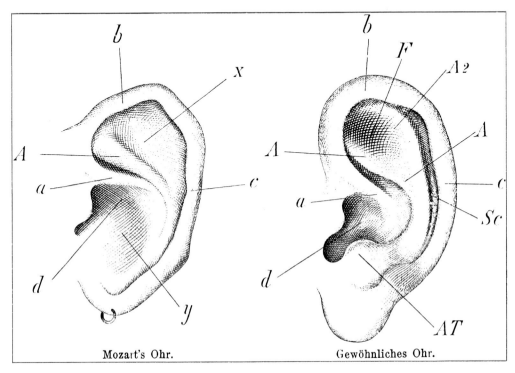

Mozart's Ohr.   Gewöhnliches Ohr.

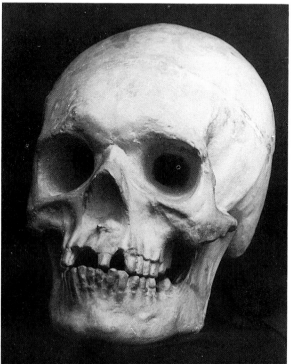

3. Beethoven on his deathbed.
Lithograph by Joseph Danhauser from
his own drawing. The composer's
emaciation is apparent.

4. Photograph of a plaster
reconstruction of Beethoven's skull.
Beethoven's body was exhumed on
13 October 1863. The skull, which was
in pieces, was carefully reconstructed
by the sculptor Alois Wittman who also
made this plaster cast. Precise
measurements were recorded and the
skeleton was reinterred in a zinc casket
on 23 October 1863.

5. Paganini (1819) by Ingres. A highly romanticized portrait executed in the year before Paganini's mercury treatment.

6. Weber by Ludwig Mauer.

7. Rossini. Engraving by Gustave Doré from sketches made on 14 November 1868, the day after Rossini's death.

8. Schubert. Pencil drawing by Leopold Kupelwieser (1821).

9. Schubert's skull. Photograph made by J.B. Rottmayer after the bodies of Beethoven and Schubert were exhumed in 1863.

10. Schumann. Drawing by J.J.B.Laurens (1853).

11. Chopin. Photograph *c.* 1847.

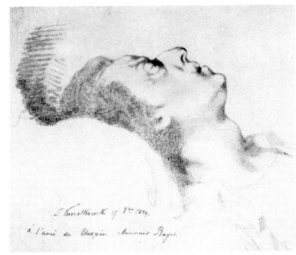

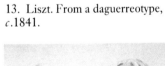

12. Chopin on his deathbed. Drawing by T.Kwiatkowski.

13. Liszt. From a daguerreotype, *c.*1841.

14. Liszt. Engraving by Charles Renouard after sketches from life. Reproduced in *The Graphic*, 10 April 1886.

15. Grieg seated in his garden at Troldhaugen, August 1907. His debility is evident at this stage.

16. Mahler in 1907.

17. Percy and Ella Grainger with Frederick and Jelka Delius, 1 July 1929.

18. The last photo of Delius, at home in Grez sur Loing, March 1934.

19. Percy Grainger and his mother, Rose, White Plains, New York, 1921.

20. Scott Joplin.

21. George Gershwin.

Paganini obviously had a tendency towards a hypochondriacal exaggeration of his symptoms. He was justifiably frightened when he was told that he would soon die of 'consumption' or syphilis. He obviously believed his physicians; he took mercury to treat a cough and minor laryngeal symptoms unaware that mercury was actually aggravating his symptoms and causing both severe bowel and upper airways disease. Francesco Benati saw Paganini's illness in its correct perspective and tried to prohibit the abuse of mercury and laxatives. Paganini's iatrogenic illness was well established by this stage and he disregarded the doctor's advice. He persisted with calomel and 'Leroy'. His violin technique disintegrated and he disappeared from public life to die a recluse in 1840.

Paganini may have had a masochistic personality disorder. He had a veritable obsession with painful remedies and he seems to have been the victim of these remedies so often that one wonders if more than an element of chance was involved in both his choice of doctors and his treatment. Certainly he ignored the more rational members of the medical profession who warned him against the dangerous medication that he took. Much of his correspondence is concerned with pain and its control. He once confidently wrote to Germi that 'like Mucius Scaevola I have finally conquered pain'.

TABLE 1 CHRONOLOGY OF PAGANINI'S ILLNESSES (1820–1840)

	Symptoms	Diagnosis/Doctor	Treatment
1820	Chronic cough, loss of weight	Consumption	'Roob'
1823	Chronic cough, loss of weight	'Hidden syphilis' (Sira Borda)	Mercury Opium
1824	Abdominal pain, gingivitis, stomatitis	Gastro-intestinal disease secondary to mercury poisoning	'Leroy'
1828	Gingivitis, oral pain	Dental abscess/osteomyelitis of jaw (Vergani)	Dental extraction Opium
1828	Dysphonia, intermittent dysuria	'Nervous constitution'	Mercury
1832	Salivation, loss of weight Deteriorating eyesight Movement disorder?, tunnel vision	'Mercury poisoning' (Francesco Benati)	Ceased 'Leroy' continued Narcotics continued
1832	Personality change, difficulty with mentation		
1834–1837	Last concert appearances (Belgium, Liverpool, Nice); poor reviews		Final retirement as virtuoso violinist
1837	Lethargy, urinary retention		
1838	Aphonia/dependent oedema, 'suffocation', tremor	'Inflammation of the bladder' (Spitzer)	Catheterization
1840	Haemoptysis, death		

REFERENCES

General

1. W. Cullen, *A Treatise on the Materia Medica* (Edinburgh, 1789), vol. 2, pp. 214–15
2. F. Benati, 'Notice physiologique et pathologique sur Paganini', *Revue de Paris*, 11 (1831), pp. 113–16
3. Anon., *Grand Dictionnaire universel du XIXe siècle* (Paris, 1870), vol. 7, p. 366
4. F. J. Fétis, *Biographical Notice of Paganini*, Eng. trans., 2nd edn (London, 1876)
5. S. Sitwell, *Liszt* (London, 1934, reprinted 1965), pp. 119–30
6. G. I. C. De Courcy, *Paginini, the Genoese*, 2 vols (Norman, Oklahoma, 1957)
7. G. I. C. De Courcy, *Chronology of Nicolo Paganini's Life* (Wiesbaden, 1961)
8. A. J. Kantarijan, 'A Syndrome Resembling Amyotrophic Lateral Sclerosis following Chronic Mercurialism', *Neurology*, 11 (1961), pp. 639–44
9. R. D. Smith and J. W. Worthington, 'Paganini: The Riddle and Connective Tissue', *Journal of the American Medical Association*, 199 (1967), pp. 820–4
10. C. J. Polson and R. N. Tattershall, *Clinical Toxicology* (London, 1969), pp. 224–41
11. W. J. Brown, *Syphilis and Other Venereal Diseases* (Cambridge, Mass., 1970)
12. V. A. McKusick, *Heritable Disorders of Connective Tissue*, 2nd edn (St Louis, 1970)
13. L. Shepphard and H. R. Axelrod, *Paganini* (Neptune, N.J., 1979)
14. K. K. Holmes (ed.), *Sexually Transmitted Diseases* (New York, 1984), pp. 288–380
15. J. G. O'Shea, 'A Medical History of Franz Liszt', *Medical Journal of Australia*, 145 (1986), pp. 625–30
16. J. G. O'Shea, 'Medical Aspects of Paganini's Life', *Liszt Saeculum*, 41–2 (1988), pp. 23–8
17. J. G. O'Shea, 'The Death of Paganini', *Journal of the Royal College of Physicians of London*, 22 (1988), p. 104
18. J. G. O'Shea, 'Was Paganini Poisoned with Mercury?', *Journal of the Royal Society of Medicine*, 81 (1988), p. 594
19. J. P. Friel (ed.), *Dorland's Illustrated Medical Dictionary*, 25th edn (Philadelphia, 1982), pp. 807, 1382

Paganini's Hands

20. G. I. C. De Courcy, *Paganini, the Genoese* (Norman, Oklahoma, 1957)
21. D. Kerner, 'Nicolò Paganini, the "Diabolic Violinist", on the 126th

Anniversary of his Death on May 25, 1840', *Folia-Clinic International* (Barc), 167 (1966), pp. 377–83

22. R. D. Smith and J. W. Worthington, 'Paganini: The Riddle and Connective Tissue', *Journal of the American Medical Association*, 199 (1967), pp. 820–4

23. J. Eskenhasy, 'Lefthandedness of Nicolò Paganini', *Neurologia, Psihiatria, Neurochirurgia*, 13/2 (1968), pp. 175–82

24. J. Camp, 'Paganini', *Orvosi-Hetilap*, 110 (1969), pp. 2230–1

25. A. S. MacNalty, 'Paganini: Master Violinist', *Nursing Mirror*, 128/4 (1969), pp. 24–5

26. J. M. Bruner, 'Moto perpetuo (Paganini): A Theme for Surgery of the Hand', *Hand*, 6/2 (1974), pp. 115–20

27. M. R. Schoenfeld, 'Nicolo Paganini: Magical Musician and Marfan Mutant?', *Journal of the American Medical Association*, 239 (1978), pp. 40–2

28. 'Paganini' [letter], *Journal of the American Medical Association*, 239 (1978), p. 1845

29. M. R. Schoenfeld, 'Nicolo Paganini - Magical Musician and Marfan Mutant?', *Medical Times*, 108/11 (1980), pp. 117–18, 120, 125

30. R. D. Smith, 'Paganini's Hand', *Arthritis and Rheumatism*, 25 (1982), pp. 1385–6

Carl Maria von Weber
(1786–1826)

INTRODUCTION: TUBERCULOSIS IN THE NINETEENTH CENTURY

Death was a frequent visitor to the nineteenth-century household. In the early part of the century the life expectancy of the urban dweller was only about thirty-eight years. This short life expectancy was due to many factors, including poor standards of medical and obstetric care, malnutrition and the ever present threat of infectious disease.

A new constellation of respiratory diseases accompanied the growing industrial revolution. These included occupational lung diseases such as silicosis and asbestosis, diseases related to increased tobacco consumption by the prosperous middle classes such as emphysema and lung cancer, and diseases related to industrial air pollution. It took many years for the medical profession fully to evaluate and differentiate these illnesses. The disease which commanded most of the attention of the medical profession in the early nineteenth century was tuberculosis. Indeed much superstition and mythology surrounded 'consumption' or 'phthisis' (as tuberculosis was also known), an illness justly dreaded by both the medical profession and the public. In the nineteenth century remarkable progress was made in determining the natural history of tuberculosis.

In London in 1840 conservative physicians estimated that 14.3% of the population died of tuberculosis. Sir James Clark, an influential Scottish physician who studied with Laennec in Paris and who treated John Keats for tuberculosis estimated that a third of deaths in Britain occurring in the 1830s were due to 'consumption' (2).

In Paris it was estimated that 18% of the population died of

89

tuberculosis. Many of those who died were children or young adults. The rising incidence of the disease in Vienna peaked in 1870 at 800/100,000 (4, 5, 7).

Although the disease had been known from ancient times, the cause of tuberculosis eluded medical science for centuries. In 1546 Girolamo Fracastoro hypothesized that the disease was actually an infectious one. The definitive proof of his hypothesis came only in 1882 when Robert Koch isolated the causative organism, mycobacterium tuberculosis. Even after this breakthrough many were sceptical about the infectious nature of tuberculosis (3, 10).

René Laennec, who did much to evaluate the pathology of tuberculosis, believed in its hereditary nature. Retrospective studies have shown that over 80% of the European population had some evidence of tubercular infection, although many did not die of the disorder. It was therefore difficult, if not impossible, to perceive transmission of the disorder without knowing its precise cause. The disease tended to occur within the same household and within families – hence assumed evidence of its hereditary nature. Some families were actually labelled as being 'consumptive'. (The Habsburgs and the Brontës are examples of families where the idea of a 'hereditary tubercular diathesis' being responsible for illnesses is still receiving currency in biographies written today (3, 4).)

Laennec perceived correctly that the urban environment and indeed industrialization somehow favoured the development of tuberculosis. The great Celtic physician, a native of rural Brittany where the disease was rarer than in Paris, felt that country air might contain substances which repressed tuberculosis. He brought seaweed from Brittany to his hospital in Paris where he piled it in the wards in a vain but scientifically valid attempt to repress the disease. Laennec conducted over two hundred autopsies on patients with tuberculosis and described the 'tubercule' – the characteristic nodule indicating the presence of the disease. His simple invention, the stethoscope, allowed doctors to diagnose tuberculosis more accurately by listening for tuberculous cavities at the apexes of the lungs (1).

Laennec published his findings in his famous *Treatise on ... Auscultation*, which appeared in London in 1834, in a translation by his British disciple John Forbes. The work was widely influential throughout the United Kingdom but some of the more conservative elements of the medical profession remained cynical detractors of the stethoscope. (In 1840, twenty-two years after the original publication of Laennec's book,

David Livingstone nearly failed his final medical examination in Glasgow because his enthusiasm for the stethoscope was not shared by his examiners (8).)

Laennec's work and that of his colleagues added immeasurably to mankind's knowledge of tuberculosis and its prognosis, but they had no effective therapeutic answer to it. The treatment offered was mostly innocuous placebos such as the lichens given to Chopin. These substances provided the patient with much psychological comfort but did nothing to alter the long-term course of the disease. By the late nineteenth century Koch and Pasteur were developing vaccines based on their microbiological studies, and these were of considerable efficacy in preventing the disease. Today, chemotherapy with antibiotics affords a good chance of actual cure (3, 12).

The disease occupied a central place in the Romantic imagination. It was widely believed that consumption could actually enhance creativity. This is well documented in René Dubos's famous monograph on tuberculosis (5). The sufferers of tuberculosis were said to be possessed of unique strength of mind called the 'spes phthisica'. This was a state of hopefulness and creativity which belied a patient's debilitated and frail condition due to tuberculosis.

The notion that tuberculosis and genius are associated is foreign to the modern medical mind. Dubos tells us that the idea of 'spes phthisica' is an ancient one; he ascribes it to the Greeks and records the observations of the Cappadocian Aretaeus which show definitively that the idea was entrenched in the medical literature in AD 200 (5, p. 59). The idea of a 'spes phthisica' reached its zenith in Paris in the 1820s and 1830s when 'consumption' became a fashionable disease (5, p. 58). Dubos contends that tuberculous enlargement of the lymph glands of the neck made the cravat and high neckwear fashionable. The early nineteenth century was an age of revolution, opium eating and early death which paradoxically spawned great advances in the arts and sciences. Although tuberculosis continues to be an underrated scourge of the twentieth century, particularly in the underdeveloped countries, it is to the last century that it belongs emotively.

CARL MARIA VON WEBER

Weber's tuberculosis is very well documented: he undoubtedly died from slowly progressing cavitating tuberculosis. His respiratory symptoms began in 1812, when he was twenty-five years of age, and gradually worsened until his death in 1826 at the age of thirty-nine. Weber's medical history and his autopsy indicate that he was infected at an early age, many years before the onset of respiratory symptoms.

Carl Maria von Weber was born at Eutin, twenty miles north of Lübeck, in 1786. There is some doubt as to the actual date of birth, but he was baptized on 20 November. His father was the director of an itinerant provincial acting troupe, the Weber Theatre Company.

Weber's first recorded medical condition is a damaged right hip which caused a permanent limp. Several medical biographers have concluded that this was due to a tubercular lesion. The condition (which was present from before the age of eight) was very probably due to tuberculosis. The hip used to cause pain at night and when the lad was tired, a cardinal symptom of tubercular osteomyelitis. Mechanical orthopaedic conditions such as congenital dislocation or Perthe's disease may also have caused the indisposition.

Weber's mother, Genovefa, died of tuberculosis on 13 March 1798. The young Carl Maria was described as a frail and sickly child and suffered from frequent respiratory illness. His first contact with tuberculosis, the primary infection, is not recorded; it is likely to have occurred in childhood or adolescence. Primary tuberculosis is often an insidious disease: the lesion heals clinically and infection with tuberculosis becomes apparent only when the disease is reactivated in later life. Often the symptoms of primary tuberculosis are so innocuous that it is dismissed as a minor respiratory illness. However, it is possible that Weber's first encounter with tuberculosis was a stormy one and that it has not been recorded by his biographers. The autopsy provides evidence of a very long-standing illness.

Weber's early life was characterized by outstanding progress in his chosen vocation. It has been reliably documented that his father, Franz Anton, hoped for a 'second Mozart' among his progeny. He goaded Carl Maria and his brother Max Maria into early piano lessons and was a strict disciplinarian. After a few initial difficulties it was apparent that Carl Maria had unusual aptitude. The Webers spent years wandering around Bavaria. The itinerant life paid high dividends musically: Max Maria recorded that many of his brother's tunes were based on popular melodies and folktunes which he heard while roving around Germany. Like Mozart and Liszt, he was an itinerant musician with a keen ear for local musical styles.

As a young man Carl Maria was lively and perceptive, and seems to have dominated his small circle of companions. He was small – he stood about 157 cm tall – and of slight frame. He had a long thin neck, narrow shoulders and large, expressive hands. His face was thin and aquiline, not handsome but nevertheless attractive because of his lively disposition. There was a faintly reddish tinge to his brown hair. He had a brilliant piano technique, and was said to be able to span a tenth with ease.

Wagner penned a vivid description of the composer in *Mein Leben*: 'his fine narrow face with its lively yet often heavily veiled eyes made a powerful impression on me, while his pronounced limp, which I had often observed as he passed on his way home from exhausting rehearsals, impressed on my imagination the picture of the great composer as an exceptional, supernatural being'.

In 1810, after the family had fallen into debt and been banished from Württemberg, Carl Maria went to Darmstadt, where he studied with the Abbé Vogler. Like many of his successors, he earned a substantial living as a music critic while composing. From this period comes the Piano Concerto no. 1 in C and the Six Progressive Sonatas. Even at this early stage it was apparent that Weber was to be a fountainhead of the Romantic movement. Liszt and Wagner acknowledged their debt to him, and his influence is also apparent in the music of Chopin and Schumann.

The years 1811–17 were again spent by Weber as an itinerant conductor-composer. He established a brilliant reputation as he moved through many of the principal cities of German-speaking Europe, finally settling in Dresden. He courted the soprano Caroline Brandt in Vienna and Prague. The couple were married in Prague on 4 November 1817, soon after Weber had taken up the relatively secure position of director of the opera house at Dresden. Many of his most important works stem from these middle years, including the clarinet concertos, the Second Piano Concerto, the Piano Sonata no. 1 and many songs. During his tenure in Dresden, Weber began to compose works of a larger and more ambitious nature. He is best remembered today for his operas *Euryanthe, Der Freischütz* and *Oberon*.

WEBER'S ILLNESS

The first symptoms of Weber's illness appeared in January 1812. He complained of sharp chest pains which he referred to as 'rheumatism'. The trouble recurred later that summer. He collapsed in Prague in 1813 and in 1817 he suffered from stomach trouble and from haemorrhoids which bled and gave him pain. Also in 1817 he suffered from a painful throat condition which did not clear up for several weeks.

In 1819 he found himself unwell with recurrent fevers; he became extremely pessimistic about his health and consulted a Dr Bienitz, who decided that Weber had an 'abdominal condition'. The composer was not happy with this opinion and consulted a younger doctor, Weigel, who concluded that the composer had a 'chest complaint'. Whether these diffuse symptoms were due to tuberculosis remains debatable. Certainly that diagnosis was not made by his physicians and it would certainly have been inappropriate for them to do so. Cavitating tuberculosis often begins insidiously.

In Dresden in 1821 Weber had his first pulmonary haemorrhage (haemoptysis). He recorded the event in his diary of 6 July 1821 and also noted that he felt 'very tired and ill'. The haemorrhage coincided with the rejection of his opera *Die drei Pintos*, and he became deeply depressed and pessimistic about his health and work. His diary now recorded a chronic cough and intermittent haemorrhage. In Vienna he laconically wrote: 'I cough a bit but no more than I do at home and after I've been talking.'

Weber's pupil Julius Benedict gives a graphic description of the evolution of Weber's disease (Dresden, 26 October 1823):

He seemed to have grown older by ten years in those few weeks, his former strength of mind, his love of art had all forsaken him. Sunken eyes, general apathy and a dry, hectic cough bespoke clearly the precarious condition of his health. He attended official duties as before with the most scrupulous punctuality, but his creative powers were at a complete standstill (9).

By March 1824 he began to experience severe shortness of breath and his cough became more painful. He was forced to give up his daily walk. In August his delicate health obliged him to take a water cure at Marienbad. When he returned to Dresden he received a letter from Charles Kemble, the manager of the Royal Opera House, Covent Garden, commissioning an opera. This commission was to make him a respected international figure at a time when he was obviously terminally ill. It would potentially alter his precarious financial situation for the better. Because of his fluctuating health, Weber was initially apathetic about the commission, but he realized that he needed to provide for his family in the event of his early death. He consulted a Dr Hedenus, who told him that he might live for six years in the warm climate of Italy but would succumb within months or weeks in England.

He began to learn English from a man named Carey. He took 153 lessons, filled a note-book with carefully written English exercises and learned to correspond in English with considerable accuracy. There were some financial problems connected with the Covent Garden commission. However, during the latter part of 1824 he decided both to undertake the commission of an opera – *Oberon* – and to accept the offer of a trip to England in order to conduct and rehearse it himself.

By December 1824 Weber was complaining of a severe depression provoked, no doubt, by both debt and disease. His mood was elevated by the birth of a son, Alexander, on 6 January 1825. (His son evidently showed great artistic promise but died prematurely of tuberculosis at nineteen years of age in Dresden in 1844.) The rest of the year was spent preparing *Oberon*. Weber set out for London in February 1826. He wrote to Frederick Gubitz: 'My dear Friend, I shall earn a great deal of money in England – I owe it to my family, I'm going to London to die. Be silent: I know it!'

WEBER'S DEATH IN LONDON

Weber travelled to London by coach via Paris. At the first posting station on the way to Paris he sent back his horses and his coachman; as the last link with Dresden was gone he was visibly holding back the tears. In Paris he paid a call on Rossini, who was shocked to find him so pale and wasted and coughing frantically with the effort of climbing the stairs. He left Paris on 1 March 1826, travelling to Calais via Amiens. He crossed the channel on the English steamboat *Fury*, then took the express coach to London and reached his lodgings at 91 (now 103) Great Portland Street. He was installed on the second floor with an excellent grand piano. Sir George Smart, the director of the Royal Opera House, oversaw his domestic care to the extent of providing servants and a warm bath – a luxury in those days – for the ailing composer. He received a £500 commission fee for *Oberon* and a further £225 for conducting four concerts. His letters express a warm enthusiasm for English hospitality and for the high standard of the opera house orchestra.

Rehearsals for *Oberon* began on 9 March. Anne Coward, a twenty-two-year-old soprano, recalled that 'he was the most perfect gentleman I met, and his sad face and fragile appearance excited much sympathy from all of us on stage'. In the months that followed Weber attended concerts and aristocratic dinners, doing his best to conceal his debilitated condition from the public.

His breathlessness was worsening, he began to experience diarrhoea and his ankles began to swell; despite this, he gave of his best at his last performance (25 May), as the musician J.E.Cox noted in his diary:

> I had seen him, whilst conducting his music, throwing his whole heart and soul into the work, ... and manifesting an energy that would have wearied a man in rude health ... But on passing to his private room ... as I then saw him panting for breath, torn to pieces by a hacking consumptive cough, and reeking with cold perspiration, all the delight I had experienced vanished. How gratefully would he recognize with a weary smile any slight attempt to minister some small relief to the excruciating agony of the half-suffocation against which he struggled with all the determination of his energetic spirit!

Those in the audience who perceived the state of his health sent a flood of home remedies to the composer. Great Portland Street was inundated with lozenges, jellies and cough cures.

Ominously, Weber's feet began to swell so much that he could not put on his best shoes and stockings. He wrote that he was shocked by the amount of blood he had coughed up. His complexion was pale; he was consumed with anguish and homesickness, and his hands began to shake from fever. His diarrhoea became intractable; he wrote in his diary, 'I am now a broken machine.' Weber consulted a Dr P.M. Kind, who recommended inhalations of prussic acid for his lung condition. Weber refused to submit to this dangerous régime.

His health continued to deteriorate: on 28 May he had an acute attack of breathlessness which left him exhausted; on the following day, after a benefit concert for the *Oberon* soprano, he had a severe haemorrhage in his carriage and had to be carried up the stairs by Smart. His letters now betrayed the weakness of a failing hand. He could no longer walk unaided. He began to plan his journey home along the Rhine to Dresden, but his condition continued to decline inexorably. His diarrhoea no longer responded to the opium which had been prescribed to control it.

On 1 June he had another serious episode of expectoration of blood. Dr Kind applied a mustard plaster. Although this strictly had no therapeutic efficacy it supplied comfort and seemed to relieve Weber's breathing. He wrote optimistically to his wife telling of his plans to return home. Throughout his illness he had taken great pains not to alarm his family.

On 4 June, the night before he died, he dined once more with Sir George Smart. He drank three glasses of port and spent the evening reclining on a sofa and talking about the journey home. He was persuaded to go to bed at 10 o'clock. Anton Fürstenau, who had accompanied Weber to England, tried to persuade the ailing composer to sleep in his room. Weber declined the offer but agreed to leave the door of his room unlocked. Fürstenau applied a plaster to his chest, and Weber retired, after which his friends discussed ways of trying to stop his journey home.

On the morning of Monday, 5 June 1826, the harp maker Conrad Stumpff called on Weber at 6.50. He got no answer from Weber's room and so roused the servants. Lucy Hall, the housekeeper, tried the door. It was locked. Alarmed, they raised Smart and the pianist Moscheles. Fürstenau bought locksmith's tools and together they forced the door. When they tore the bedcurtains back they found Weber lying still with his head resting on his left hand and a calm expression on his face. A physician was summoned to open a vein; he raised Weber's hand and then let it fall saying, 'It is all useless, this man has been dead these five or six hours.' In the afternoon a postmortem was held and a medical certificate issued. The body was embalmed and put into a lead coffin, which was sealed.

At 9.30 a.m. on 21 June a funeral procession was held and the hearse drawn by six black horses made its way to the Catholic chapel at Moorfields where twelve eminent musicians carried the coffin to the vault. Fourteen years after Weber's death, his coffin was discovered among an enormous pile of accumulating coffins. In 1844 Richard Wagner and Giacomo Meyerbeer arranged its return to Dresden. It was reinterred in the Catholic cemetery to funeral music specially arranged from Weber's operas by Wagner, who was profoundly moved by the occasion.

WEBER'S AUTOPSY AND THE CLINICAL EXPLANATION OF HIS DEATH

Weber's death certificate and postmortem report are now in the British Library (Additional MS 41778). The report by the doctors reads as follows:

On examining the body of C.M. von Weber we found an ulcer on the left side of the larynx, the lungs almost universally diseased, filled with tubercles, of which many were in a state of suppuration with two vomicae one of them about the size of a common egg, the other smaller. The which was a quite sufficient cause of death.

F.Jenkins, M.D., Chas.F.Forbes, M.D., P.M.Kind, M.D., Wm.Robinson, Surgeon.

91, Great Portland Street, 5th of June, 5 o'clock.

Forbes also wrote privately to Sir George Smart that evening; the letter contains considerably more detail than the death certificate.

My dear Sir,
The appearances which presented themselves on examining the body of Carl Maria von Weber were as follows. An ulcer in the larynx, left side, the lungs full of tubercles large and small, many of them in a state of suppuration – two vomicae[1] in the left lung – the one about the size of a hen's egg, the other rather smaller – on the upper surface of the left lung were two bladder-like appearances which I at first took for Hydatids[2] – the one as large as a walnut, the other rather larger than a hazel nut. They arose from a rupture of the air cells of the lungs; the investing membrane became consequently distended with air. This appearance is frequently seen in the lungs of a broken-winded horse.

Believe me, my dear sir,
Yours faithfully,
Chas.F.Forbes.

Monday evening, June 5, 1826.

There can be no doubt that tuberculosis was responsible for Weber's death.

Pulmonary tuberculosis is due to infection with mycobacterium tuberculosis. The disease is transmitted from person to person; it has been estimated that one person with 'open' tuberculosis infects ten new cases each year (12). The disease is still a very serious problem in many underdeveloped countries (12). The infection develops in two stages. In the primary stage it commonly involves the middle lobe of the lung and the local lymph glands. Often the disease heals at this stage, to

[1] cysts – hollow lesions with central cavities
[2] tumour-like lesions, extremely common in the nineteenth century, caused by the tapeworm echinococcus granulosis

98

reactivate later. (Healing coincides with the development of immunity.) In cases where such reactivation occurs the cavitating picture, 'secondary tuberculosis', common in adults, is seen. Primary tuberculosis is common in children. Often it causes no severe illness. Occasionally the bacterium disseminates via the blood stream to other organs during the primary stage, often causing severe disease. It is likely that Weber's diseased hip was due to a disseminated primary tuberculosis (12).

That Weber's tuberculosis was of long standing is evidenced by apical emphysema. The 'vomicae' are actually air cysts of bullous emphysema, and the appearance at the apex of the left lung resembling the 'lungs of a broken-winded horse' suggests apical emphysema. Emphysema is caused by loss of the alveoli, the respiratory units. Apical compensatory emphysema is frequently seen with old, long-standing tuberculous scarring. The scarring may have occurred during the primary phase and the infection may have lain dormant for many years before reactivating. (Emphysema in the left lung may be indicative of an extensive primary focus in that lung which healed by scarring many years before.) Weber had considerable evidence of reactivation tuberculosis. The 'suppurating tubercules' and the ulcer on the larynx strongly suggest active secondary disease. In secondary tuberculosis the characteristic cavitating lesions with central caseation[3] occur. These are clearly described in the autopsy report by Charles Forbes.

Some medical biographers have related the ulcer on Weber's larynx to the famous incident when he ruined his singing voice by accidentally drinking engraving acid in Breslau in 1805. However, it seems more likely that the ulcer relates to reactivation tuberculosis, although it is a little surprising that his associates did not report the voice change and difficulty in swallowing which is characteristic of tubercular laryngitis.

Weber's diarrhoea probably relates to dissemination of tuberculosis to the gastro-intestinal tract which, like tubercular laryngitis, commonly occurs in the terminal phase of cavitating pulmonary tuberculosis. The swelling of Weber's ankles probably relates to the strain imposed upon the heart by extensive lung disease but may also have been due to the deposition of a protein called amyloid in the heart muscle causing heart failure. This sometimes occurs in long-standing tuberculosis.

Weber's pallor was caused by anaemia due to loss of blood and to chronic disease.

---

[3] a characteristic cheesy appearance in the centre of the cavity

Tuberculosis claimed the lives of many of the members of Weber's immediate family. The case of the Weber family, where many members were struck down from one generation to another, serves as a reminder of the considerable philosophical and scientific difficulties which attended the demonstration of the infectious nature of tuberculosis.

REFERENCES

1. R. Laennec, *A Treatise on Diseases of the Chest* (London, 1834, trans. J. Forbes), pp. 100–12, 163–70, 253–341
2. J. Clark, *A Treatise on Pulmonary Consumption* (London, 1835), pp. 146–7, 161–3, 221–36, 240–1, 288–99
3. R. Koch, *The Cure of Consumption* (London, 1890)
4. R. H. Major, *Classic Descriptions of Disease* (London, 1932), pp. 8–10, 37–9
5. R. Dubos, *The White Plague* (Boston, 1952), pp. 44–6
6. R. Kervan, *Laennec: His Life and Times* (New York, 1960)
7. S. A. Waksman, *The Conquest of Tuberculosis* (Berkeley, 1964)
8. D. Kerner, 'Carl Maria von Weber als Patient', *Münchener medizinische Wochenschrift*, 116 (1967), p. 903
9. J. Warrack, *Carl Maria von Weber* (London, 1968), pp. 30–5, 55, 83–104, 263–307
10. G. Shepperson, 'David Livingstone 1813–1873', *British Medical Journal* (1973), pp. 2, 232
11. C. E. Abbot, 'Composers and Tuberculosis: The Effects on Creativity', *Journal of The Canadian Medical Association*, 126 (1982), pp. 534–44
12. D. J. Weatherall (ed.), *Oxford Textbook of Medicine*, 2nd edn (Oxford, 1986), vol. 1, section 5, pp. 278–303

Gioachino Rossini
(1792–1868)

INTRODUCTION

Rossini died in Paris in November 1868, at the age of seventy-six, of the complications of an operation performed for a tumour of the rectum. He had suffered for many years from the stigmata of multiple, chronic indispositions. Rossini officially 'retired' from composing soon after his greatest success, the opera *William Tell*, premièred in Paris in August 1829. He was a wealthy man, and he was renowned for his witticisms and his brilliant musical soirées and banquets, which were attended by many of the great artists and statesmen of the time. There was, however, a darker side behind this façade of high living.

CHRONIC GONORRHOEA

Rossini suffered from chronic gonorrhoea and his correspondence is full of reference to this painful condition. He contracted the disease from a prostitute and fell seriously ill with the complaint in 1832. He experienced many years of a painful discharge, haemorrhage and dysuria[1] due to gonococcal cystitis.[2] Rossini's physicians were well aware of the venereal nature of his complaint, as was the composer himself, who suffered intense feelings of guilt and shame. Rossini's physician tells us in a surviving medical report (published by Riboli: see below) that the composer lived a life of 'determined celibacy' after contracting gonorrhoea: 'At the age of forty-four he mitigated his

[1] pain on urination
[2] an infection of the bladder

101

passion for women and abandoned the use of liquors and overheating foods. But already haemorrhoids manifested themselves and during the periods of losses of blood from them his health was much improved' (7). Rossini developed a urethral stricture which obstructed the flow of urine. He learned to treat this stricture himself by the daily use of a tin catheter to relieve the obstruction. In the medical report the disease was called blennorrhoeal urethritis, a contemporary medical synonym for gonorrhoea. Gonorrhoea is a disease with a long history: it was described and named by the Roman physician Galen in AD 130, and there are even references to it in the Old Testament. The disease now responds well to antibiotic therapy. It is caused by the bacterium neisseria gonorrhoea. In the nineteenth century the only effective treatment of chronic gonococcal urethral stricturing was obtained by surgical means; today, chemotherapy with antibiotics aims to halt the disease before strictures of the urethra develop.

The Parisian venereologist Philippe Ricord differentiated gonorrhoea from syphilis in 1838. He demonstrated that the disease was caused by a different agent from syphilis by inoculating 667 subjects with gonococcal pus; none of them developed syphilis. It is unlikely that Rossini was treated with mercury: after the publication of Ricord's paper it was not customary to give 'mineral specifics' for gonorrhoea.

The comprehensive knowledge we have of Rossini's medical history comes from two principal sources: L.S.Silvestri detailed the effects of Rossini's bladder ailment in his life of the composer (5) and in 1954 Bruno Riboli published his penetrating 'medical–psychological profile' in *La Rassegna musicale* (7). Riboli's work is based on a letter from an unknown physician at Bologna to Jean Civiale, the Parisian urologist whom Rossini consulted in May 1843. (This document was unearthed in 1947.) The letter was written in passable French.

Jean Civiale was the most acclaimed of the Parisian urologists. He was noted for his manual dexterity with catheterization and for his skill with the lithotrite, a device inserted per urethra which could crush bladder stones. (Bladder stones were extremely common in the nineteenth century.) The lithotrite made hazardous and painful perineal lithotomies unnecessary and doubtless saved many lives.

Civiale claimed the invention of the lithotrite as his own. He wrote many urological papers on the instrument (e.g. 2, 4), which he exhibited to the Royal Academy of Sciences in Paris in 1824. It consisted of a very thin catheter tube, a transmission rod and a three-pronged forceps. The tube was introduced into the bladder; the forceps then opened and grasped the stone, which was broken up by a drill system and subsequently removed in small pieces.

Civiale's skill with the catheter undoubtedly spared Rossini an unenviable demise by bladder obstruction. After consulting him, Rossini was confined to his home for three months. He lay in his darkened bedroom obsessed with thoughts of death while Civiale treated him both medically and surgically. Olympe Pelissier, Rossini's second wife, nursed him devotedly. Rossini's illness does not fully explain his subsequent mental and physical prostration nor his probable manic–depressive illness.

After his convalescence Rossini penned approximately 180 vocal and instrumental pieces, collectively called *Péchés de vieillesse* (sins of old age). Some of them have bizarre titles suggestive of the sufferings and hypochondriacal leanings of the composer's later years: *Prélude convulsif*, *Étude asthmatique, Mon Prélude hygiénique du matin, Valse torturée.*

BIPOLAR AFFECTIVE DISORDER (MANIC–DEPRESSIVE ILLNESS)

There is considerable evidence to support the suggestion that Rossini suffered from manic–depressive illness. Riboli classifies Rossini as having the pyknic bodily habitus and notes the periods of profound depression which characterized Rossini's later life (7). (The pyknic body conformation is a squat, heavy build which was thought to be associated with manic–depressive illness.) 'In reality the chronic urethritis itself, though in a grave and painful form, does not alone suffice to explain the strong physical and psychic prostration into which Rossini fell.' Rossini experienced a bewildering variety of symptoms including loss of weight, chronic diarrhoea, auditory hallucinations and suicidal ideation. In later years, according to his own testimony, he suffered from a profound dementing illness. If mercury was used to treat Rossini's venereal disease it may have exacerbated the psychiatric illness, but it is doubtful that it was the actual cause of it (1, 6, 8); in any case, as was previously stated, it is unlikely that Rossini received mercury.

RESPIRATORY AND CARDIOVASCULAR DISEASES

Rossini suffered from numerous aggravating physical disorders. He became pathologically obese and by 1865 he found walking difficult. He confined himself to his home and was often obsessed with thoughts of death. Rossini showed evidence of chronic bronchitis and emphysema, no doubt due to cigar smoking. He became short of breath and complained of a chronic cough with winter exacerbation. In December 1866 he suffered a stroke and was immobilized in bed for several months. The old man unexpectedly made a full recovery and regained 'so much of his former strength that no sign of the attack showed'. He celebrated his seventy-fifth birthday on 28 February 1867 (his actual birthday was 29 February). Rossini was not above joking about his health: once, when giving a reception for Liszt, he ran his fingers through Liszt's long hair, which fell like a mane to his shoulders; 'Les beaux cheveux – sont-ils à vous?' he asked. He then pointed sadly to his own wig and remarked ironically that he would soon have neither teeth nor legs of his own. Rossini suffered from pains in the legs and the hands. His painfully swollen hands may have been due to chronic Raynaud's disease, and the weakness and pain in his legs which grew worse on walking were due to peripheral vascular disease,[3] again a consequence of cigar smoking.

ROSSINI'S FATAL CARCINOMA

Rossini was troubled by rectal bleeding and pain in 1868. He consulted Dr Vio Bonato who examined him and found what he thought to be a rectal fistula. Rossini was by now bedridden and frail. He was uncommunicative and spoke only when questioned or when he needed assistance. Bonato routinely re-examined the composer several months later and revised his diagnosis. He felt that an operation would help the composer. It was evident by now that Rossini was suffering from a rapidly growing carcinoma of the rectum or anal canal. Rossini's bronchitis improved in early November, and Bonato consulted Auguste Nelaton,[4] who scheduled the operation for 3 November 1868. He planned to remove as much of the tumour as possible by operating per ano.

Because of the chronic bronchitis and evident cardiac failure, Nelaton correctly perceived Rossini as a poor anaesthetic risk and planned the operation so that the composer would be under chloroform for no longer than five minutes. He removed as much as possible of the cancerous tissue and patched the area with cotton bandages to stop haemorrhaging. Olympe dressed the wound herself and would allow no one else to

[3] caused by hardening and narrowing of the arteries of the legs
[4] Auguste Nelaton, professor of surgery at the Hôpital St Louis, was a pioneer of abdominal surgery and the inventor of the flexible rubber catheter.

touch the ailing musician. Nelaton returned on 5 November and, alarmed by the appearance of the wound, decided upon a second operation. After this operation he was optimistic about the healing of the wound and was heard to say, 'I think we shall save him.' This, alas, was not to be.

Rossini's condition soon began to deteriorate precipitously. He was maddened by pain and disorientated in place and time because of an acute brain syndrome. He began to fight with and abuse the four medical interns who were to lift the heavy man and change his bed-linen. He became febrile and constantly requested ice which was forbidden by his physician. When one of his attendants gave him ice he caressed the young man's head in gratitude. A fatal wound infection developed. This was called erysipelas by Rossini's early biographers, and we have no reason to doubt the validity of the diagnosis. (Erysipelas is a surgical infection. In Rossini's case it undoubtedly resulted from the use of an unsterile scalpel.) The infection quickly spread over the entire lower half of the composer's body. He became delirious with fever and pain and lapsed into a coma. A priest was sent for and Extreme Unction hastily given. Rossini died on 13 November 1868.

On Saturday morning, 14 November 1868, Gustave Doré made two sketches of Rossini on his death-bed. The corpse was embalmed by a Dr Falcony, who had invented a liquid which he grandly said would 'hold back corruption for ever'. A Requiem Mass attended by a crowd of three thousand was held in the Madeleine. Olympe Rossini lived until 22 March 1878. After her death, her remains were returned to Italy with those of her husband. They now rest together in the church of Santa Croce in Florence. The creeping paralysis of Rossini's faculties and the slow decline of his health was an unfitting sequel to the years of brilliant success of a man who was once the world's most popular composer of opera.

A COMPLICATION OF SURGERY

Erysipelas is a rapidly spreading infection of the skin and subcutaneous tissues usually caused by the organism streptococcus pyogenes. This organism produces an enzyme called hyaluronidase which breaks down connective tissues and allows it to spread quickly through tissue planes. The condition is characterized by a raised, indurated red area with a sharply demarcated border. It is acutely painful and is accompanied by a high fever. Death results from a metabolic toxaemia or septicaemia.

In the era before antiseptic technique epidemics of erysipelas were common as the infection was spread from patient to patient by unwashed or imperfectly cleaned instruments. It was one of the principal causes of death in the infamous Scutari Hospital during the Crimean campaign, and also in the hospitals of the American Civil War. Ironically, Lister's epoch-making paper describing antiseptic technique, which revolutionized surgery and ushered in the modern surgical era, appeared in 1867 in the *Lancet* – the year before Rossini's death. If Nelaton had adopted Lister's methods, it is conceivable that the fatal infection could have been prevented. It was many years before the medical profession accepted the methods of Lister and the doctrines of Pasteur and Koch.

PRESENT-DAY TREATMENT
OF BOWEL TUMOURS

The local operation was of course inadequate to deal with a large primary tumour of the bowel and to prevent local recurrence, and it seems that Rossini was at least spared a slow death from obstruction of the bowel. Modern operations involve an abdominal approach to the tumour, and if the tumour is located low down in the rectum or the anal canal, as Rossini's must have been, diversion of the bowel and the fashioning of a colostomy is undertaken. The rate of local recurrence of the tumour is still high. Local recurrence or spread to the liver are the principal causes of death in carcinoma of the rectum. The tumour does not respond well to chemotherapy and surgery still affords the only mode of possible cure.

In the early part of the nineteenth century laparotomy and opening of the peritoneum spelt almost inevitable death, but by the 1880s, after antiseptic techniques were more widely adopted, laparotomy was becoming a common and reasonably safe procedure. The development of blood-banking procedures and effective antibiotic cover (which dates only from the 1940s) have greatly added to the safety of abdominal surgery in the twentieth century, as have dramatic advances in technology relating to anaesthesia.

Carcinoma of the colon is a common tumour among the elderly and is particularly prevalent in Western society. Dietary factors are blamed for the high incidence of the tumour and these include, *inter alia*, insufficient dietary fibre and high consumption of meat. The tumour is derived from the surface epithelium of the bowel and often presents as a polyp or an ulcer. If Rossini's cancer was located in the peri-anal region, it is most likely to have been a squamous cell carcinoma. This grows as a flat, hard, shield-like lesion. It has a poor prognosis (10).

TABLE 1
SUMMARY OF ROSSINI'S ILLNESSES

Carcinoma of the Rectum
Cause of death: wound infection, probably erysipelas, occurring after attempted local excision of a carcinoma of the rectum or anal canal.

Other Illnesses
chronic gonorrhoea
congestive cardiac failure
chronic obstructive airways disease
tobacco abuse
cerebrovascular accident

Probable Illnesses
senile dementia
bipolar affective disorder
   Dr Riboli contends that Rossini's psychological symptoms are referable to manic–depressive illness. However, it is possible that chronic illness, chronic pain and senile dementia combined to produce the dark state of mind that was a feature of his later years. Rossini's psychological condition and, especially, the factors which prompted his early abandonment of opera are poorly documented by his biographers.

peripheral vascular disease

REFERENCES

 1. Stendhal [H. Beyle], *Vie de Rossini*, 2 vols (Paris, 1824; rev. 2nd edn, 1922)
 2. J. Civiale, *De la Lithotrite ou Broiement de la pierre dans la vessie* (Paris, 1827)
 3. A. Zanolini, *Biografia di Gioachino Rossini* (Paris, 1836; rev. 2nd edn, Bologna, 1875)
 4. J. Civiale, *Collection de calculs urinaires et d'instruments de chirurgie* (Paris, 1869)
 5. S. Silvestri, *Della Vita e delle Opere di Gioachino Rossini* (Milan, 1874)

6. G. H. J. Derwent, *Rossini and some Forgotten Nightingales* (London, 1934)
7. B. Riboli, 'Profilo medico-psicologico di G. Rossini', *La Rassegna musicale*, 24 (1954), p. 292
8. H. Weinstock, *Rossini: a Biography* (New York, 1968)
9. J. Sabiston (ed.), *Textbook of Surgery: The Biological Basis of Modern Surgical Practice*, 13th edn (London, 1986), pp. 277, 1003–11, 1035–52
10. R. W. Talbot, 'The Changing Nature of Anal Cancer', *British Medical Journal*, 297 (1988), p. 239

Franz Schubert
(1797–1828)

Franz Schubert was born on 31 January 1797, the twelfth of fourteen children of whom five survived infancy. His father was an enterprising schoolmaster who owned his own school. From 1808 Schubert received his education in the Imperial and Royal Seminary. By the age of 12 he had become a proficient composer, violinist and pianist. He attempted to become a schoolmaster like his father, but loathed the work and gradually turned towards his principal goal of composing. By 1818 the sole source of his income – meagre as it was – was composition.

Physically he was unimpressive – about 155 cm tall. He was stumpy with a stubby, rounded nose, an oval face and a deeply cleft chin. He was near-sighted and wore glasses. His hair was brown and curly. Although eager to play the piano at parties, he was quiet and uncommunicative. He often smoked and drank heavily. Karl Beethoven made a remark about Schubert's reclusiveness in the conversation book of 1823; Schubert and Beethoven met only briefly when Beethoven was on his deathbed. Liszt, who was later to become a great champion of the composer, is said not to have met the retiring musician, although he was studying in Vienna at the time.

Through the efforts of Anna Milder and Johann Vogl, popular singers of the era, Schubert gradually became known to a small and select audience in Vienna and the famous evenings known as Schubertiads were organized. Schubert's enthusiastic admirers would present evenings of his songs and instrumental pieces, often with the composer himself accompanying the performers. Schubert made little effort to court this spontaneous and appreciative audience.

Like Mozart, he was an amazingly fast composer who could conceive complete scores in his head and simply write them down. According to contemporary testimony Schubert wrote down the ballad *Erlkönig* within minutes of receiving the poem. He preferred to compose without a piano, claiming that it was not necessary and actually disturbed his train of thought – indeed, he never owned a piano.

Why a man so gifted remained a private figure is a mystery. Schubert's personality may have contributed to the public's neglect of his music. He himself wrote, 'I have come into the world for no purpose but to compose', and although he fulfilled this mission superbly, he seems to have lacked the impetus to get his music publicly performed and was neglectful in even keeping his scores for posterity to judge them. There have been numerous theories as to why Schubert so shunned conventional society, and perhaps we shall never know entirely why he failed to gain the recognition due to him. Some of the reasons, however, are obvious, not least Schubert's unfavourable physical appearance: he was a competent musician but not an interesting figure at the keyboard. He was a poor and unassertive businessman and had little interest in financial matters, living from day to day with little regard for the future and for money.

SCHUBERT CONTRACTS SYPHILIS

The circumstances in which Schubert contracted syphilis are unknown, although it is commonly believed that he contracted it from a prostitute about six years before his death. Josef Kenner, a close friend, noted that 'anyone who knew Schubert knows that he has two natures foreign to each other and how powerfully the craving for pleasure dragged his soul down to the slough of moral degradation'. Kenner's comment, stripped of its pious moralizing, may indicate that Schubert had a vigorous, clandestine sexual life that we do not know about.

It seems that he associated frequently with prostitutes and was a dark figure to many of his contemporaries. A profound sense of shame pervaded his life which was heightened when he contracted syphilis. The disease was not fatal to him and did not impair his physical health or mental abilities – he contracted it only a few years before he died, and the tertiary stage of the disease which is characterized by tissue destruction and progressive and often fatal neurological illness had not manifested itself. Schubert suffered from the stigmata of recurrent secondary-stage disease which, while not fatal, were embarrassing and boded ill for his future with their implication of later serious physical and mental illness. The most humiliating effect of the disease was on his skin and hair: his body was often entirely covered by a recurrent red rash. When it was present he confined himself to his house and hid from his friends. Schubert's hair began to fall out in a patchy manner because of the disease, and he bought himself a wig. In his last year he also suffered from dizziness and headaches. His depression, remorse and guilt were heartfelt. The haunting song cycle *Winterreise* and the last piano sonatas were composed when Schubert was well aware of his illness and its fatal complications. The melancholy in these last works is said by many of his biographers and by many music critics to reflect his state of mind and his shame and dejection at the progress of the disease. Schubert does not once mention syphilis directly in his correspondence.

However, it was not syphilis but another, more acute, infectious disease which killed Schubert. The cause of his death is given as 'typhus' on his death certificate. (This is probably not the disease that modern physicians refer to as 'typhus', which is a specific illness caused by a rickettsia, a micro-organism similar to a bacterium.) In the early nineteenth century 'typhus' was a generic term applied to illnesses which caused fever and clouding of consciousness. Indeed, Schubert's illness is more typical of typhoid fever,[1] which we know was endemic in Europe at the time and outbreaks of which were frequent. Schubert died in such an epidemic. (It is impossible to determine precisely how he died. In Schubert's day, even the diagnosis of 'fever' was a subjective one, as the clinical thermometer had not been invented.[2])

Schubert's death was untimely and unexpected, although in the preceding years his health had not been good. He died on 19 November 1828, at 3.00 p.m., having not quite reached his thirty-second birthday.

THE PSYCHOLOGICAL AFTERMATH OF SYPHILIS

Schubert was admitted to Vienna General Hospital in 1824 for the treatment of the rash. He experienced an improvement of it, and he no longer needed to wear a wig. His friend Moritz von Schwind writes of the composer's improved condition: 'He says that after a few days

[1] The two diseases were differentiated by the American physician W. W. Gerhard in 1836.
[2] K. A. Wunderlich popularized the thermometer with an essay published in Leipzig in 1868.

of the new treatment he felt how his complaint broke up and how every-thing was different. He still lives one day on panada [boiled bread flavoured with sugar and cinnamon] and the next on cutlets; he lavishly drinks tea and goes bathing a good deal and is still superhumanly indus-trious. A new quartet is to be performed at Schuppanzigh's ... He has now long been at work on an octet with the greatest zeal.' (1) Schubert complains in letters of the side effects of his medications, and it may be that some of the morbidity of his illness was actually due to them. On the positive side, his physicians imparted to him a new optimism about his illness, taking the correct line – that his condition would not inevitably lead to mental disease.

During the year of his death Schubert seems to have been in a latent stage of his disease, with very few of the stigmata present. The dizziness from which he suffered may have been the first manifestation of men-ingovascular syphilis, an early part of the tertiary neurosyphilis complex, although this is by no means certain. Schubert was almost certainly given mercury, but we cannot know to what extent this agent damaged his health.

The best-known study of the chronic effects of syphilis is the Oslo Study, which was conducted from 1910 to 1951, in the era before penicil-lin was used to cure the disease. The study showed that one-third of patients with untreated syphilis develop clinical evidence of tertiary syphilis and that about 15% of patients actually die of the condition. Sero-logical studies conducted at the turn of the century showed that syphilis was far commoner among the socio-economically deprived and that prostitution was an important vector in the transmission of the disease.

Interestingly, the study noted that there was an additional excess of mortality which was not directly attributable to syphilis in people known to have the disease. Untreated syphilis may make people susceptible to other infectious diseases: chronic illness is known to cause immuno-suppression, and it is likely that chronic untreated syphilis did so. Alter-natively, those who contract syphilis may, coincidentally, be more sus-ceptible to other diseases, perhaps because of socio-economic or social factors undisclosed in the study. In short, Schubert's future was by no means assured and was made more uncertain by the fact that he had syphilis. The life of the average urban dweller in the early nineteenth century was in any case a precarious one, and the threat of infectious disease was ever present; it is not true, however, that Schubert would inevitably have died or developed mental disease because he had second-ary syphilis.

Syphilis is becoming rarer in Western communities thanks to the advent of the penicillins which cure the condition. Antibiotics do not reverse the damage which is done chronically in the tertiary stage. Tertiary lesions often cause irreversible tissue destruction. Thus, changes – which include damage to heart valves, to the brain and to the skeletal system – remain after treatment but, with adequate antibiotic treatment, progress no further. The organism remains sensitive to penicillin.

SCHUBERT'S FINAL ILLNESS

Schubert contracted his last illness shortly after moving to his brother Ferdinand's house in the Vienna suburb of Neue Wieden. His doctor, the court physician Ernst von Rinna, thought that this change of climate, namely, fresh air and the country environment, would do him good. However, sanitary conditions in the suburbs were often crude and insufficient. Despite the pressures of moving into a new house, Schubert took long walks in the countryside and this had the effect of invigorating his health and his spirits.

In late October 1828 a new illness began. This was not thought by von Rinna to be a manifestation of syphilis. Schubert's brother, Ferdinand, describes how the symptoms commenced[3]:

> Then on the last day of October, when he wished to eat some fish in the evening, he suddenly drew his knife and fork on the plate as soon as he had tasted the first morsel, suggesting that he found his food immensely repellent and he felt just as though he had taken poison. From that moment he hardly ate or drank anything more, taking nothing but medicines. He tried to find relief by moving in the fresh air and therefore took a few walks.

Over the next weeks, despite intermittent bouts of nausea, he was 'very cheerful, in fact almost unrestrained in his gaiety'.

On 12 November, Schubert wrote his last letter to his friend, Schober:

> Dear Schober, I am ill, I have eaten nothing for eleven days and have drunk nothing. I totter feebly and shakily from my chair to bed and back again. Rinna is treating me; if I ever take anything I bring it up at once.

Schubert was then racked with intermittent bouts of fever and nausea.

[3] All quotations in this section are taken from Deutsch (1).

He was lovingly and carefully nursed by his family but, despite this, his condition continued to worsen. He took his medicines punctually and kept a watch beside his bed for the purpose. Josef von Spaun writes:

> I found him ill in bed although his condition did not seem to me at all serious. He corrected my copy in bed and was glad to see me and said, 'there is really nothing the matter with me, I'm so exhausted I feel as if I were going to fall through the bed'. He was cared for most affectionately by a charming thirteen-year-old sister whom he praised very highly to me. I left him without any anxiety at all and it came as a thunderbolt when, a few days later, I heard of his death.

Lachner, who visited Schubert on 17 November, noted:

> When I came into his room he was lying with his face turned to the wall in the deepest, feverish delirium. Added to this was scanty nursing and a badly heated room on the walls of which the damp was running down! During a lucid moment I took my leave of him and I told him I hoped to be back in four days, but when I returned to Vienna on 21 November, Schubert was already in his grave.

Schober's story is consistent with this. He saw Schubert several times on 17 November. At times his mind seemed lucid and the patient seemed well orientated, but by the evening a delirium set in. Schubert's breathing became laboured and he was raving violently and distractedly.

Ferdinand described Schubert's last hours in a letter to his father, written two days after Schubert's death:

> For on the evening before his death, though only half-conscious, he still said to me, 'I implore you to transfer me to my room, not to leave me here in this corner under the earth. Do I, then, deserve no place above the earth?' I answered him, dear Franz, rest assured, believe me, believe your brother Ferdinand, whom you have always trusted and who loves you so much, you are in the room which you have always been in so far and lie in your bed, and Franz said, 'No, it is not true, Beethoven does not lie here'. Could this be anything but an indication of his inmost wish to repose by the side of Beethoven whom he so greatly revered?

Schubert became disorientated, imagining that he was in some strange and frightening place. He thought of his beloved Beethoven who had been a model for his own career and whose musical ideals he had emulated so well. Ferdinand did his best to quieten and reassure the restless patient: 'A few hours later the doctor appeared who persuaded him in similar words. Schubert looked fixedly into the doctor's eyes and grasped the wall with a feeble hand and he said slowly and seriously: "Here, here is my end."' Schubert died shortly after this. 'Typhus abdominalis' (typhoid fever) was recorded as the cause of death(1).

THE NATURAL HISTORY OF TYPHOID FEVER

Typhoid fever is an acute systemic disease resulting from infection by a bacterium called salmonella typhi, which gains access to the body by the oral route and is in almost all cases a consequence of the ingestion of contaminated food, water or milk. Humans are the only species affected by salmonella typhi, and convalescent patients or chronic carriers serve as the ultimate source of infection. Continuing improvements in socio-economic conditions are thought to be a major factor in the decline of the disease over the last two centuries. To these should be added effective sewage disposal and the securing of a safe water supply, and the detection of chronic carriers of the disease. It is still endemic in Third World countries, and international travellers are often recommended to have typhoid immunization injections. The disease is characterized by malaise, fever, abdominal discomfort and pain, and a transient rash with rose spots on the abdomen. An increase in the size of the spleen and a decreased white blood cell count are also characteristic.

The salmonella bacterium invades the body through the gastro-intestinal tract, and the disease follows a characteristic progression which is seen in the case of Franz Schubert. Initially there is nausea and intermittent fever; frequently the fever increases gradually as the illness develops. Abdominal pain, discomfort and bloating are also common during this early phase. A dry cough and nose-bleeds often occur and may complicate the diagnosis. In the second week a characteristic rash is often observed and the liver and spleen are often enlarged. The mode of death is often due to bowel perforation with peritonitis or by intestinal haemorrhage. There are, of course, many other diagnostic possibilities, and definitive diagnosis at this stage is not possible. Typhoid fever, then, an extremely common illness, best fits the known facts.

Schubert now lies in Vienna cemetery next to Beethoven, his idol and 'role model'. The physician's fee and the funeral were a great expense to his family, who none the less bore it out of a deep affection for the dead composer. His estate amounted to a few sets of clothes and a few sheets of music. The manuscripts of his music were scattered all over Austria and were mainly held in the possession of his loyal friends.

POSTHUMOUS IMPRESSIONS OF THE COMPOSER

In 1863, when Schubert had long been recognized as a musical genius, his remains were exhumed, along with those of Beethoven. The advanced state of decay of the skeleton was held to be due to the presence of syphilitic disease of bone, or possibly to mercurial damage to the skeleton caused by medication. In 1888, the bodies found their final resting-place in metal coffins in the Musicians' Grove of the newly laid-out Central Cemetery in Vienna. The bodies of Beethoven and Schubert lie next to a monument to Mozart. Before the body was reinterred it was again exhumed and further decay of the skeleton was noted. (There was little left of the skull and the long bones.)

The musical world clamoured for anecdotes and images of the now renowned composer. Von Spaun criticized the contemporary portraits of Schubert, saying that they did little justice to his charm and physical characteristics and that they made him look ugly:

> Just as little can one say that Schubert was handsome, but he was well formed and when he spoke pleasantly or smiled, his features were full of charm, and when he was working, full of enthusiasm and burning with zeal. His features then appeared sublimated and almost beautiful. So far as his body is concerned, one might imagine him as a fat lump from the descriptions in his biography but these are entirely incorrect. Schubert had a solidly built, thick-set body, but there was no question of being fat or having a paunch.

Although he was shy and certainly disliked the public's attention, and had little regard for social status or economic advancement, his character was generally attractive to most people. Bauernfeld, who noted occasional outbursts of temper, remarked that Schubert was

> amiable and modest, devoted to his friends from the bottom of his heart and acknowledging with affection the achievements of others, as was shown, for example, with his ever recurring delight over each little drawing done by our highly gifted Schwind. For what was evil and false, on the other hand, he had a veritable hatred. There are also times when a black-winged demon of sorrow and melancholy forced its way into

Schubert's vicinity, not altogether an evil spirit, it is true, since in the dark consecrated hours it often brought out songs of the most agonizing beauty. The conflict between unrestrained and boisterous living and the restless activity of spiritual creation is always exhausting if no balance exists in the soul. Fortunately, in our friend's case, an idealized love was at work, mediating, reconciling, compensating.

Only thirty-one years old at the time of his death, unrecognized and living in inauspicious circumstances, Schubert kept up a truly prodigious output of spellbinding music without apparent regard for prosperity, financial gain or, indeed, even the performance of his music. We know little about his personal life and he may have well been an unhappy, isolated and stigmatized man. The music, however, remains fresh and miraculous, and the famous epitaph on Schubert's tombstone remains succinct and appropriate: 'Music here entombed a rich possession but even fairer hopes.'

TABLE 1

SUMMARY OF SCHUBERT'S ILLNESSES

Cause of Death: Endemic Typhoid Fever ('Typhus Abdominalis'): documented history of food poisoning in an area where Typhoid was endemic; symptoms compatible with Typhoid.

Probable premorbid conditions:
(i) *Syphilis*
   Evidence suggests that the disease was in an early or latent stage. However, recurring headaches and nausea may mean that the composer suffered from a low-grade syphilitic inflammation of the meninges (the connective tissue coverings of the brain).
(ii) *Alcoholism* – high alcohol intake is documented by the composer's friends and relations making alcoholism a strong possibility (1).

REFERENCES

1. O. E. Deutsch, *Schubert: A Documentary Biography* (London, 1946) [Ger. original, Munich, 1914]
2. A. Einstein, *Schubert* (London, 1951)
3. W. J. Brown, *Syphilis and Other Venereal Diseases* (Cambridge, Mass., 1970)
4. P. Woodford, *Schubert* (London, 1978)

The Mendelssohn Family

Felix Mendelssohn's family was one of the most distinguished in Europe. His grandfather, Moses, was a clever businessman who founded the family bank and was also a noted philosopher. Mendelssohn's father, Abraham, was an astute businessman who further consolidated the family's financial interests. Both Felix and his sister were musical child prodigies. Tragically, all were to die of strokes, a condition that was to be known as the 'curse of the Mendelssohns'.

Felix was the son of Moses' second child, Abraham, who undoubtedly contributed his share to the wellbeing and stature of the Mendelssohn family (though he thought of himself with undue modesty as a 'mere dash' between the more famous grandfather and grandson). The Mendelssohns were almost fanatical in the furtherance of their children's education: Felix was provided with his own symphony orchestra to try out his compositions in his teens. The Mendelssohn children received a well-rounded education in music, languages, literature and art; Felix was a gifted draughtsman and landscape artist and, like his grandfather, had a noted ability at languages. He differed from many composers in having a good general education, wealth, status and a supportive and close family life(1) – indeed, it was said by his critics that he did not develop to his full extent as a composer because he had no profound negative experiences to draw on in his art.

To many people Felix Mendelssohn represented an ideal for the past, present and future. He composed in a pleasantly lyrical style within a romantic but somewhat conservative framework, playing no part in the evolution of musical form which was taking place under the hands of many of his contemporaries. His later compositions, which included

118

the oratorios *St Paul* and *Elijah*, found immediate favour with the general public, a condition many of his peers must have envied. The *Songs without Words* were immensely popular during the Victorian era. Mendelssohn himself wrote that he loved clarity and definition in his work.

Both as a composer and as a person he was well respected by his colleagues. Mendelssohn was handsome, with strikingly regular features. He had a graceful figure and though not tall (he was 162 cm in height) was impressive at the podium. His conversation was witty and refined. Mendelssohn had an eye for pretty women and was a popular escort at social events. When he finally married, it was the beautiful Cécile Jeanrenaud he chose. He was a privileged man but one who worked hard to further the arts and who was universally admired for his generosity (1, 3, 5). He held a special place in the affections of the British and formed a close friendship with Queen Victoria and Prince Albert, who were grief-stricken at his early death.

THE EARLY DEATHS
OF THE MENDELSSOHNS

Both Mendelssohn's father and his grandmother were in their sixth decade when they died suddenly after lapsing into unconsciousness. Their death certificates recorded 'cerebral apoplexy' as the cause of death. Today we would call the condition a cerebrovascular accident or stroke. In the elderly, hypertension and atherosclerosis – hardening of the blood vessels – presage a cerebrovascular accident. Hypertension is a hereditary condition and it is likely that both Felix and his sister Fanny also suffered from it, although there was no way of recording blood pressure in Mendelssohn's day. (The sphygmomanometer, which measures blood pressure, was invented only in 1876, by Ritter von Basch.)

Felix's sister Fanny was a fine pianist who married the painter Wilhelm Hensel. She and her brother died suddenly within a year of one another, probably from cerebral haemorrhage of subarachnoid or hypertensive type.

In individuals predisposed to subarachnoid haemorrhage, the walls of the arteries at the base of the brain are defective: their elastic lining is missing. When the blood pressure is chronically raised, as in systemic hypertension, the blood vessels dilate to form balloon-like swellings called 'aneurisms'. They resemble berries and are known as congenital berry aneurisms; the condition, like hypertension, runs in families (6). The aneurisms are a weak area in the artery wall, and if the blood pressure increases they are prone to grow and to rupture suddenly, with potentially catastrophic results. The aneurisms commonly rupture into the subarachnoid space, producing a subarachnoid haemorrhage. If the bleed is large enough, the only manifestation may be sudden death. Often the condition is marked by a blinding headache followed by clouding of consciousness, with severe neck stiffness setting in. A lesser degree of haemorrhage is called a 'warning bleed'. Physicians today would aim to diagnose a cerebral haemorrhage at this early stage so that neurosurgical intervention, which involves clipping off the balloon-shaped aneurism, can be planned. Careful lowering of raised blood pressure can also prevent the extension of a subarachnoid haemorrhage.

THE DEATH OF FANNY MENDELSSOHN

Fanny was 42, an accomplished musician as well as a wife and mother. She had had a busy day and had been organizing a female choir to sing at the local church that morning. Like all of the Mendelssohn family, she maintained a hectic schedule despite having recently noticed a decline in her health. She saw a doctor who could find nothing specifically wrong with her but advised rest and gave some medication to treat nose-bleeds.

At about 2.00 p.m. on 14 May 1847, Fanny became suddenly pale, sweaty and nauseated, and her hands felt numb and heavy. She mumbled incoherently. Her brother Paul managed to put her to bed and rushed off for the doctor. When the doctor arrived Fanny was unconscious; she died at 11.00 p.m. Her death was typical of a large intracerebral haemorrhage (1, p. 334; 3).

The death of Fanny Mendelssohn plunged the close-knit family into grief. They accompanied her husband, Wilhelm Hensel, to Switzerland for a vacation. Felix was the most severely affected: he became profoundly depressed, and although he kept up his busy schedule of composing and performing all that year, thoughts of death and of his beloved sister were not far from his mind. Moscheles wrote that when Mendelssohn returned to Leipzig at the end of September, he had changed in his looks, appearing aged, frail and as if 'marked by death'. Mentally, he was agile and still a marvellous friend; bodily, he was weak and his walk was much slower than before (1, 3).

THE DEATH OF FELIX MENDELSSOHN

Mendelssohn's death in November 1847 followed closely the pattern of his sister's last illness, although it was somewhat more protracted. It began with the same non-specific illness characterized by lethargy, tiredness and depression. It is probable that this illness was hypertension.

On 9 October, Mendelssohn had symptoms suggestive of intracerebral bleeding. He developed a severe headache of sudden onset. When his physician examined him, he found Felix's pulse extremely slow, about 40 beats per minute. The patient was agitated, cold and clammy and very anxious but not yet irrational. A diagnosis was made – that of a 'stomach ailment'. Leeches were prescribed as a curative. Mendelssohn felt a little better a few days later, and on 28 October was able to take a short walk. Taken in the context of the illness that was soon to evolve, this episode represented a 'warning bleed' or a small bleed from a blood vessel at the base of the brain. Mendelssohn had experienced a similar episode seven years before.

On 1 November 1847, Mendelssohn's condition rapidly deteriorated. He experienced the first of a series of strokes. We are told the stroke left him conscious but much weakened. He lay in his bed for two days until, on 3 November, the final haemorrhage came. At 2.00 p.m. he rose from his bed screaming because of the terrible pain in his head and neck. Later that afternoon he lay in a stuporous sleep, and when his wife Cécile asked him how he was, he managed to say only, 'tired ... very tired'. His condition deteriorated, his breathing becoming laboured and heavy. He died at 9.24 that evening (1, p. 339; 3).

The brother and sister virtuosi thus tragically died suddenly within a year of one another probably because of an inherited, familial condition. Mendelssohn was much missed by his many friends and contemporaries, to whom he was the embodiment of enlightenment, generosity and education.

DIFFERENTIAL DIAGNOSIS

In Felix's generation three family members suffered early strokes, characterized by blinding headaches, signs of raised intracranial pressure and, in Felix's case, a 'warning bleed'. (Rebecca Mendelssohn also died of a stroke in her fourth decade.) Many of the descendants of the Mendelssohns succumbed to early strokes (1, p. 345; 3).

Congenital aneurisms of the arteries at the base of the brain, associated with hypertension, is the most likely diagnostic possibility for the illness which so frequently affected the Mendelssohn family. There is no evidence that the Mendelssohns had the polycystic kidneys sometimes associated with these aneurisms. Hypertension, alone, may have caused the strokes, and it is the principal differential diagnosis.

None of the younger Mendelssohns inherited the spinal deformity of Moses Mendelssohn who was born with a thoracic kyphoscoliosis which gave him a hunchbacked appearance.

TABLE 1

POSSIBLE CAUSES OF MENDELSSOHN'S DEATH

1. Subarachnoid haemorrhage (prefigured by hypertension)
2. Hypertensive cerebral haemorrhage (stroke)
3. Myocardial infarction (heart attack)
4. Other:
    Intracranial malignancy
    Hereditary vascular defect

REFERENCES

1. S. Hensel, *The Mendelssohn Family (1729–1847)*, trans. C. Klingemann (London, 1882), vol. 2, pp. 324–36
2. H. Kupferberg, *The Mendelssohns: Three Generations of Genius* (New York and London, 1972)
3. G. R. Marek, *Gentle Genius: The Story of Felix Mendelssohn* (New York, 1972; London, 1973), pp. 350–65
4. A. Altman, *Moses Mendelssohn: A Biographical Study* (London, 1973)
5. W. R. Blunt, *On Wings of Song* (New York, 1974), pp. 14–19, 179–207, 231, 259–70
6. J. G. Greenfield, *Neuropathology*, 3rd edn (Baltimore, 1976), pp. 136, 138–9, 417–19, 725

7. E. Braunewald, R. G. Petersdorf, R. D. Adams *et al.* (eds), *Harrison's Principles of Internal Medicine*, 11th edn (New York, 1987)
8. A. Saifuddin and J. R. E. Dathan, 'Adult Polycystic Kidney Disease and Intracranial Aneurisms', *British Medical Journal*, 295 (1987), p. 526

Robert Schumann
(1810–56)

Robert Schumann was born on 8 June 1810 in the little town of Zwickau in Thuringia. Thuringia, largely rural, has a rich musical heritage; the aristocracy had been noted patrons of the arts for many centuries. Goethe and Schiller had revitalized German literature under the patronage of the Grand Duke of Weimar. Bach was born at Eisenach and spent much of his adult life at Weimar and Leipzig. The Wartburg, a beautiful medieval castle, is associated with the Tannhäuser legend: it was in the music hall that Tannhäuser sang of Venus and was banished from Germany. Mindful of this rich artistic and musical heritage and ambitious to make his own contribution to it, Thuringia's new-born son was destined to become one of the best-loved and most productive composers of the Romantic era.

Schumann's interest in the arts extended beyond music: he was widely read and steeped in the Romantic literary tradition of Jean Paul. Schumann distinguished himself as an essayist and a music critic; he helped to found the *Neue Zeitschrift für Musik*, and was widely known for perceptive and laudatory reviews of the up-and-coming musical figures of his day, including Chopin, Brahms and Mendelssohn.

Despite consistent productivity and accomplishment over three decades, Schumann's life was guided by a dark star; the spectre of madness haunted the sensitive musician. His mental breakdowns dated from his early twenties, and there was a strong history of mental illness in the Schumann family. Throughout his life Schumann's mood swings and behaviour patterns altered in a way not entirely accounted for by his immediate circumstances. At times he exhibited frankly psychotic behaviour. The last five of his forty-six years were spent as an in-patient at a mental asylum following a suicide attempt. The cause of his death was probably self-starvation.

In the preceding years his genius shone brightly, and at times his productivity was almost superhuman, perhaps owing to the mood elevation which was a part of his illness. The precise diagnosis of Robert Schumann's affliction remains impossible today because we lack the necessary information supplied by laboratory tests, X-rays and serology. Even Schumann's autopsy report is imprecise by modern standards, and the documentation of his final decline is patchy indeed.

Schumann is of great interest to the medical biographers because, as with Van Gogh, it is possible to see the influence of an unusual state of mind and being on his art. The composer documented his moods and anxieties with unusual precision and obsessiveness in his diaries, and it is fascinating to review his career in the light of modern medical knowledge, although our conclusions cannot be too precise because the relevant investigations were not carried out by contemporary doctors. The principal question to be resolved is whether the condition that led to the final disintegration of Schumann's personality and to his terminal illness was due to an organic brain lesion or to a 'primary' psychiatric illness.

In bipolar affective disorders (formerly known as manic-depressive illness) there are mood swings from profound elation to deepest depression. This diagnosis has been brought forward to explain Schumann's symptomatology. Many organic lesions of the brain – which include syphilis, Alzheimer's disease and tumours – also alter behaviour over the long term and could indeed have been responsible for some of Schumann's mental problems. Let us then briefly review his life, noting the medical and psychological milestones and the problems as they evolved.

SCHUMANN'S EARLY YEARS

Schumann showed musical talent from the age of seven. He received little systematic musical instruction during his early years and his parents did not regard music as a suitable career. Schumann's ability to improvise was present from a very early age and it is said that he had an almost uncanny ability to make musical portraits of his acquaintances at the piano – he could produce music which subtly suggested movements and mannerisms, and even physical appearance. He did not possess the gift of 'perfect pitch', unlike many of the great composers.

It is said that he was so sensitive that he would cry if he heard a beautiful series of chords. He also showed a marked ability for languages. In his teens he became engrossed with the literature of the contemporary Romantic writers, most notably Jean Paul. Schumann, then, was a sensitive and intellectually well-developed youth. He was a noted extrovert and apparently popular because of the wide range of his dramatic and artistic talents.

The boy's father was a publisher who lavished praise on his diversely talented son. When Robert was nine he was given a beautiful Viennese grand piano. His father was also noted to be of a somewhat depressive and hypochondriacal personality, and Robert may have inherited something of his later behaviour from his father. Robert remained close to his beloved mother throughout his life, and from his later teens there were to be inner conflicts of dependence versus independence in relation to her.

When Robert was fifteen, two deaths in the immediate family, separated by only ten months, were to change his personality precipitously and disrupt its development. He first lost his sister, Emilie, who was four years older than himself. We know that she suffered from a severe, chronic skin disease. She is said to have committed suicide by jumping from a window and may have been ill for several months before her death. The precise details of Emilie's death and her final illness have been lost to us; there may have been a deliberate attempt by the Schumann family to conceal unpleasant and embarrassing aspects of the unfortunate girl's life and early demise.

Ten months after Emilie's death, Robert's father died suddenly at the age of 53. It was noted that after these incidents Schumann became taciturn, meditative and quiet; he developed anxieties in company. Despite his unprepossessing nature, Schumann was determined to become famous; he worked doggedly at poetry and writing. The creative impulse served a therapeutic and a consolatory function as well as providing a vocation for the zealous young man. Schumann may have sublimated his fears about death into a relentless quest for artistic immortality.

Schumann attended the university at Leipzig. He studied law without much enthusiasm; he was apparently very unhappy and felt abandoned by both his friends and family. As a release from his situation and his recriminations about the lack of direction of his life he experimented with alcohol and casual sex. He was intermittently plagued with depression and sleep disturbance, and he experienced frequent severe anxiety attacks, often associated with palpitations and sometimes with frank derealization.[1] Schumann found stability in the rich intellectual and cultural life of Leipzig. He soon acquired a piano teacher, a man who was to change his destiny and whose daughter was to become his confidant, lover and intellectual soulmate. This man was Friedrich Wieck. He noted the young man's promise as a virtuoso and guided his efforts in composition.

In the early 1830s, Schumann invented his two imaginary companions, Florestan and Eusebius. The two appeared as 'characters' in some of his review articles. Eusebius represented the dreamy side of Schumann's character; Florestan was the man of action, an achiever. They were literary contrivances by which Schumann acquainted his readers with diverse aspects of his personality, and they served to underline its contrasting elements. Moreover, these imaginary figures probably helped to dissipate conflicts and anxieties generated by action and inactivity respectively: Schumann as an adult retained a rich fantasy life which seems in some way childlike and which some psychiatrists have seen as evidence of mental disorder. Beyond any doubt, however, that fantasy life was an adaptive and an important process in his creativity.

Unlike Beethoven, Schumann did not proceed from sketchbooks, and he almost wilfully combined the logical with the emotive. Schumann's creativity grew out of a complicated process of dreamlike auditory and emotional experiences combined with the well-documented mood swings which marked the beginning of a creative period, and it is more difficult to comprehend than Beethoven's because it is the product of an unusual state of being and feeling which is not entirely rationally comprehensible. We can perhaps best understand Schumann's state of mind by listening to his music – the emotional feelings contained within it pervaded his very life. (Beethoven's music began often with a simple idea and grew by a logical process to a point where the composition reflected his emotional and inner life as well as his artistic aspirations.)

The 1830s were to see the beginning of Schumann's creative output as well as the end of his career as a virtuoso owing to a hand injury, the gradual development of a union with Clara, and his estrangement from Wieck. They were also the years of the *Papillons*, the Symphonic Études, *Carnaval*, the piano sonatas and the *Davidsbündlertänze*. The end of the 1830s showed an almost abrupt transition from piano music to lieder as his favoured means of artistic expression.

---

[1] A mental state characterized by a change in awareness of the external world, creating a feeling of unreality. It is commonly associated with states of extreme anxiety.

SCHUMANN'S HAND INJURY

Most accounts of Schumann's life say that his blossoming virtuoso career was ended abruptly by an injury to the third or fourth finger of the right hand, said to have been caused or exacerbated by a mechanical weighted aid used in piano practising; it is difficult today to determine the precise nature of the injury. Accounts written by contemporary doctors name different fingers and differ in other important ways – for example, as to whether sensation was lost or not. Most accounts talk of weakness or paralysis in the symptomatology of the disease. It may be that the injury was a tenosynovitis produced by cumulative strains. On occasion afterwards, Schumann was certainly able to play with full use of his right hand.

It may also be that the 'injury' was a non-anatomical one, that it was psychogenic in origin. In a conversion neurosis a patient develops a pain due to injury and its symptomatology allows a 'secondary gain' – that is, the injury itself changes the patient's lifestyle in some way favourable to the patient. The secondary gain in Schumann's case could have been that he was not drafted into the local militia or that he abandoned his time-consuming and stressful career in favour of his preferred one: composition. Certainly he took little time in coming to terms with his incapacity and quickly turned his abundant energy into new fields. If Schumann had seriously contemplated becoming a virtuoso the loss would have been much more devastating than it actually was.

It is extremely unlikely that this injury was an early manifestation of neurosyphilis, as has been suggested by some authors (7).

MARRIAGE TO CLARA WIECK

Schumann's relationship with Clara (whom he had known since she was 12) developed over the same period and culminated in their marriage in September 1840, despite the disapproval of Clara's father. The story of the struggle between the two men over Clara – Wieck did not want his daughter to marry the aloof and eccentric musician – and their court battle is well known and detailed by many biographers. Initially rivals at the keyboard and for the acclaim of the public, the two musicians became lovers and a mutually artistically and romantically productive union resulted.

Themes representing Clara, and musical reminiscences of her personality and their love, appear in Schumann's compositions. The couple had their share of marital problems – Schumann confessed to a 'desire for debauchery', and his sexual frustration and alcoholism probably strained the marriage. Mutual ambition and heightened artistic productivity probably held the relationship together.

Clara still had a deep regard for her father but saw him only infrequently because of Schumann's possessiveness and the hot rivalry and dislike that now existed between the two parties. One feels pity for the way that Clara was dominated by the often moody and irascible Schumann; on the other hand, the pair enjoyed a satisfying artistic friendship and an intimate symbolic fantasy life, and there seems little doubt that at the deepest level these two supremely gifted beings loved one another.

SCHUMANN'S MENTAL DISORDER

Schumann had always experienced phobias and mood swings. In September 1844, he experienced a 'violent nervous attack'. This compelled him to seek medical help. He consulted Carl Carus, an eminent Dresden physician. Schumann appeared profoundly depressed and complained vociferously about his health, especially about his eyes – he was extremely near-sighted. He also complained about many phobic symptoms, including a fear of heights. It is difficult to relate lifelong phobias to organic disease; they usually have a psychological cause.

In his youth Schumann had attempted suicide by throwing himself out of a building. Perhaps from the fear of a sudden suicidal impulse, he always lived on the ground floor of any house. (When visiting the pianist Henselt, he refused to climb a tower and aggressively forbade Clara to go alone: 'she does not go where I do not go'.) He also had a fear of being poisoned and lived for many years with an obsessional fear of death. The anniversary of Beethoven's death affected him profoundly, initiating a depressive episode that lasted for several months. Schumann sublimated the symptoms of his psychological disorder by plunging into hard work – in this case the six fugues on B-A-C-H, which were finally published in 1846.

From about 1844 on, there were to be repeated bouts of depression, often at intervals of several months or years. There were also periods when Schumann's productivity and creativity were heightened to an astounding level. The Fantasy in C Major was composed in five days, the Violin Concerto in less than a fortnight. Schumann's moods clearly showed cyclical swings from depression to profound elation and creativity.

It is difficult to date the onset of the mental disturbance which brought about Schumann's decline and death. He sometimes heard 'inner voices' which urged him to compose, for instance during the composition of *Kreisleriana*. Additionally, the intensity of Schumann's musical imagination was remarkable, that the 'music was with him all the time'. It was felt by his friends that this was a factor in his withdrawal from the world. To use Berlioz's phrase, he was a man 'haunted by genius'.

Prior to the onset of the condition that led up to Schumann's suicide attempt, he developed full-blown psychotic symptoms for about two months. He had auditory hallucinations of a musical note being played in his head; initially this disturbed only his nights, but eventually it plagued him during the day as well. Schumann later told his friend Rupert Becker that he heard wondrously beautiful music fully formed and complete: 'The sound is like distant brasses, underscored by the most magnificent harmonies.'

Schumann's psychotic delirium intensified, and he told Clara that angels were singing a beautiful melody, which he attempted to write down. Clara writes that 'it was his fixed belief that angels were hovering around him offering the most glorious revelations, all this in wonderful music; they called to welcome us and before the end of the year we would both be united with them' (11). Schumann's delusional frame of mind soon turned from exaltation to terror. Clara wrote that 'the angels' voices transformed themselves into the voices of demons with horrible music. They told him he was a sinner and that they wanted to throw him into hell. In short, his condition grew into a nervous paroxysm, he screamed in anguish because the embodiments of tigers and hyenas were rushing forward to seize him.'

By 19 February, Schumann would not allow himself to be talked out of the belief that supernatural creatures were soaring about him. The next day, he again listened to his angels. He worried intensely about harming Clara and his family as his psychotic delusions intensified. His mood ranged from exaltation to abject misery, associated with his delusional state.

ATTEMPTED SUICIDE
AND HOSPITALIZATION (1854–6)

Schumann's mental disarray was brought to the attention of the public by a suicide attempt on 27 February 1854. Suffering from a severe depressive episode, Schumann, who was then living in Düsseldorf, left his home clad only in a thin robe and slippers and walked towards the Rhine. When he reached the toll-bridge he suddenly flung himself into the freezing waters. After a determined struggle, some fishermen managed to bring him ashore. Schumann was removed from his home to a mental asylum at Endenich, a Bonn suburb. The dishevelled man did not say goodbye to his wife or his family and voluntarily accepted his hospitalization. Clara did not see him again until the day of his death over two years later. In the main, Schumann remained depressed and withdrawn during his stay in hospital. He did not compose another substantial piece of music. For reasons which are still not understood, his behaviour and mental functioning underwent a relatively abrupt and profound change, and he never recovered his former level of activity.

Endenich was a nine-acre private mental institution run by Franz Richarz, an 'organicist' psychiatrist. The official medical history detailing Schumann's admission has been lost, and we can only speculate about the standard of care given to him.

Organicists looked for pharmaceutical cures for mental disease, namely, herbs and drugs, and believed that mental disease stemmed from either a circulatory or a cerebral disturbance. They held that interpersonal and emotional factors were not of prime importance in the causation of mental illness. Certainly the staff did not seem to pay much attention to the personal difficulties in the composer's life. They did not encourage him to communicate with his family.

Schumann was very fearful and withdrawn, and he continued to hear voices. Sometimes he would overcome his fear and converse with his attendants. From friends who visited Schumann Clara gleaned information about his well-being. He seldom talked about his wife and family, becoming withdrawn from all interpersonal relationships. It remains unclear as to whether Schumann was suffering from dementia due to an organic illness or to 'pseudodementia' due to 'psychotic' depression exacerbated by over-medication and enforced isolation. Such illnesses can be profound and are often difficult to differentiate from true dementia.

Schumann's health initially followed a fluctuating course in the asylum. At times he wrote affectionate letters to his wife and family; at other times his behaviour was clearly delusional and pathological. He complained of a speech problem – difficulty in articulating his words. By early 1856 he was unable to speak intelligibly; he spoke in monosyllables which were seldom recognizable as words. Both organic disorders of the brain and profound depression are associated with changes in the pattern of speech. Without a precise description of Schumann's speech deficit, a definitive diagnosis of the condition cannot be made. The once brilliant composer was so withdrawn (or demented) that he refused even to eat. Despite attempts by the hospital staff to forcefeed him or to feed him via nasogastric tubes, his health continued to decline inexorably.

Towards the end, Schumann's feet began to swell – a possible sign of cardiac failure due to severe malnutrition. Clara visited Schumann shortly before he died and he embraced her with the greatest effort. The next day Clara fed the composer, apparently with some success, but in his emaciated state the outcome was inevitable; the unhappy man died on 29 July 1856.

The quality of Schumann's care at Endenich is highly questionable. The poor documentation of his stay is not only suspect but also frustrating for biographers, who would like to know much more about the progression of his disease and its symptoms and signs in order to determine its aetiology. It also implies that Schumann's physicians were only superficially interested in his illness and may have incorrectly concluded that the inevitable outcome of his illness was madness and death. In isolating a depressed patient from his family and friends in a grim asylum they may have exacerbated his illness. When Schumann's behaviour reached an adaptive level no attempt was made to discharge him. Certainly his friends were critical that the psychiatrists were not making an effort to communicate with Schumann and to explain and rationalize his disease with him. This view has some validity when we consider that Dr Richarz, the superintendent, considered organic determinants responsible for Schumann's disease. Schumann may have been over-medicated or incorrectly medicated, adding iatrogenic[2] illness to his afflictions. Finally, Clara Schumann herself seems to have made little attempt to visit her husband. She may have been preoccupied by her friendship with the young Brahms (who had developed a passionate attachment to her) and had no desire to resurrect the relationship with her eccentric husband, whose psychotic behaviour was now public knowledge. It is thus open to speculation that with better care Schumann might have been successfully discharged and might for a time have resumed life with his family.

[2] caused by his doctors

SCHUMANN'S AUTOPSY AND THE MEDICAL LITERATURE ON HIS ILLNESS

An autopsy was performed on Schumann's body. The brain was examined both micro- and macroscopically but no convincing evidence of an organic lesion was found. The lungs were found to be congested in a patchy fashion – probably evidence of bronchopneumonia, or pulmonary oedema, a terminal event in Schumann's deterioration. Dr Richarz, who performed the autopsy, had little training in autopsy procedures and his report is often vague and contradictory. He felt that Schumann had an organic brain disease, but his statements must be regarded with caution because his basic medical philosophy was that all mental illnesses were due to organic disease of the brain. Neuropathologists consulted by the author feel that the remaining information is too vague for definite conclusions to be drawn as to the aetiology of the composer's illness.

POSSIBLE NEUROSYPHILIS

The cause of Schumann's madness has been hotly debated in the medical literature for several decades. Eliot Slater has suggested that syphilis was responsible. The evidence for neurosyphilis is compelling but not conclusive. Several authors base their diagnoses of syphilis on a lesion which was present on Schumann's foreskin during his teenage years; they relate it to a primary syphilitic chancre and equate Richarz's postmortem diagnosis of Schumann's madness, 'incomplete general paralysis', with 'general paralysis of the insane', a part of the tertiary neurosyphilis complex. The two diagnoses are not necessarily the same (7, 11).

Samples of Schumann's hair examined chemically by Ostwald showed small traces of mercury. This may be because Schumann received mercury for syphilis, or it may relate to the use of mercury for felt hat-bands. Schumann was a noted hypochondriac. He kept many medications, and his room in Wieck's house was said to resemble 'a chemistry shop'. It is likely that he took mercury, which was a proprietary medication and used for many other diseases besides syphilis. The long-term side effects of its use can be disastrous: it causes both dementia and illnesses resembling madness. Mercury may have been a co-factor with other agents including alcohol and hypertension in producing an organic brain disease. It was often given in error to treat illnesses other than syphilis.

Schumann's 'wound' on his foreskin appears to have been a tear associated with vigorous sexual intercourse and not a painless syphilitic chancre (11). Late photographs of Schumann examined by the author do not show constricted Argyll-Robertson pupils, which are common in sufferers of neurosyphilis. 'Incomplete general paralysis' is a late nineteenth-century diagnosis and does not necessarily relate to neurosyphilis. One must be very careful about nineteenth-century diagnoses of syphilis; they should be treated with caution, as they are often unreliable. It was not until 1905 that Schaudin and Hoffman demonstrated that the micro-organism treponema pallidum caused syphilis. In 1913, the organism was isolated from the brains of sufferers of neurosyphilis by Noguchi (1). The Oslo Study, which began in 1910 and continued until 1951, prognosticated primary syphilis and demonstrated the development of secondary and tertiary neurosyphilis. Richarz was not thinking of neurosyphilis when he formulated Schumann's diagnosis, but it is of course possible that the composer suffered from this then common condition.

The one objective finding of Richarz's postmortem is that Schumann's brain weighed approximately 1,340 grams. This is a little low but falls within two standard deviations from the mean for measurements of brain weight and thus cannot be regarded as compatible with evidence of syphilitic 'general paralysis', which characteristically causes more profound loss of brain mass. Also, Richarz, who had an intimate knowledge of Schumann's medical history, emphatically denied that the composer manifested any of the known stigmata of syphilis (commonly a multi-system disease). All in all it would appear that syphilis was not the most likely cause of Schumann's decline, although it cannot be entirely discounted since diagnostic medicine was in its infancy in the mid-nineteenth century. That the brain weight was slightly low was probably due to poor autopsy technique, e.g. tardy removal of the brain after evisceration of the cadaver. Finally, syphilitic dementia does not usually present with the florid symptomatology that characterized the final phase of Schumann's illness.

POSSIBLE PSYCHIATRIC ILLNESS

Schizophrenia has been advanced as the cause of Schumann's condition, for reasons which are not entirely logical. Musicologists citing schizophrenia as the cause of Schumann's madness often refer to the characters in his reviews, Florestan and Eusebius, as evidence of multiple personalities, hence schizophrenia. But schizophrenia is not a disease characterized by multiple personalities: it is one which causes chronic deterioration of the personality, withdrawal and blunting of the emotions. It is associated with a formal thought disorder and is accompanied by auditory hallucinations, which were admittedly a prominent part of Schumann's symptomatology. These auditory hallucinations and some of the delusions associated with schizophrenia respond to modern psychotropic drugs such as the major tranquillizers which are commonly used to treat the condition, but many aspects of it are refractory to medical therapy. The insidious 'negative features' of schizophrenia – personality deterioration and withdrawal – seem to progress despite therapy. Schumann's frame of mind was clearly delusional in the last phase of his illness, but evidence of a formal thought disorder is lacking.

Some features of Schumann's illness may suggest that it had a schizophreniform component. The decline in his mental health, which has usually been designated as due to dementia or endogenous depression, could be seen as personality deterioration due to chronic schizophrenia. Moreover, Schumann's repeated auditory hallucinations in Endenich, when his mood was not elevated, his persistent withdrawal, paranoia, ideas of reference (themes dictated by angels and devils) and disordered, automatic behaviour (he played the piano in Endenich 'like a machine whose springs are broken but which still tries to work') present a strong prima facie case for this diagnosis. However, Ostwald (see below) has documented Schumann's mood swings so meticulously that it is difficult to dismiss them as exacerbations of schizophrenia ('schizophrenic excitement'). Perhaps the best formulation of Schumann's illness is that he suffered from a schizo-affective disorder.

Schumann's psychiatrists would not have perceived the significance of a thought disorder. Any of Schumann's correspondence which betrayed evidence of schizophrenia may have been destroyed by Clara or his medical attendants.

That the composer suffered from schizophrenia was proposed as early as 1856 by Dr Paul Mobius, who corresponded with Richarz. As the science of neuropathology advances it is becoming clear that schizophrenia and the affective disorders probably have an organic, biochemical basis. As the autopsy report is too imprecise to be a source of hard information, we must rely on accounts of Schumann's symptomatology to reach a differential diagnosis. Here again much essential information

135

is not available; however, recent authors have provided several satisfactory hypotheses to explain Schumann's mental and physical deterioration.

The most authoritative investigations into the causes of Schumann's 'madness' have been made by the American psychiatrist Peter Ostwald. His book on Schumann, *Music and Madness*, provides considerable evidence that the composer's mental disorder was due to a primary psychiatric illness (11). Ostwald considers that illness in the light of modern medical knowledge about mental diseases and provides a very good insight into the mind of the great composer. He equates Schumann's madness with a manic-depressive disorder. He notes the many years of mood swings which the composer experienced and the corresponding fluctuations in his musical and written output.

Exacerbating this manic-depressive illness was a personality disorder, or at least a highly unusual premorbid personality. Schumann's personality shows several strange elements which deserve further comment. He was a highly obsessional man, and perhaps obsession with greatness is common in people who achieve the stature of Schumann. From his early teens he was driven by an intense desire to succeed, first as a writer, then as a virtuoso pianist, and lastly as a composer. Schumann made the transition from writing to music at the age of nineteen, a rather late career choice. Concomitant with this striving for artistic immortality was an intense fear of death and also of obscurity.

A second feature of his personality was an intensely divided self and the conflicts which ensued as a result. Perhaps partly to overcome the divisions of his personality Schumann created the literary figures Florestan and Eusebius, under whose names he would write reviews in his music journal. The heroic Florestan derived his name from a character in Beethoven's opera *Fidelio*; Eusebius was an early Christian martyr. Both are illustrated musically in the piano composition *Carnaval*. The music certainly underlines the polarities in Schumann's personality. Florestan and Eusebius were such profound creations of Schumann's mind, and so important in his elaborate fantasy life, that he told his friends that when he became intoxicated with alcohol they actually appeared to talk to him. Ostwald also noted strong paranoid and histrionic components to Schumann's character.

Analysis of Schumann's letters by Ostwald provides evidence that his mental faculties were probably well preserved until shortly before his death, although his behaviour was clearly disturbed. This is further evidence against a dementing illness or an organic brain lesion.

136

Schumann did not show the loosening of mental associations, common to schizophrenics, in his last letters.

ORGANIC CO-FACTORS IN SCHUMANN'S MENTAL ILLNESS

Finally, Schumann had a series of physical disorders which are worthy of comment. He was obese and presumably hypertensive. He was a heavy drinker of alcohol, and noted that alcohol would heighten and intensify the auditory sensations which often became the basis of his compositions. Although he often found being intoxicated a frightening experience, he valued the heightened creativity that it generated. He would supplement alcohol with caffeine and strong cigars to achieve a state of emotional euphoria and increased sensitivity. Alcohol and tobacco were likely co-factors in Schumann's mental and physical deterioration. Mercury is also a possible co-factor.

Schumann was thus a man of exquisite sensitivity but with a paradoxical ambition and drive. He created his music at times with a manic productivity that often left him emotionally and psychologically bereft. Despite ill-health and mental illness he achieved through his music the lasting recognition for which he strove.

TABLE 1

CAUSES OF ROBERT SCHUMANN'S MENTAL ILLNESS AS POSTULATED BY HIS BIOGRAPHERS

Franz Richarz (1856): Incomplete general paralysis

Paul Mobius (1856): dementia praecox (schizophrenia)

Hans Gruhle (1856), Eric Sams (1972), Eliot Slater (1972): Neuro-syphilis (general paralysis of the insane)

Hans Martin Sutermeister (1959): Involutional and situational depression

Peter F. Ostwald (1985):

Axis 1   Mental disorder: bipolar affective disorder (manic-depressive illness)

Axis 2   Personality disorder: unusual personality characterized by histrionic, obsessive, compulsive elements and 'divided self'

Axis 3   Physical disorders:
> alcohol abuse
> obesity
> possible hypertension, cardiovascular disease and other occult organic illness
> iatrogenic illness – inappropriate medication by medical attendants

Axis 4   Psycho-social stress factors:
> difficult relationship with wife, Clara
> isolation at Endenich
> failure of career as pianist
> loss of creativity as a composer

Axis 5   Highest level of adaptation recently achieved

Letters and communications from Schumann during his stay at Endenich do not indicate that he suffered from a dementing disorder. Schumann was unsuited to his position as music director at Düsseldorf by temperament and because of recurring illness. Failure in this position was a key factor in precipitating his final depression.

Dieter Kerner (1963): Hypertensive encephalopathy

Other: Psychosis of mercurialism
> Chronic alcoholic hallucinosis

REFERENCES

1. H. Noguchi and J. W. Moore, *Journal of Experimental Medicine* (1913), 17, pp. 232–8
2. F. Niecks, *Robert Schumann: A Supplementary and Corrective Biography* (London and New York, 1925)
3. A. Meyer and E. Slater, 'Contributions to a Pathography of the Musicians: I Robert Schumann', *Confina psychiatrica*, 2 (1959), p. 65
4. D. Kerner, 'Robert Schumann', *Krankheiten grosser Musiker* (Stuttgart, 1963), pp. 103–26
5. C. J. Polson and R. N. Tattershall, *Clinical Toxicology* (London, 1969), pp. 224–41
6. E. Sams, 'Schumann's Hand Injury', *The Musical Times*, 112 (1971), p.1156; 113 (1972), p. 456
7. E. Slater, 'Schumann's Illness', in A. Walker (ed.), *Robert Schumann: The Man and his Music* (London, 1972), pp. 406–13
8. J. G. Greenfield, *Neuropathology*, 3rd edn (Baltimore, 1976)
9. R. A. Henson and H. Ulrich, 'Schumann's Hand Injury', *British Medical Journal* (1978), pp. 900–3
10. R. Taylor, *Robert Schumann: His Life and Work* (London, 1982), pp. 281–328
11. P. F. Ostwald, *Schumann: Music and Madness* (London, 1985)
12. W. Jänisch *et al.*, 'Autopsy Report of the Corpse of Robert Schumann: Publication and Interpretation of a Rediscovered Document', *Zentralblatt für allgemeine Pathologie und pathologische Anatomie*, 132 (1986), pp. 129–36
13. R. L. Spitzer and J. B. Williams (eds), *Diagnostic and Statistical Manual of Mental Disorders*, 3rd (rev.) edn (Washington, 1987), pp. 97–165, 187–205, 208–13
14. J. G. O'Shea, 'Robert Schumann', *Liszt Saeculum*, 41–2 (1988), pp. 16–22

Frédéric Chopin
(1810–49)

Chopin suffered from a debilitating lung disease which caused his untimely death in Paris in 1849 at the age of thirty-nine years. Although his reclusive nature and his poor health conspired to make his public concerts infrequent, he was hailed as among the foremost piano virtuosos of his era. In his last years Chopin lived the life of an invalid, the victim of a slowly progressive lung disease. Despite advanced disease, however, he undertook a demanding tour of Great Britain in 1848, but this severely sapped his strength: when he returned to Paris he had but eleven months to live. Chopin's lung disease is commonly attributed to tuberculosis, but thorough examination of his medical history shows that other disease entities may have been responsible for his condition. In this chapter the reconstructed medical history of the composer will be reviewed and the recent medical literature on him considered.

MEDICAL HISTORY

Chopin had an unusual bodily habitus. Although 170 cm tall, he actually weighed less than 45 kg in 1840 – that is, nine years before his death. His frailty and emaciation were remarked on from his teenage years (15, pp. 39, 44, 56, 62). In later life Chopin grew markedly barrel-chested. This feature of his bodily habitus is clearly seen in a caricature executed by his friend Pauline Viardot in 1844 (16, p. 116). Almost all observers remarked on the unusual slenderness of his limbs. When travelling in horse-drawn carriages, Chopin had a fear of fracturing his frail limbs. This is perhaps unremarkable in concert pianists, but may have significance when seen in the context of his illness. During

140

the terminal phase Chopin developed severe pains in his wrists and ankles which were partially relieved by massage; these may have been due to pulmonary hypertrophic osteoarthropathy, a type of arthritis associated with long-standing chest diseases.

EXERCISE TOLERANCE

From his late teenage years it was observed that Chopin's exercise tolerance was remarkably poor, so much so that it was constantly remarked on by his peers. In 1828, when Chopin was 18, he held an audience entranced with his spontaneous improvisations at the piano at an inn in Sulechów. After this performance he was so exhausted that he had to be carried to his coach; this cannot be regarded as normal for a young man who was used to playing the piano. Chopin could never produce a true *forte*, even on the light-actioned pianos of his day, and seldom played above *mezzoforte* (22). In 1826 he went for a series of adventurous walks in the Silesian countryside despite being 'puffed out and exhausted'. Because his health was so delicate, his Parisian friends managed most of his daily affairs, to the extent of shopping for him and buying wallpaper and furniture for his home. George Sand tried to stop sexual relations with him in 1838 because she feared the toll on his health (2, p. 483). Chopin's respiratory illness affected him for at least thirty years: Liszt and Sand state that it was present before the onset of puberty.

DIETARY HABITS

There is considerable evidence that Chopin suffered from a form of gastrointestinal disease, the most telling being his extreme emaciation. Careful study of his dietary habits shows that he had a preference for a high carbohydrate diet, and assiduously avoided fatty foods. We know that he subsisted on bread and confectionery and supplemented this diet with fish or lean chicken, which was not the staple diet of the people of northern Europe. Moreover in his fifteenth year, when he lost a great deal of weight following a respiratory illness, his doctor found that putting him on a high-carbohydrate diet allowed him to regain weight. Chopin developed a polyphagia[1] for carbohydrates (16, p. 40). George Sand relates that one of the unfortunate consequences of the couple's isolation on Majorca was that it was impossible to find the correct food for Chopin: at one stage the only food available was

[1] excessive appetite

pork. On eating it he immediately developed diarrhoea and abdominal pain (6, 9). Sand overcame the problem by preparing most of Chopin's food herself and forbidding the servants to use pork fat because it upset his digestion so much. In the last year of his life Chopin suffered from intractable diarrhoea due either to *cor pulmonale*[2] or to pancreatic insufficiency. Chopin often wrote to his family that he was 'watching his diet' to prevent indigestion and diarrhoea (16). He took belladonna to control both his gastrointestinal problems and his cough.

FERTILITY

Chopin never fathered a child, despite frequent sexual liaisons, especially during his early years in Paris. He wrote to many of his mistresses discussing the possibility of having children (4, p. 129) and had a deep love of children and of family life. He had a protracted relationship with George Sand, who had had many lovers but had no children after the end of her marriage, which had produced two; it is therefore likely that she practised some form of contraception. It is not known whether the couple had considered having children in their many years together. No speculation about 'natural' children fathered by Chopin has ever reached us, and there is thus good reason to think that Chopin may have been infertile. (Chronic lung disease can cause subfertility, but there is a particularly strong association between subfertility and cystic fibrosis and Kartagener's syndrome).[3]

FAMILY HISTORY

Chopin's sister, Emily, died at the age of 14 of a respiratory illness. Her terminal illness lasted for more than one year and was characterized by severe weight loss, haemorrhage and terminal pneumonia. Like Chopin, Emily had a long history of respiratory infection and was often confined to her bed. Chopin's earlier medical biographers have dismissed Emily's illness as miliary tuberculosis, noting only her final, catastrophic decline, but in view of the prolonged nature of her illness this diagnosis seems unlikely to have been the correct one. They have also stated that Chopin acquired his infection from his sister. Cavitating

[2] heart disease occurring as a consequence of advanced respiratory disease
[3] a rare inherited disorder, the cardinal features of which are sinusitis, middle-ear disease, bronchiectasis and infertility

tuberculosis is comparatively rare in children, but it does occur. Other paediatric illnesses, such as cystic fibrosis, may explain her condition.

PATTERN OF RESPIRATORY SYMPTOMS

Chopin suffered from a chronic cough from an early age. Respiratory pathology was present by the time he was fifteen, and he was never without some evidence of respiratory disease throughout his life. Chopin's correspondence reveals an obsession with the weather: foggy or wintry weather would provoke both respiratory disease and paroxysms of coughing. He often left Paris during the winter to avoid the winter pollution. The famous haemorrhages of his later years were preceded by a chronic cough of many years' duration. This cough was often productive and was loose in the morning: Chopin was in the habit of clearing his chest at 10.00 a.m. For the last ten years of his life he took opium on sugar to suppress this intractable cough (6). Auscultation of his chest did not disclose a cavitating lesion. Chopin had several large pulmonary haemorrhages at Palma in 1838; more often his sputum would be streaked with scanty blood or mucopurulent, suggestive of suppurative lung disease.

RESPIRATORY ILLNESSES

Let us now review the long history of respiratory disease which beset Chopin. Contemporary biographers are emphatic that his illness began long before the famous Majorca voyage. Liszt tells us that Chopin's illness was present from the latter years of his childhood. He describes the young composer as 'sickly and delicate; the attentions of his family were always concentrated upon his health ... The little fellow was indeed seen to be suffering but was always trying to smile and to all seemed happy.' He also says that Chopin 'lacked normal muscular development' – an obvious reference to early emaciation. Most major biographers agree that Chopin's illness was well established by 1830 but that the composer and his friends scarcely wrote about his ill-health in their correspondence to his family in order to allay their justifiable anxiety (4, 5, 9, 15, 17). Each year was usually attended by some manifestation of respiratory illness. In 1826 Chopin had an illness which lasted six months; it was marked by frontal headache and cervical adenopathy,[4] and was slow to resolve. In 1830 in Vienna his nose swelled up embarrassingly

[4] swelling of the lymph glands in the neck

with a prolonged cold, forcing him to cancel his concerts. In Paris in 1831, when he was 21, Chopin had an episode of haemoptysis (coughing blood) and fever. His boyhood friend Dr Jan Matuszyński recommended several weeks of bedrest. Chopin recovered his health quickly and resumed his hectic life of teaching and composition. He was not labelled consumptive at the time. Haemoptysis was a new symptom which occasionally occurred with winter chest infections. Chopin also suffered from painful, chronic sinusitis. It was in 1832 in Paris that the Irish composer-pianist John Field made his famous remark about Chopin: 'He is a sickroom talent'; the chronic stigmata of his disease were clearly visible by this stage.

In 1835, Chopin had a bout of bronchitis and laryngitis; the latter resolved but was to recur often. These early bouts of recurrent suppurative laryngitis cast considerable doubt on the diagnosis of tubercular laryngitis recorded by many Chopin biographers. The illness of 1835 interrupted his correspondence for two months; he was actually reported dead in Warsaw (6). After recurrences of the symptoms in 1836 and 1837 Chopin consulted Dr Pierre Gaubert, an allopathist and a friend of George Sand. Chopin was worried that he might be 'consumptive' in view of his family history of respiratory disease. Gaubert assured Chopin that he was not 'consumptive' and recommended the warmer climate of the south. Chopin, George Sand and her two children, Solange and Maurice, left Paris to escape the winter of 1838, arriving in Majorca in November.

At the outset, the move was a great success. Chopin wrote rapturously, 'Here I am in Palma in the shade of the palm trees, cedars, aloes, oranges, lemons, fig trees and pomegranates. The sky is of a turquoise blue ... the mountains of emerald, the air is as it must be in heaven! Everybody goes about in summer clothes and it is hot ... in short a delicious existence.' Initially the trip was marred only by a bout of heat exhaustion on Chopin's part. The couple rented a villa several miles outside Palma and, although local society was suspicious of the eccentric group, the pair were happy because both Chopin and Maurice enjoyed such good health.

The weather broke in early December, and with it Chopin's health. The summer house they had rented was ill-equipped to stand the winter rains. Chopin's respiratory symptoms worsened: he began to cough blood-flecked sputum and became febrile and breathless. Sand sent for doctors and three arrived. They soon became preoccupied by Chopin's sputum. Chopin recorded the experience laconically, 'I have been sick as a dog these two weeks, the doctors – the best on the island – have examined me. One sniffed at what I spat, another tapped at the place whence I spat it, the third poked and listened while I spat. The first said I would die. The second, that I was dying, and the third said I was dead already!' Sand writes that Chopin was now coughing sputum 'by the bowlful' (9). The doctors recommended bleeding; this Chopin refused to submit to. He was sceptical of the value of this aggressive treatment, having seen no therapeutic benefit in his sister Emily's case. The doctors recommended milk which, however, could not be found in any quantity on the island, and Chopin's treatment consisted in toto of poultices applied at irregular intervals.

Spanish law required that cases of 'consumption' be notified to the proper authorities. The doctors complied with this law. Attitudes and medical opinion in relation to tuberculosis differed widely in northern and southern Europe. In Paris, tuberculosis was not generally regarded as an infectious disease. In contrast, the Italian Girolamo Fracastoro, who published the first modern description of tuberculosis in 1546, clearly labelled the disease a contagious one. The belief held sway in southern Europe from that time on. In northern Europe, where the population density was greater, it was noted that tuberculosis tended to occur in the same house and family. Children who had a tubercular parent often became consumptive, and this was taken to be clear evidence of the hereditary nature of the disease. Chopin's physicians all held this view: Sir James Clark, Laennec's English disciple, tells us in his famous treatise that contagion 'has absolutely no part in the spread of tuberculosis' (2, p. 220). In Spain, however, Chopin and Sand were having trouble with the local authorities, who clearly believed in the infectious nature of tuberculosis. Chopin was ostracized by the islanders. George Sand wrote that they had become objects of 'horror and terror for the local population'. Life was difficult for the couple and they withdrew to the sombre Charterhouse at Valldemosa, where Chopin composed some of his preludes. On one occasion in Palma he haemorrhaged badly all over the pavement. They left Majorca in February for Marseille.

In France Chopin regained much of his strength; he stopped coughing blood and started to gain weight. A chronic cough and shortness of breath were the main stigmata of the disease for the next few years. Sand wrote, however, that Chopin was 'never really well' and there was a slow, progressive decline in his health. After his return from Majorca, Chopin was repeatedly examined by doctors who were well versed in the use of Laennec's stethoscope. They reassured him that he did not have a discrete lung lesion consistent with tuberculosis. He was often wheezy (14, pp. 483, 533) but according to his testimony suffered seldom from fevers and never from night sweats.

For the last four years of his life the composer lived as an invalid. He became so dependent on his friends that George Sand now unmaliciously referred to him as her son. Chopin employed a servant to carry him upstairs, and conducted his piano lessons reclining on a couch. His mornings were interrupted by bouts of productive coughing and his sputum was streaked with blood. The cough was now so severe that even heavy doses of opium were of little value in suppressing it (15). He began to experience ghastly nightmares and nocturnal disorientation, probably due to the emergence of respiratory failure (9, 14).

After Chopin's estrangement from Sand in 1847, his health underwent a precipitous decline, exacerbated by the cold weather and fog during a disastrous trip to Scotland in 1848. Chopin entered into another relationship, again characterized by both dependency and resentment, this time with Jane Stirling, a Scottish heiress. His creativity had dried up completely and he could no longer compose. He suffered a bout of deep depression during the trip, which compounded his medical problems. When the idea of marriage was broached, Chopin replied that it would be unfair if Stirling married 'a corpse'. He returned to Paris in November 1848 prostrated with exhaustion, and with only eleven months to live.

THE LAST MONTHS

The existing accounts of Chopin's final illness are based on the combined observations of three authors: Chopin's pupils Adolf Gutman and Charles Gavard, and Franz Liszt. Neither Gutman nor Liszt was an eyewitness to Chopin's death. There is some evidence that their accounts were influenced by discussion with contemporary medical practitioners because they list symptoms and signs that a nineteenth-century practitioner would try to elicit, and often ignore what a first-hand observer would see and what a medical practitioner would look for today. Liszt consulted Jane Stirling for first-hand information and we know she discussed the case extensively with Jean Cruveilhier, Chopin's most famous physician. All sources relate that Chopin remained conscious and capable of speech until he died. There were no rigors and none of the disorientation suggestive of an acute brain syndrome which one

146

would expect in a pneumonic process. On the contrary, he was conscious, alert, and able to answer questions and talk to his friends, although his voice was painfully weak. The diagnosis of tubercular pneumonia and laryngitis is thus unlikely to have been correct; it is probable that Chopin died of heart disease secondary to his lung condition.

Much has been made of Chopin's laryngitis, which was regarded by nineteenth-century doctors as having a special association with tuberculosis (2) – a view now discredited. The symptom is thus given undue importance by contemporary biographers, who dutifully consulted their medical practitioners before writing their accounts. Chopin had suffered from episodic bouts of laryngitis in the past and his biographers do not mention any difficulty in swallowing, which is a prominent symptom of tubercular laryngitis. The weakness of his voice was probably due to frailty and respiratory failure alone.

Chopin's last illness was characterized by increasing weakness, diarrhoea and gross oedema (swelling) of the lower extremities. His face was so congested before his death that his features were almost unrecognizable, probably because of venous hypertension. Liszt remarked that his face returned to its usual appearance soon after his death. Gavard noticed that Chopin's face was 'blackened', suggesting central cyanosis. (The possible presence of pulmonary hypertrophic osteoarthropathy has also been commented on.)

It became clear to all that Chopin's health was failing in February 1849. His cough was now suffocating. Pauline Viardot wrote, 'His health is slowly declining; with fairly good days he can go out in his carriage. There are other days during which he coughs blood and suffers spells of coughing which choke him.' By early July his ankles had become grossly swollen, and his weight loss and cachexia[5] accelerated alarmingly. On 25 July he wrote that he could no longer walk, even with assistance. Earlier he had sent for his family in Poland, and on 25 June he wrote to his sister, Louisa, in Warsaw, 'My dearest, if you possibly can, please come. I am very weak and no doctor will do me half as much good as you will. If you are short of money borrow some. When I am better I shall easily make enough to pay back whoever will have lent it to you.' Chopin's legs became swollen right up to the calves. He could no longer breathe while lying down and had to be propped up at all times.

One of Chopin's physicians was a Dr Fraenkel, who prescribed emetics

---

[5] weakness and emaciation

in an effort to release the bad humour from the composer's body. In Chopin's words to his friend Wojciech Grzymała he 'did not spare them' and offered little practical advice. Unhappy with this regime, under which he suffered badly, Chopin consulted Jean Baptiste Cruveilhier, widely considered Paris's foremost expert on 'pulmonary phthisis'. (Cruveilhier (1791–1874), a distinguished physician and pathologist, was the author of the historically important *Anatomie pathologique du corps humain*, for many years the definitive pathology atlas in France.) Cruveilhier ended the more aggressive treatment Chopin had been having, recommending what amounted to a placebo plus further rest and a light diet. Chopin was impressed with the physician and became more optimistic in his outlook. Louisa arrived in Paris in August, which added to his happiness. In September she consulted Cruveilhier, who informed her confidentially of the diagnosis and its impending outcome. He told the Chopin family what the other doctors were loth to say: that his patient was indeed 'consumptive'. Chopin had expected Cruveilhier's diagnosis because he had been given lichens, a herbal remedy for tuberculosis which was common at the time.

Chopin's deterioration was irreversible and progressive, and he died suddenly after a bout of coughing on 17 October 1849, at 2.00 a.m. Cruveilhier put a mirror to his mouth and illuminated his pupils with a candle to confirm that the frail musician was dead. Before his death, Chopin's apartment had been the scene of great social activity. Pauline Viardot remarked that 'all the great ladies came to his room to faint'. A photographer was refused permission to photograph Chopin on his deathbed. A contemporary cartoon of a weeping woman was captioned, 'The Only Countess In Whose Arms Chopin Did Not Die'.

POSTMORTEM CONTROVERSY

After his death all Paris clamoured to know the cause of Chopin's untimely demise. He had asked that his body be opened; Cruveilhier performed an autopsy and the body was afterwards embalmed, including the heart which was sent to Warsaw for burial. Chopin's body was buried in Paris after a moving public funeral at the Madeleine.

The precise findings of the autopsy are not known. Jane Stirling, in response to a letter from Liszt, quoted Cruveilhier as saying, 'The autopsy did nothing to disclose the cause of death but it appeared that the lungs were affected less than the heart' – a statement regarded by earlier medical biographers as an attempt to disguise the fact that Chopin had pulmonary tuberculosis, which is an infectious disease. This is incongruous because few people in Paris would have believed that tuberculosis was infectious (2, p. 220). A considerable amount of controversy surrounds the issue of the autopsy report allegedly produced by Cruveilhier. The report has certainly not been seen in modern times, and it has been described as having been 'destroyed in a fire'. Despite this, it is frequently quoted in the medical literature pertaining to Chopin (e.g. 13, p. 2937)! It has not been possible either to find or to reconstruct the original. The relevant documents may have been destroyed by the German Army during the war years (16, p. 10) or in the fire which attended the destruction of the Paris commune in 1871, in which Chopin's death certificate is known to have been destroyed.

A surviving letter from Wojciech Grzymała supports the view that Chopin's autopsy did not disclose pulmonary tuberculosis and, indeed, that Chopin's disease was one that had not been encountered earlier by medical science. Grzymała wrote to Auguste Leo from Paris in October 1849: 'He [Chopin] gave instructions for his body to be opened, being convinced that medical science had never understood his disease, and in fact it was found that the cause of death had been different from what was thought but that nevertheless he could not have lived.' (11, p. 375)

DIAGNOSTIC POSSIBILITIES

The most commonly accepted interpretation of Chopin's illness is that it was caused by tuberculosis. A recent scholarly paper by Dr Czesław Sielużycki in *Rocznik Chopinowski* (27), the magazine of the Chopin Society of Warsaw, upholds this view. Sielużycki contends that Cruveilhier's autopsy disclosed cavitating tuberculosis and pericarditis as well as other diverse pathology. However, the statements are based on secondary sources and are not authenticated. (It is also said that Cruveilhier told another of Chopin's circle that he suffered from an unknown lung disease of thirty years' duration; another unauthenticated statement holds that Chopin suffered from a lung disease complicated by extensive pleurisy.) It would seem that Cruveilhier and Chopin's circle of friends have succeeded in maintaining secrecy regarding the postmortem findings. It is not possible to dismiss tuberculosis as a possible cause of Chopin's manifestations, and any scholar who wishes accurately to reconstruct Chopin's medical history must engage in deciding what is possible, what is impossible, what is hearsay and what is simply legend (7, 12, 27).

Several clinicians have doubted that Chopin suffered from tuberculosis. One eminent American cardiologist who gave credence to Chopin's own statement that his heart rather than his lungs was diseased decided that the composer suffered from mitral stenosis. There is certainly enough evidence to support the view that Chopin suffered from lung disease, whereas mitral stenosis is unlikely to cause a twenty-two-year history of pulmonary haemorrhage. Certain factors militate against a diagnosis of uncomplicated tuberculosis. The illness at Majorca is unlikely to have been due to tuberculosis: it is extremely unlikely that Chopin would have recovered spontaneously from an episode consisting of transient respiratory failure, gross weight loss and massive pulmonary haemorrhage if these had been caused by tuberculosis. The large amount of sputum produced is not consistent with the disease.

Chopin obviously had at least an element of suppurative lung disease. The suppurative lung diseases are those that feature chronic bacterial infection. The commonest is bronchiectasis, which results from pathological dilatation of the airways with consequent infection of them. The first case was described by René Laennec (1) (coincidentally, his patient was a music teacher). The disease may be associated with tuberculosis or other infective diseases or it may occur insidiously without prior cause. It was considerably more common in the nineteenth century, probably nearly as common as tuberculosis itself. In the opinion of this author, a suppurative lung disease more convincingly explains Chopin's complex symptomatology. Bronchiectasis can certainly cause recurrent pulmonary haemorrhage (20, 21).

Another possibility is that Chopin suffered from the hereditary suppurative lung disease cystic fibrosis (26), which affects approximately one in two thousand children born to Caucasian parents. Chopin's pathological emaciation, dietary problems and prostration after exercise are consistent with this disease. Children affected by the disease commonly died around the onset of puberty in the pre-antibiotic era (as did Chopin's sister Emily). Chopin's 'barrel-chestedness', a feature of later photographs and drawings, is consistent with an obstructive lung disease (16, p. 116; 27, p. 112). The disease was first described in 1932 and was thus unknown to Chopin's doctors. That sufferers of cystic fibrosis could survive to a reasonable age in the pre-antibiotic era is well documented: the disease is very variable in its clinical presentation. Marks and Anderson in 1960 reported the case of a patient with cystic fibrosis who was born in 1913 (10). He went on to live to the age of 66.

A final point of interest is whether Chopin actually suffered from digital clubbing. This is a deformity of the fingertips seen in long-standing respiratory disease. Clessinger took several casts of the death mask and of Chopin's left hand before arriving at the final version. The original cast of the death mask, recently discovered in Paris, is gruesome and vividly shows the extent of Chopin's sufferings. It is possible that the cast of the left hand has similarly been altered. The probable presence of a sympathetic arthritis makes it likely that Chopin had the condition. However, the presence of the condition is not necessary to prove that Chopin had cystic fibrosis. (Marks's patient did not show the condition when he presented with cystic fibrosis at the age of 46.)

While some doubt remains about the cause of Chopin's illness, there is little doubt that it severely affected the composer for most of his adult life. The ramifications of the disease to his career and his personal life are deep: indeed, Liszt wrote poignantly that Chopin 'used his art to reflect on the tragedy of his life'.

TABLE 1

SUMMARY OF CHOPIN'S MEDICAL HISTORY — COMPARATIVE EVIDENCE FOR AND AGAINST TUBERCULOSIS

1. *Evidence for Cystic Fibrosis or Bronchiectasis*

Chopin was ill from his later childhood years. He was noticeably emaciated. His exercise tolerance was below that of his peers (Liszt, Sand, Stirling, Field). Cruveilhier himself noted that Chopin's illness was of at least thirty years' duration.

Chopin had a suppurative lung disease marked by chronic productive cough, winter exacerbations and occasional haemoptysis (Chopin, Sand, Liszt).

Chopin may have died of respiratory failure and cor pulmonale (Liszt, Gutman, Gavard).

Chopin had intermittent, suppurative upper airways disease, sinusitis, laryngitis, etc (Chopin, Sand).

Chopin lost weight after dietary indiscretion. He restricted his intake of fatty foods. He lost weight after respiratory illnesses (Sand, Chopin).

Chopin's weight loss occurred very early in the course of his disease (Chopin, Sand, Liszt).

Chopin suffered from heat prostration (Sand).

Chopin had no offspring.

Chopin's sister may have died of cystic fibrosis.

2. *Evidence for Tuberculosis*

Chopin had a chronic cough and multiple haemoptyses, suggesting slowly progressive cavitating tuberculosis (Chopin, Sand, Liszt, Gutman). A history of twenty years of haemoptyses is not unknown with tuberculosis but it makes the disease unlikely.

Chopin may have died of respiratory failure and pericarditis causing right heart failure both ultimately due to secondary tuberculosis.

Chopin's sister, Emily, may have died of tuberculosis (although not of miliary tuberculosis).

Tuberculosis complicated by bronchiectasis would account for many of the composer's symptoms.

TABLE 2
CHOPIN'S PHYSICIANS

Warsaw (1810–30): F. Girardot, F. Roemer, W. Malcz
Vienna (1830–1): G. Malfatti
Paris – early years (from 1831): A. Hofman, J. Matuszyński, P. M. Gaubert, G. Papet, J. H. Coste
England and Scotland (1848): Sir James Clark, A. Lyszczyński
Paris – final illness (1848–9): L. F. Simon, Fraenkel, J. F. Koreff, J. B. Cruveilhier, P. Louis, D. Roth

REFERENCES

1. R. Laennec, *A Treatise on Diseases of the Chest* (London, 1834, trans. J. Forbes), pp. 100–12
2. J. Clark, *A Treatise on Pulmonary Consumption: A Comprehending Enquiry into the Causes, Nature and Prevention of Tuberculosis and Scrofulous Diseases in General* (London, 1835)
3. F. Liszt, *Frederic Chopin* (revised edition)[6] (London, 1877, trans. J. Broadhouse)
4. M. Karasowski, *Life and Letters of Chopin* (London, 1879)
5. F. Niecks, *Frederick Chopin as a Man and Musician*, 2 vols (London, 1887)
6. W. D. Murdoch, *Chopin: His Life* (London, 1934), pp. 27, 150, 244
7. E. Ganche, *Souffrances de Frédéric Chopin* (Paris, 1935)
8. L. Brown, *The Story of Clinical Pulmonary Tuberculosis* (Baltimore, 1941), pp. 109–33, 141–2, 156–7
9. G. Sand, *Winter in Majorca* (Palma de Mallorca, 1956, trans. R. Graves), pp. 18, 27, 48, 49, 115, 116, 137–9, 149–50, 167–74
10. B. L. Marks and C. M. Anderson, 'Fibrocystic Disease of the Pancreas in a Man aged 46', *Lancet* (1960), pp. 365–7
11. A. Hedley (ed.), *Selected Correspondence of Fryderyk Chopin* (London, 1962), pp. 372–5
12. A. Harasowski, *The Skein of Legends around Chopin* (Glasgow, 1967)
13. F. Mullam, 'The Sickness of Frederic Chopin: A Study of Disease and Society', *Rocky Mountain Medical Journal*, 70 (1973), p. 2934
14. C. Cate, *George Sand: A Biography* (New York, 1975), pp. 441–567
15. R. Jordan, *Nocturne: A Life of Chopin* (London, 1978)
16. G. R. Marek, *Chopin* (New York, 1978)
17. G. Sand, *My Life* (New York, 1979, trans. D. Hofstader), pp. 229–39

[6] This edition was revised, to its detriment, by Princess Carolyne Sayn-Wittgenstein.

18. T. Higgins, 'Delphina Potocka and Frederic Chopin', *Journal of The American Liszt Society*, 9 (1981), p. 71

19. C. E. Abbot, 'Composers and Tuberculosis: The Effects on Creativity', *Journal of the Canadian Medical Association*, 126 (1982), pp. 534–44

20. R. E. Behrman (ed.), *Nelson's Textbook of Paediatrics*, 12th edn (Philadelphia, 1982), pp. 708–26, 1071–2, 1086–99

21. J. G. Wyngaarden (ed.), *Cecil's Textbook of Medicine*, 16th edn (Philadelphia, 1982), pp. 386–8, 1542–8

22. W. von Lenz, *The Great Piano Virtuosos of our Time* (London, 1983, trans. P. Reder) [Ger. original Berlin, 1872]

23. A. Walker, *Franz Liszt: The Virtuoso Years 1811–1847* (London, 1983)

24. J. G. O'Shea, 'A Medical History of Franz Liszt', *Medical Journal of Australia*, 145 (1986), pp. 625–30

25. D. L. Mein, 'A Selective Advantage for Cystic Fibrosis Heterozygotes', *American Journal of Physical Anthropology*, 74 (1987), pp. 39–45

26. J. G. O'Shea, 'Was Frederic Chopin's Illness Actually Cystic Fibrosis?', *Medical Journal of Australia*, 147 (1987), p. 586

27. C. Sielużycki, 'Ozdowiu Chopina', *Rocznik Chopinowski*, 15 (1987), pp. 69–117

Franz Liszt
(1811–86)

CHILDHOOD YEARS

Franz Liszt was born in Raiding, near Sopron, on 22 October 1811. The progenitor of the legend that grew around him was, to some extent, not Liszt himself but his father. Adam Liszt was a clever man and a talented amateur musician who chafed at his 'exile' to Raiding, where he held the humble post of steward to Prince Nikolaus Esterházy. In this small, provincial village he longed for advancement and the stimulation of the life at court. It was not to come. At first it did not seem that the birth of a son would do much to change his life. Franz, a frail, sickly infant, seemed unlikely to survive. He suffered fevers and convulsions so frequently that it has been proposed he was epileptic. It is more probable, however, that frequent acute infections, combined with poor nutrition and housing conditions, were the cause of his problems. When he was six years old the young Liszt was profoundly ill after his smallpox vaccination. (Edward Jenner's technique of vaccination to immunize against the disease had been lately introduced.) Liszt bore no stigma of chronic infection or epileptic condition in his adult life; he grew to a strapping young man of about 180 cm in height, rather tall for the era.

It is an established fact that musical talent runs in families, and there have been several who have numbered numerous musical prodigies among their offspring – the Bachs, the Mozarts, the Mendelssohns. Liszt's family, too, had its share of brilliant musical talent. His cousin Eduard was highly gifted and toyed with the idea of becoming a virtuoso. He eventually forged a distinguished career in law, reaching the post of Imperial Prosecutor in Vienna. Both of Liszt's daughters, Cosima and Blandine, were reckoned musically precocious by Wagner and Von Bülow.

When young Franz had recovered sufficient health to demonstrate his phenomenal musical talent, Adam Liszt was quick to encourage him so that he could avoid the crushing monotony of provincial life that had been his own lot. Adam Liszt, a devout man who had served for a time in a Franciscan seminary, was responsible for young Franz's religious education, which included reading the *Lives of the Saints* and Thomas à Kempis's *Imitation of Christ*. Liszt's fascination with mystical Christianity was to provide a programme for many of his later compositions.

During his childhood, Franz made phenomenal musical progress. He was playing well by the end of his fifth year. At eight he was improvising and, according to his father's testimony, could read the most difficult pieces by contemporary musicians at sight. He composed his first piece of music, a *Tantum ergo* (now lost), at ten. He composed a one-act opera, *Don Sanche*, at the age of twelve, an achievement that shows his remarkable aptitude for composition. The opera failed to win public acclaim because of its poor libretto.

By the age of twelve or thirteen, Liszt was reckoned among the foremost virtuosi in Europe. His early aptitude for composition flowered; at fourteen he composed an advanced set of technical exercises which later became the *Transcendental Studies* (he had already written two piano concertos and several piano sonatas which unfortunately are now lost). His prowess was not without cost, however. The Liszts were extremely strained financially when they moved to Vienna. Franz was often ill through hard work, poor accommodation and travel. He was also now in the equivocal position of being the family wage-earner. His father died of typhoid fever just before the composer's sixteenth birthday.

EFFECTS OF CAREER ON HEALTH

Liszt's health and his playing were, of course, intertwined. In his youth, Franz's extraordinary motivation may have pushed him beyond his physical capacity. Each summer, during the concert season, there were episodes when his hand shook uncontrollably for a few days. At a concert in Paris in 1835 Liszt actually collapsed. The incident has been cited by his detractors as an example of his most cynical and blatant showmanship: it has been suggested that Liszt feigned a collapse to lead his

156

audience into a frenzy. The incident as described by Henry Reeve in his extravagant nineteenth-century prose certainly has comic overtones.

Liszt had already played a great Fantasia of his own and Beethoven's 27th Sonata. After the latter piece he gasped with emotion as I shook his hand and thanked him for the divine energy he had shed forth. My chair was on the same board as the piano when the final piece began. It was a duet for two instruments beginning with Mendelssohn's 'Chants Sans Paroles' and proceeding to a work of his own. We had already passed that delicious chime of the song written in a Gondola and the gay tendrils of sound in another piece which always remind me of an Italian vine. As the closing strains began I saw Liszt's countenance assume that agony of expression mingled with radiant smiles of joy, which I never saw on any other human face except in the paintings of our saviour by some of the early masters. The floor on which I sat shook like a wire and the whole audience were wrapped in sound, when the hand and frame of the artist gave way. He fainted into the arms of a friend who was turning over the pages for him and we bore him out in a strong fit of hysterics. The effect of the scene was really dreadful. The whole room sat breathless with fear until Hiller came forward and announced that Liszt was already restored to consciousness and was comparatively well again. As I handed Madame de Circcoutt to her carriage we both trembled and I tremble scarcely less as I write this.

It is probable that the fit in question was neither epilepsy nor a deliberate attempt by Liszt to frighten his audience but possibly a simple vasovagal attack. Liszt was then 24, working hard on acquiring his 'transcendental technique' and practising many hours a day as well as living a hectic social life. The vasovagal attack, or faint, may be seen as a reaction to stress and the ensuing 'fit of hysterics' may have been a rare moment of emotional release or even a phenomenon resembling an epileptiform seizure which often accompanies vasovagal attacks. The incident may have also been somewhat exaggerated in contemporary reports, and there are no other accounts of 'convulsions' during Liszt's adult years.

The strain of travel often made inroads on Liszt's health. In Bonn he suffered from a 'brilliant jaundice' (possibly infectious hepatitis – a common complaint among tourists today) and took a water cure at Baden Baden. He occasionally resorted to alcohol on tour. As his coordination and health were not impaired by his drinking, it was probably more episodic than his contemporaries imagined. During a tour of Britain in 1840, however, Liszt drank rather heavily; this is well documented in the diary of John Orlando Parry who accompanied the pianist on the tour. In the last few years of his life, after the death of his children, and because of problems in his relationship with the Princess Sayn-Wittgenstein, he did sometimes drink heavily. The direct effects on his health are speculative.

A prominent feature in the later portraits of Liszt are the moles or 'grains of genius', as they were facetiously called by the popular press (one Roman journalist remarked that Liszt's ability as a composer was increasing as the number of moles was increasing). The 'moles' were molles naevi (soft moles); these are common in the middle-aged and are not the product of or associated with organic disease. They occur on the face and the back of the hands. They are harmless and are today excised for cosmetic reasons. The Roman journalists saw Liszt as a source of endless material for their gossip columns and were ceaselessly dissecting his foibles and running articles about such trivia as his penchant for black coffee and smoked oysters. Reports by palmists and fortune tellers concerning Liszt's hands and the 'phrenology' of the bumps on his head also made for undistinguished reading in the contemporary press.

SLOW ONSET OF CHRONIC ILLNESS

Liszt suffered from serious health problems in his later years, although such was his public bearing they were overlooked. His health declined progressively after 1880 but until 1882 he still enjoyed relatively long periods of good health – Borodin found the virtuoso in fine form when he visited Weimar in 1881. After 1881 congestive heart failure was manifest and it sorely affected Liszt. In 1883 Liszt's daughter Cosima noted his frail appearance and remarked, sorrowfully, that she felt that his death was near. In the last year of his life he was rendered almost blind by cataracts. In her memoirs, published in 1908, Jenny Churchill writes rather cruelly of the old man and tells how she had to help him eat his asparagus at a public banquet during his last visit to London in April 1886.

Poor vision and physical frailty sometimes impaired Liszt's playing towards the end of his life but we are told by Alexander Ziloti and Frederic Lamond, among others, that, on the occasions when his health was good, his playing was still incomparable, although it probably did not reach the heights of his technical achievement in the virtuoso years (38). Liszt practised hardly at all after his 'retirement' from the concert stage in 1847, but such was his aptitude that his technique still remained astonishing despite years of neglect of practice. His power to move an audience as no other musician could remained until his death.

Osteoarthritis may also have affected Liszt's hands in the later years. We are told by Jenny Churchill of the 'gouty' swellings on the tips of his fingers which occasionally impaired his playing (though late photographs of his hands do not show tophaceous gout). From Carl Lachmund comes the testimony that Liszt could span barely a tenth in his last year (38). (We know that in his youth he played the Henselt Piano Concerto, which requires a twelfth.) The explanation for the painfully swollen hands and the decline in the hand span could be that osteoarthritis affected the digits and the carpo-metacarpal joint of the thumb. This is borne out by photographs of Liszt's hands taken in 1886 which reveal the presence of Heberden's nodes (swellings at the fingertips), a clear indication that he suffered from osteoarthritis (33), though the degree to which this affected his playing cannot be established. Liszt limped because of osteoarthritis in his hip and painful 'dropsy' affecting his feet. To cope with his blindness and hand disease, Felix Weingartner noted (38), Liszt now kept his hands close to the keyboard, in contrast to the high position adopted during the virtuoso years.

Before his last tour of England, Liszt apologized for not intending to play publicly because his '75-year-old fingers' were not up to the task. As it turned out the old artist arrived in England in unexpectedly good health and played often and well in public. The long journeys of the last years often left Liszt prostrated with exhaustion – after a long and eventful life, and suffering from untreated heart failure and chronic respiratory disease, he must have been pushed to the limits of human endurance by long and often physically uncomfortable journeys.

The best accounts of Liszt in his old age come from the written reminiscences of A.W.Gottschalg, the court organist at Weimar (38), Lina Schmalhausen, a pupil who acted as Liszt's private secretary (2) and the conductor Felix Weingartner (38). All relate that despite advanced illness Liszt kept up a busy schedule of teaching and useful work.

ILLNESSES OF LISZT'S LAST YEARS (1880–1886)

Like many old people Liszt was affected by multiple illnesses which were the result of physiological decline, occupational illness and the habits of a lifetime. These illnesses were overlooked for two reasons: firstly, because of the composer's magnificent public bearing which forced his contemporaries to concentrate on aspects of his personality rather than his physical and personal well-being. Secondly, although these illnesses were of considerable severity – so severe in fact that Liszt was near death many times in the last few years of his life – the miracle of Liszt's piano playing was still preserved right up until the time of his death, despite disease of the lungs, heart, eyes and the skeletomuscular system.

Liszt's last illness was due to long-standing disease of the lungs and the cardiovascular system. The key aetiological factor in this disease was tobacco abuse – Liszt was an inveterate smoker of cigars and pipes. He frequently rose at 4.00 a.m. and commenced chain smoking while working steadily at his compositions. After evening dinner there would be further rounds of cigars – Liszt preferred the cheapest and strongest Havana cigars available. He had begun to smoke during his teenage years in Paris. Nicotine improves alertness and fine motor co-ordination and may have helped Liszt's playing, particularly the arduous periods of practice. Ultimately tobacco was responsible for his death.

We can see evidence of advancing disease of the lung and heart in the last photographs of Liszt. His chest has assumed a prominent barrel shape and in some portraits his body is swollen with 'dropsy' or oedema fluid, a legacy of right-sided heart failure. This fluid is labile and accounts for the great variation in Liszt's physical appearance in the last photographs. Like the famous photographs of Robert E. Lee in his old age, one can trace the progression of Liszt's illness through the later photographs. Adelheid von Schorn wrote of Liszt in her memoirs (October 1882):

> When I first saw him I was shocked. His face was pale, his features bloated, his hands were swollen and he had become quite corpulent. His mood varied with the fluctuations in his physical condition and he was tired practically the whole time. He scarcely ever left his rooms but sat at his desk and worked, often dropping off to sleep in his chair. (38)

This is a fine description of the symptoms of right heart failure.

By 1886, Liszt's 'dropsy' was such that his legs were chronically swollen right up to the knees. He was prone to frequent bouts of deep fatigue and depression and his personality seemed subdued. This is certainly due largely to the progress of his right heart disease. Many of the later photographs of Liszt show the hyperinflated chest of chronic airways disease. In his last months and during his last illness Liszt suffered from painful 'heart spasms' undoubtedly caused by coronary artery disease. These were episodes of crushing chest pain located behind the sternum (breast bone).

Heart failure is a term used by physicians to describe a cardiac output that is insufficient to meet the physiological needs of the body. The heart itself consists of two pumps in parallel; the right side pumps blood through the lungs, and failure of its action causes blood to pool before it reaches the lungs. Hence the collection of oedema fluid in the dependent areas of the body. In the last few months of his life, Liszt experienced the symptoms of left heart failure, with pooling of the blood in the lungs themselves. This left heart failure initially manifested as a chronic cough, but it progressed to respiratory embarrassment and was probably a synergistic cause of Liszt's death along with bronchopneumonia. Left heart failure causes congestion of the lungs by fluid (pulmonary oedema). The photographic studies for Munkacsy's famous portrait of Liszt taken in 1882 show the peripheral oedema fluid well.

The reason that right heart failure appeared first was probably due to the fact that Liszt's lungs were heavily damaged by cigarette smoking. The disease of the lungs produced by cigarette smoking is now called chronic obstructive airways disease and this entity is a combination of chronic bronchitis (inflammation of the respiratory passages) and emphysema (destruction of the respiratory cells themselves). When these cells die, their blood vessels die along with them, increasing the resistance of the pulmonary vascular tree and placing a strain on the right side of the heart. Factors which led to the development of left-sided heart failure in Liszt's case probably included disease of the arteries and hypertension (high blood pressure). Visible in the full-face photographs by Nadar is the so-called 'arcus senilis', a ring of cholesterol deposits around Liszt's cornea. The 'arcus' is sometimes associated with disease of the arteries.

Alcohol is also associated with acceleration of vascular disease. We are told that Liszt had something of a problem with alcohol in the last two or three years of his life. He had consumed alcohol since his early years in Paris, but he seldom drank more than he could handle. His drinking occurred mainly in a social context, was balanced by a good diet and did Liszt's health little harm. However, by 1883 his students were becoming alarmed by an increase in Liszt's alcohol intake. There are two possible reasons for it: firstly, those who suffer from loneliness, depression or chronic illness often drink heavily to allay their sufferings.

Secondly, Liszt may have had congestive liver disease secondary to right-sided heart failure, and this disease entity would have caused a marked decline in his alcohol tolerance. In later photographs Liszt's abdomen is grossly distended, presumably because of the collection of ascitic fluid probably caused by heart failure or cirrhosis of the liver.

Other subtle manifestations of cardiac failure would have included the 'cardiac cachexia' or generalized weakness associated with the condition. Ziloti tells us that Liszt played the 'Moonlight' Sonata of Beethoven in response to a challenge by a student that he could not play it better than Rubinstein (38). His playing of the first two movements was incomparable, but he soon became fatigued playing the last movement and gave it up as soon as he had impressed the class with his abilities. Despite such advanced disease, Liszt managed to put up a bold front and played many times in public in 1886. Diehl, MacKenzie and Stavenhagen testify that, although little more than a trace of the fiery virtuosity of his youth remained, his playing still held its magical technical and musical qualities (4, 7, 38).

LISZT'S HEALTH IN 1886

A feature of chronic bronchitis is that its sufferers are prone to minor respiratory infections which may exacerbate the disease and lead to serious complications. Thus a simple cold may progress to pneumonia in an elderly person with chronically damaged lungs. This is because of the damaged disease-fighting and immune mechanisms in the walls of the respiratory passages, the bronchi. Liszt's physical condition deteriorated rapidly in 1886 with the progress of his long-standing lung and heart disease, and it was apparent to all that his end was not far away. The year was to mark the seventy-fifth anniversary of Liszt's birth and the composer, despite his illness, planned a long tour including England, France, Belgium and the Netherlands; anniversary celebrations had been planned throughout the Continent.

The year did not begin well, however. In February the Hungarian winter was particularly heavy, with violent snow storms and lashing rain, and Liszt, who was staying in Budapest, caught a bad cold which resulted in prostration and respiratory embarrassment for him and took a great toll on his health. He was eager to attend the planned celebrations, though he was well aware that little time remained to him and alluded to this fact frequently in his last letters. He therefore took great care of himself during his illness and made a slow and steady recovery.

This fastidiousness was uncharacteristic, and Liszt's adoption of the Franciscan spirit of self-abnegation probably prolonged his life by several months.

Liszt was absent from public life for over a month but he did not neglect his piano teaching, which he now considered to be his most important obligation. When he left Budapest for the last time in early March, his friends were dismayed at the sight of the frail, emaciated figure embarking on what was to be his last journey. He took the night train from the city after a farewell dinner and a concert given in his honour. He was now white-haired and haggard, his eventful life almost at a close. His once tall figure was hunched and his gait impaired by arthritis and poor vision. His body was often swollen by the dropsy, or oedema fluid, which was a legacy of his heart disease. He had few teeth of his own and his jaw sagged. Yet whenever he played the piano or appeared in public the old charisma remained and the audience was once more overwhelmed. The old man was a phenomenon, a ghost from the past who had been a friend of Chopin, Wagner and Berlioz. He was so obviously near death, yet still played uniquely and magnificently.

The terminal phase of Liszt's illness lasted for about ten days, from 21 July, when he arrived in Bayreuth, until the 31st when he died. He took refuge in rented rooms near the Villa Wahnfried, where his daughter Cosima lived, and his debilitated condition was evident to all in his circle. He had had to be helped from his carriage for several months before he died and was now so frail that he could not walk without assistance. (He had had difficulty with stairs for several years; his poor mobility would thus seem to have been a long-standing problem.) Death was probably due to an exacerbation of congestive cardiac failure complicated by bronchopneumonia. The prodromal signs of Liszt's illness – a worsening chronic cough and increasing 'dropsy' – had been present for many months according to the testimonies of Ziloti, Adelheid von Schorn and Lina Schmalhausen (38, 2).

On the afternoon of 24 July, Adelheid von Schorn wrote:

Liszt was sitting on the sofa in his living room holding his cards in his hand and surrounded by a number of his pupils who were playing whist with him. He coughed, fell asleep for a moment, then went on playing. He hardly knew who was there and could scarcely sit upright. Deeply depressed, we both left knowing that there was nothing we could do for the master we loved. (37, 38)

163

The reason for this stuporous state was twofold: the progression of heart failure, and the fact that Liszt's doctor Landgraf had prescribed morphine for a violent cough which now plagued him day and night and was a symptom of his cardio-respiratory disease. Although morphine is a fine cough suppressant it depresses both the respiratory drive and the level of consciousness. The doctor forbade Liszt his brandy and prescribed foot baths and mustard plasters. These had no therapeutic efficacy but may have supplied much needed comfort: Liszt took to his bed the next day.

By 28 July he was confined to bed; his breathing had become more laboured, his coughing worse. Landgraf sent for a second opinion. Professor Fleischer from the University of Erlangen was consulted on the 30th. He diagnosed pneumonia of the right lung and told Cosima that her father would not recover. The pathology that Fleischer noted on his examination was probably a pleural effusion – fluid in the pleural cavity on the right side of Liszt's chest. This was probably a manifestation either of chronic pulmonary oedema or of an infective process in Liszt's lungs. The pulmonary oedema was of course a consequence of chronic heart failure. Liszt had several 'heart spasms' that day, likely manifestations of angina pectoris or of myocardial infarction. His students, who were listening outside his room, could hear his cries of pain. Liszt's illness now progressed with alarming rapidity. At 2.00 a.m. on the night of the 30th he clutched his chest as if in pain, stumbled around his room crying 'Air, air!' and jostled his servants, all of which suggest that he may have sustained a heart attack before he died. By the night of 31 July Liszt was delirious and his 'dropsy' was far worse. This suggests that progressive heart failure, perhaps due to a series of heart attacks, was responsible for his death. Bernard Stavenhagen confirms this (38). Liszt's final hours were less terrifying as he was now profoundly unconscious; he died on the evening of 31 July at 10.30 p.m. His doctor gave him camphor injections directly into the heart when he finally became still; he convulsed and fell back dead. No cause of death was recorded on the death certificate: Landgraf and Fleischer obviously had doubts.

Liszt was nearly 75 when he died, and ill-health had affected his life far less than that of many of his contemporaries. He showed great courage and determination in the face of a host of final aggravating illnesses. Many biographers fail to make allowance for these illnesses in their critical and pessimistic accounts of Liszt's last years (26, 37). There is little doubt that his final illness was not 'acute lobar pneumonia' as stated by most biographers but the terminal stage of long-standing cardiovascular and airways disease.

Liszt's body lay in state at the Villa Wahnfried. A muslin gauze was placed over the face to protect it from decomposition. Bernard Stavenhagen wrote that the condition of the body prompted the rushed funeral: the immense 'dropsy' would not allow the body to keep (38). Others believed that the funeral was hasty so that the Wagner festival would not be interrupted. Constance Bache, writing in the *Monthly Musical Record* (1 September 1886), provides details of the funeral and Requiem:

> The funeral was fixed for Tuesday, 3 August, and was a most solemn and impressive sight to those who were privileged to be present. The gathering was an immense one, filling all the large drive of Wahnfried, in the hall of which the coffin had been placed previous to its last journey to the cemetery. But the numbers would assuredly have been doubled had not the funeral been fixed for such an untimely date ... The next morning a requiem service was held in the Catholic church in Bayreuth, at which all the eminent people who were present at the funeral attended. The musical part of the service was in the highest degree unsatisfactory, and the feeling of many must have been that if nothing better than that could be done, it would have been far better to have no service at all. When the composer of the Symphonic Poems, the Gran Mass, the *St Elisabeth*, had just passed away, in the very town where the air is rife with Wagner and music, where two of the most renowned conductors and numbers of Germany's most gifted song-birds were on the spot, it does seem strange that no better memorial service could have been arranged than the nasal chanting of two or three harsh-voiced priests, in response to the very inharmonious and discordant singing and playing of an inefficient choir and organist. However, enough of this; happily, his memory does not hang upon a funeral service! [The organist was actually Anton Bruckner.]

A mortuary chapel erected above Liszt's grave was destroyed in the shelling of Bayreuth in 1944. The coffin was not damaged. The Hungarian Liszt Society paid for the restoration of Liszt's grave; it has asked that Liszt's body be reinterred in Hungary, but the request has been repeatedly turned down by the German authorities.

LISZT'S EYE DISEASE

In the last few months of his life Liszt was rendered nearly blind by cataracts. His last letters are often only brief notes in a laborious scrawl.

The left eye was affected first but gradually the vision in both eyes was reduced as the disease progressed.

Liszt had normal sight, but in middle age he became markedly presbyopic (long-sighted). An unfortunate manifestation of his eye disease was a painful condition producing a discharge from his eyes. This was probably a form of chronic blepharoconjunctivitis (a long-standing inflammation of the eyelids and the conjunctiva). The full-face photograph taken by Nadar suggests corneal scarring due to staphylococcal (bacterial) eye disease: Liszt obtained little relief from the drops prescribed by his physicians.

Liszt was reluctant to undergo cataract surgery, citing his age and physical frailty as reasons against its being undertaken. Nevertheless, the rapid deterioration of his vision made the operation a necessity. Liszt's surgeon was to be Alfred Karl Gräfe (1830–99), the most eminent of the German ophthalmic surgeons, who wrote the definitive contemporary textbook on eye surgery. Antiseptic technique had been introduced to surgery by Lister, and topical analgesia in cataract surgery by Karl Koller. In 1884 Koller wrote a paper describing topical analgesia of the eye by the instillation of cocaine drops; a technique for immobilizing the eye and its muscles of movement was as yet unknown. Cocaine as a local anaesthetic was introduced to the medical profession by Sigmund Freud but its use in Germany in 1886 was by no means universal. Gräfe's technique of cataract operations involved operative removal of the lens,[1] and a peripheral iridectomy was performed at the same time. The occurrence of major complications was in the order of 2–5% from his operation. Anterior uveitis and sympathetic ophthalmia were the most frequent of the serious complications. Intraocular infection was less frequent but a dangerous potential complication of eye surgery. Much of Gräfe's technique was based on the work of his cousin, the distinguished ophthalmic surgeon Albrecht von Gräfe (1828–70) of Berlin.

Ramann described the encounter between Liszt and Gräfe in *Lisztiana* (30). Liszt's eye problems began in his left eye, and he consulted Gräfe in 1883; by 1886 the vision in both eyes was affected. The surgeon noted that the left cataract was a 'grey cataract' and was probably a typical dense nuclear senile cataract. Since he contemplated an operation Liszt's visual acuity must have been very poor (probably down to perception of light or hand movements). By June 1886 Liszt could no longer

[1] An extracapsular lens extraction was performed by ophthalmologists of Gräfe's school.

notate music and could write only with the greatest difficulty. The spherical aphakic glasses available in the late nineteenth century could certainly restore 6/18 vision, which is needed for close vision and the notation of music. If Liszt had undergone surgery without complications he would undoubtedly have benefited from the operation.

Cataract surgery today is far more effective and safe and involves the implantation of an artificial lens into the posterior chamber of the eye. Thanks to this lens, which aids vision and obviates the necessity to wear thick and cumbersome glasses, cataract operations are performed at an earlier stage in the disease than ever before. The operation usually takes place under the operating microscope. Quite apart from the high rate of complications of cataract operations in the nineteenth century, it was very difficult to make an adequate lens once the eye's own natural lens had been removed. The thick 'pebble glasses' had a very narrow field of vision and produced considerable distortion.

Liszt's operation was to be carried out at a late stage when the eye was almost blind because of the opacified lens which covered the visual axis; surgery often provided some relief in these circumstances and with glasses he may have been able to read. Liszt's poor physical condition and the presence of an ectropion were important negative prognostic factors in the surgical treatment of his eye condition. Chloroform anaesthesia was particularly hazardous in those with chronic lung or cardiovascular disease. Liszt's death intervened before the operation, scheduled to take place in Halle in September 1886, was undertaken.

DEPRESSION IN THE ELDERLY

It is clear from a study of Liszt's medical history that much of the often discussed depression of his later years may have been due to physical illness. Advanced cardio-respiratory illness is known to be associated with psychic depression; sufferers of these disorders often sleep poorly owing to nocturnal breathlessness. Additionally, it is noted that many old people suffer from psychic depression. This has been labelled 'endogenous depression' or 'involutional melancholia' and it is not related entirely to environmental circumstances. A possible cause of this form of depression is that the aging brain does not manufacture enough catecolamine neurotransmitters; these substances are implicated in affective disorders. The poor sleeping and nocturnal ruminations that many people experience and the feeling of unsatisfied sleep which Liszt strove to capture in his nocturne *Schlaflos, Frage und Antwort*

(Sleepless, question and answer) probably has an organic as well as a psychological basis. Modern psychotropic drugs such as the tricyclic antidepressants, which appear to act by increasing the concentration of catecolamines in the brain, are used to treat depression in the elderly.

Critics of the music of Liszt's last years tend to the view that, although it is of interest for its experimental harmonic writing, its lack of form, simple themes and general inconclusiveness make it ultimately unsatisfying. But it would surely not be fanciful to view these late works as programme music in which Liszt recreates the feelings and state of mind of many elderly people. The sometimes undefined anxiety which the approach of death inevitably provokes is mirrored in these works. Past happiness is evoked nostalgically in the *Valses oubliées*. Often these return to original form after a series of complex variations – much like the rumination of any elderly person recalling the past. It is a highly personal music of involution, uncertainty and loss.

TABLE 1

SUMMARY OF LISZT'S ILLNESSES

Cause of death
Exacerbation of chronic obstructive airways disease and chronic congestive cardiac failure. A probable myocardial infarction in the terminal phase of the illness precipitated death due to cardiogenic shock. (Diagnosis of right lobar pneumonia made by physicians attending composer is doubtful.) The pathology of myocardial infarction was elaborated by René Marie only in 1896 (25).

Antecedent causes
   Chronic obstructive airways disease (due to tobacco)
   Chronic congestive cardiac failure
   Ischaemic heart disease (coronary artery disease)

Other illnesses
   Cataracts
   Chronic blepharoconjunctivitis
   Infective pyoderma
   Dental caries, gingivitis
   Osteoarthritis (spine, hips, hands)
   Respiratory illness due to tobacco abuse

Possible illnesses
   Gout
   Childhood epilepsy (unlikely)
   Chronic hepato-cellular failure

Associated conditions
   Postural deformity due to piano playing
   (stooped neck and shoulders)
   Molles naevi (soft moles)

REFERENCES

1. G. Sand, *Lettres d'un voyageur* (Paris, 1862)
2. L. Schmalhausen, MS diary, 1886 (Liszt Museum, Weimar)
3. *The Musical Times*, 27 (1886), pp. 65, 89, 253–60, 513–30
4. J. Wohl, *Franz Liszt: Souvenirs d'une compatriote* (Paris, 1887)
5. A. M. Diehl, *Musical Memories* (London, 1897), p. 271
6. 'Un hommage peu banal', *La chronique médicale*, 18 (1911), p. 688

7. E. Jentsch, 'Die Lokalisation der musikalischen Anlage am Schadel', *Zeitschrift für die gesamte Neurologie und Psychiatrie*, no. 48 (1919), pp. 263–93

8. R. Klose, Letters of Franz Liszt, in 'Das Gehirn eines Wunderkindes (des Pianisten Goswin Sokeland)', *Monatsschrift für Psychiatrie und Neurologie*, 48 (1920), pp. 76–8

9. A. MacKenzie, *A Musician's Narrative* (London, 1927)

10. M. d'Aymeric, 'Gluck et Liszt', *La chronique médicale*, 39 (1932), p. 297

11. R. Quero, *Franz Liszt: Étude psychopathologique*, Thesis, no. 84 (Bordeaux, 1932)

12. Stauffer, 'Gluck et Liszt', *La chronique médicale*, 39 (1932), p. 324

13. L. Pérignon, 'Gluck et Liszt', *ibid.*, 40 (1933), p. 40

14. R. Sebillotte, 'Gluck et Liszt', *ibid.*, p. 98

15. R. Schramek, 'Franz Liszt: Eine psychologische Untersuchung über Leben und Werk', *Archiv für die gesamte Psychologie*, 92 (1934), pp. 45–84

16. S. Sitwell, *Liszt* (London, 1934, reprinted 1965), pp. 320–6

17. L. J. Karnosh, 'The Insanities of Famous Men', *Journal of the Indiana State Medical Association*, 29 (1936), pp. 4–5

18. H. E. Hugo (ed.), *The Letters of Franz Liszt to Marie zu Sayn-Wittgenstein* (Cambridge, Mass., 1953)

19. H. Searle, *The Music of Liszt* (London, 1954, rev. New York, 1966)

20. D. Davila Bethoud, *Fils de Liszt? Sa vie, son oeuvre, le secret de ses origines d'après ses lettres, les documents réunis par sa fille, la générale Perticari, et quelques sources nouvelles* (Neuchâtel, 1956)

21. B. Szabolcsi, *Liszt Ferenc estéje* (The twilight of Liszt) (Budapest, 1956)

22. G. B. Gilbert, *Disease and Destiny* (London, 1962), p. 304

23. E. Gurlt and A. Wernich (eds.), *Biographisches Lexicon der hervorragenden Ärzte* (Munich, 1962)

24. S. Duke-Elder, *System of Ophthalmology*, vol. 11: *Diseases of the Lens and Vitreous Humour* (London, 1965)

25. A. D. Morgan, 'Some Forms of Undiagnosed Coronary Artery Disease in Nineteenth Century England', *Medical History*, 12 (1968), p. 344

26. E. Newman, *The Man Liszt*, 2nd edn (London, 1970)

27. D. Kerner, 'Liszt's Tod in Bayreuth', *Münchener medizinische Wochenschrift*, 119 (1977), pp. 1311–14

28. D. Legány, *Liszt and his Country: 1869–1973* (Budapest, 1983)

29. W. von Lenz, *The Great Piano Virtuosos of our Time* (London, 1983, trans. P. Reder) [Ger. original Berlin, 1872]

30. L. Ramann, *Lisztiana* (Mainz, 1983)

31. A. Walker, *Franz Liszt*, 1: *The Virtuoso Years 1811–1847* (London, 1983), pp. 131, 136, 428–9

32. J. G. O'Shea, 'Franz Liszt: A Medical History', *Liszt Saeculum*, 36 (1985), pp. 69–72

33. E. Burger, *Franz Liszt: Eine Lebenschronik in Bildern und Dokumenten* (Munich, 1986)
34. D. Legány, 'Liszt and the Budapest Musical Scene', *New Hungarian Quarterly*, 27 (1986), p. 119
35. J. G. O'Shea, 'A Medical History of Franz Liszt', *Medical Journal of Australia*, 145 (1986), pp. 625–39
36. J. G. O'Shea, 'The Abbé and his Church', *Liszt Saeculum*, 38 (1986), p. 90
37. R. Taylor, *Liszt the Man and the Musician* (London, 1986), pp. 228–57
38. A. Williams (compiler), '1886: Liszt's Last Months and Death', *Liszt Society Journal* (December 1986), pp. 102–10
39. A. Williams, 'The Last Visit to London', *New Hungarian Quarterly*, 27 (1986), p. 131
40. J. G. O'Shea, 'Liszt's Last Illness', *Hungarian Observer*, 2/2 (1987), p. 19
41. J. G. O'Shea, 'Liszt utolso betegsége' (Liszt's last illness), *Nemzeti ujsag*, 4 (December 1987), p. 16
42. J. G. O'Shea, 'The Abbé and his Alcohol', *Liszt Saeculum*, 40 (1987), 12–15
43. J. G. O'Shea, 'Liszt utolso betegsége' (Liszt's last illness), *Orvosi Hetilap*, 129 (1988), 1059–60
44. S. Rocchietta, 'Liszt's Last Years', *Minerva medicina*, 79 (1988), pp. 153–4

Edvard Grieg
(1843–1907)

INTRODUCTION

Edvard Grieg was born on 15 June 1843 in Bergen, Norway. The child who was destined to become Norway's greatest composer could actually trace his name and his paternal ancestry to Scotland. His greatgrandfather Alexander Grieg migrated to Bergen and obtained Norwegian citizenship in 1779. He acquired considerable wealth and was a prominent citizen of the small town. It is said that Grieg's father, Alexander, maintained a lively interest in all things British because of his illustrious ancestor. Grieg's mother Gesine Hagerup was of indigenous Bergen stock.

The young Edvard showed considerable aptitude for music and, inspired by Ole Bull, a Norwegian violin virtuoso who had obtained international success, he completed his student days in Leipzig where he studied piano with Moscheles and composition with E.F.Richter, Moritz Hauptmann and Carl Reinecke. His four-year period at the conservatory lasted from 1858 to 1862. During his student days a contemporary described him as 'a slightly built retiring youth of a typical Northern physiognomy, flaxen hair and large dreamy eyes. He was very quiet, self-absorbed and industrious. As a pianist he never laid much stress on technique but his playing was always delicate and intelligent.' He stood about 150 cm tall, and through most of his adult life his health was delicate. Leipzig provided Grieg with a well-rounded knowledge of composition and of piano playing. His first noteworthy compositions date from this period.

Grieg spent the years 1863–6 in Denmark. His activities there were connected with composition: the Poetic Tone Pictures Op. 3 and *Hjertets*

Melodier Op. 5 date from this period. He then returned to Norway; in 1870 he went to Rome, where his talents were recognized by Franz Liszt. A favourable letter from Liszt was instrumental in securing a stipend from the Norwegian Government. During his years in Christiania (1866–74) Grieg reached maturity as a composer, and the most substantial fruit of his labours there is his opera *Olav Trygvason*. The popular *Peer Gynt* suite also dates from this period: it forms the incidental music to Henrik Ibsen's play and represents a unique collaboration between these two great Scandinavian artists. The *Peer Gynt* suite and the A minor Piano Concerto Op. 16, which was written in 1869 before his trip to Rome, guarantee the composer's popularity, perhaps to the sad neglect of many other of his lyrical works.

Grieg spent most of his later years in Norway. He conducted concerts and spent much of his time composing. Grieg's fame rests mainly on miniatures like the Lyric Pieces Op. 38 and longer works of exquisite charm and delicacy and unique lyrical ideas arising from the composer's study of Norwegian folk music. The *Holberg Suite* (1884) is a work which enjoys considerable popularity. The Symphonic Dances Op. 64, the Folk Songs Op. 66 and the Folk Dances Op. 72 are typical of the steady stream of compositions of moderate length produced during the composer's later years.

Many of Grieg's letters contain evidence of the legitimate frustration of the serious creative artist, the search for perfection in form, and of his obsessive frustration with what he perceived to be a lack of musical education, which restricted him from tackling larger compositions. They also reveal a sharp tendency to self-criticism.

Grieg married Nina Hagerup, his first cousin, in 1865. On 10 April 1868 their only child, a daughter Alexandra, was born; tragically she died thirteen months later. The composer was bitterly upset by the death of his daughter, and a profound depression marred much of his middle years. Grieg was keenly interested in mountaineering and made many ascents despite worsening respiratory disease. He was also interested in the natural history of his native land. A man whose wide erudition embodied many facets of European culture and a creative artist of international importance, Edvard Grieg is justly held in high regard by posterity.

GRIEG'S ILLNESS

Edvard Grieg died on 4 September 1907. He was 64 years old. His long illness was the direct result of a severe respiratory illness contracted during adolescence. This disease led to the collapse of the composer's left lung and caused progressive lung disease.

In 1860 in Leipzig, Grieg suffered a very severe attack of 'pleurisy'. The illness was marked by fever and chest pain, which was worse on inspiration, and breathlessness. Grieg's mother came to Leipzig to nurse her son, and eventually she took him home to Bergen. Grieg was unwell for almost a year but soon returned to Leipzig to complete his studies, against his doctor's advice. Grieg's friend, the physician Klaus Hanssen, tells us of the long-term effect of this early illness. (Hanssen was later to attend Grieg in his final illness.)

> When sixteen years old, Edvard Grieg had an attack of pleurisy that led to collapse of his left lung, which never expanded again. It was permanently useless and the whole of the left half of the chest fell in. Although the shortness of breath resulting from this was a permanent inconvenience to him, he was, nevertheless, an enthusiastic mountaineer and in his earlier days a frequent visitor to the Jotunheim. On the whole, he had good health and a remarkable capacity for work. His exceptional energy was the main factor here. In the last three years his shortness of breath increased very much and his strength failed. This curtailed his mountain wanderings, but did not stop his work. Even in these years he made his strenuous concert tours. The nervous excitement of these concerts enabled him to forget his body and carried him through. (3)

Carl Abbot has ascribed this illness to tuberculosis (6). It is known from Grieg's autopsy that the primary condition failed to progress. Extensive adhesions between the pleura (the covering of the lungs) and scarring within the left lung itself suggested a tuberculous aetiology (6) and it is well documented that tuberculosis can cause a collapsed lung (7). There is also evidence that Grieg suffered from asthma prior to his illness. Throughout his life he continued to smoke cigars and this no doubt aggravated his lung condition. Grieg was indisposed by the acute lung condition until the autumn of 1861.

Pleurisy and empyema occasionally occur in primary tuberculosis. (Collapse of the lung may occur as a result of contraction of fibrous adhesions between the two layers of the pleura or through obstruction of the bronchi by extensive middle lobe disease. A fistulous connection between the bronchi and the pleura can also occur in tuberculosis and may also cause collapse.)

The slow emergence of chronic lung disease and its constitutional sequelae are well documented in Grieg's diary. He began to suffer from winter bronchitis and intermittent shortness of breath and there were considerable periods of ill-health during the 1880s. By the 1890s he was marked by shortness of breath, but his mountaineering and outdoor activities continued. His doctors marvelled at his determination and resilience.

Grieg also complained of a 'wretched rheumatism' – pains in the wrists and the hands. Late photographs of the composer, taken in 1906, show that this condition caused considerable deformity of his fingers. The condition may have been allied to his lung condition or may actually have been due to a separate disease entity. The photographs also show the presence of 'clubbing', a curvature of the nails and swelling of the finger-tips associated with respiratory disease. Examination of serial photographs indicates that the 'clubbing' was present only during the last two or three years of the composer's life.

By 1900 the composer's health was indeed very poor. He complained that the least exertion brought on bronchitis and asthma. He was often confined to bed for weeks on end. In 1900 Grieg visited the Voskenkollen sanatorium near Christiania and experienced a temporary improvement in his condition. In Copenhagen in March 1901 he was once more laid up with bronchitis. Slowly emerging respiratory failure was now manifest. He could barely sleep owing to nocturnal breathlessness, and he became disorientated at night and experienced ghastly nightmares. Grieg took heavy doses of chloral hydrate to enable him to sleep. In Copenhagen in February 1905 he wrote to his friend Frants Beyer: 'I can hardly hold my pen and am unspeakably worn out. Can hardly walk across the floor. The last two days I have been up and a little better. Last night I slept for the first time without a sleeping draught ...'.

In March 1905 he wrote: 'The last week has been melancholy with breathlessness, want of sleep at night, and nervous weakness. Either the end is drawing near or I am going to have some years so heavy that I probably won't be able to bear them.' 'Music must rest, in the name of all the gods,' he writes. A concert tour of Russia and Finland had to be given up. 'All that doesn't trouble me very much,' he continues; 'What goes to my inmost heart is the failing of courage for life and the thought of the last years' miserable existence.'

There were some happier moments during the last years. When Grieg celebrated his sixtieth birthday, on 15 June 1903, there were public festivities which lasted for several days. He was given honorary doctorates by both Oxford and Cambridge. His close friendship and artistic association with the Australian pianist Percy Grainger dates from 1906.

His diary for 1906 shows that he suffered from increasing sleepless-ness and breathlessness. His nocturnal hallucinations worsened as did his 'rheumatism'. Despite this he kept up a steady stream of correspon-dence and conducted at many concerts of his music. He wrote in his diary on 30 March 1906, 'Reaction set in as I feared. Asthma, sleepless-ness, with breathlessness, and the most dreadful hallucinations left me with but one wish: Away, away from it all. No one knows how little existence is worth in such suffering. No one understands that there is then only one friend to be found – death.' Depression is a common consequence of such advanced respiratory disease. On 5 April he wrote: 'During the night at Göteborg such an attack of asthma, breathlessness and hallucinations that I thought of going home, but went on to Copen-hagen where in the Hotel Bristol I had, thank God, a good sleep.'

Grieg also complained of swollen ankles caused, no doubt, by right heart failure. Right heart failure secondary to advanced respiratory dis-ease is known as 'cor pulmonale'. In Grieg's case, heart failure resulted from destruction of the vascular system of the lungs with consequent right heart strain. Because of the destruction of the blood vessels of the lungs the work on the right side of the heart is greater because it must work against a greater resistance. Eventually the heart begins to fail. Cor pulmonale and advanced respiratory failure undoubtedly brought about the composer's death.

GRIEG'S DEATH

Grieg had promised to take part in the Leeds Music Festival which was to be held in September 1907. He was to conduct his Piano Concerto with Percy Grainger in the solo part. His condition grew steadily worse but it did not undermine his resolution to go. Fate itself determined otherwise. The last two entries in Grieg's diary concern his deteriorating condition (Hanssen treated Grieg's condition with massage therapy to maintain muscle tone):

25 August 1907
From the 6th to the 25th has been one continuous suffering. Breathless-ness and sleeplessness increasing. The 20th, 21st and 22nd we spent with Beyers and Elisabeth at Voss. I hoped that the inland climate might bring me sleep. But no. Only of my general condition can I say that

it is a little better. We had a still, warm day of sunshine, I might almost say the only one in the whole summer, and I felt that that was what I needed. But next day it poured again and has gone on pouring since. Yesterday evening, Klaus Hanssen and his wife came up to us and, oddly enough, just at the same time as my new masseur who was to give me massage and 'packs' à la Skodsborg. Klaus examined me with the greatest kindness and superintended the whole performance. The result is that the massage is to be dropped, as it is too much for my nerves, but the packs to be continued, as they did me good and brought me a little sleep at night – at least in the first part of the night. Wretched today, the 25th, after breakfast,[1] don't understand why, it may be the strain of the massage yesterday evening. (3)

31 August 1907

27th – 30th spent in the hospital at Bergen under Klaus Hanssen's observation. Under worsening of illness, too, alas. The first night was without sleep, the 2nd and the 3rd under chloral.[2] Today, the 31st, everything impossible as the isopral had no effect whatever and I lay awake almost the whole time. The whole thing is terribly depressing. Nevertheless, we must prepare for our overland journey on the 3rd. It is a question of getting away from this climate, though the journey to England these days seems to me more than doubtful.

Here Grieg's diary ends on Saturday, 31 August (3).

By Monday, 2 September, Grieg was 'very, very ill'. His feet were grossly swollen and his lips and fingers had a bluish tinge. None the less he left the hospital and moved to the Hotel Norge in Bergen. By 3 September his condition had deteriorated so much that Hanssen had no choice but to forbid the trip. At 7.00 p.m. Frants Beyer visited Grieg in the Bergen hospital. The composer's breathing was fast and laboured, but his friend was unaware that death was near.

He looked more ill than ever before [Beyer relates], and had hardly strength to ask me to take his greetings to my wife as I held his hand in mine for good-bye. But though I was infinitely anxious about him, I did not think that death was drawing so near. I thought that his collapse came as a result of his sleeplessness and I hoped to find him better next morning. (3)

[1] Depression is often worst in the morning.
[2] chloral hydrate, a sleeping draught

By the evening Hanssen saw that there was no hope. Grieg realized it himself and remarked 'so this will be the end'. Nina Grieg was with her husband. A little after midnight Grieg said his last words to his wife 'well – if it must be so'. At 3.00 a.m. he appeared to fall asleep. Nina Grieg, who was resting in another part of the building, was hastily wakened and she attended her husband's last moments. She later wrote of that night that 'he had suffered terribly from breathlessness, but in the end fell asleep as calmly as a child' (3, 5).

On the next morning, Wednesday, 4 September 1904, Dr P.H.Lie performed an autopsy and gave an accurate summary of the cause of the composer's death:

> The unfortunate issue of the inflammation of the lungs in his youth ruined his left lung and entailed consequences which impaired the working capacity of the right lung also. This reduction in the breathing surface of the lungs could, to a very large extent, be compensated for by a powerful heart. And Grieg's heart remained strong for a surprisingly long time. But difficulties increased when the healthy lung became emphysematously enlarged and danger came when the age was reached at which, as a rule, changes which weaken the heart develop in the blood vessels. These changes had not, however, occurred in the blood vessels of the heart but to an unusual extent in the vessels of the lungs so that the circulation in the lungs became more difficult and the demands upon the heart were increased. Finally, these became too great. The nourishment of the heart suffered on account of the poor circulation of air in the lungs and paralysis of the heart supervened.

Grieg therefore died of pulmonary hypertension and secondary cor pulmonale. Respiratory failure also exacerbated his heart problems. The heart was noted to be grossly enlarged at the postmortem. The *Chronique médicale* published a short account of Grieg's illness and a synopsis of his autopsy report in 1907 (1):

> People who knew Grieg closely knew that for a long time the composer had only one lung and that his difficult personality was due to tuberculosis which slowed down his daily tasks. The postmortem also revealed other sad things. The left lung had completely collapsed and the right was also badly affected by disease. His heart was now shifted into the place of his right lung (owing to collapse of the chest wall on the left-hand side). The rib-cage was very compressed and had formed what resembled

a tight waistcoat five centimetres across. He had other anomalies equally bizarre so that the doctors were astonished that Grieg had lived so long.[3]

The Swedish author Annie Wall gives a lengthy, detailed description of the funeral ceremony in her book *People I Have Met* (3, p. 390). In April 1908, Frants Beyer completed the funeral rites by placing the urn containing Grieg's ashes in a niche in a rocky outcrop above the fiord at Troldhaugen which was well known to Grieg from the excursions of happier days.

REFERENCES

1. 'L'Autopsie d'Édouard Grieg', *La Chronique médicale*, 14 (1907), p. 749
2. *L'Indépendance belge* (24 September 1907) [letter]
3. D. Monrad-Johansen, *Edvard Grieg*, Eng. trans. (New York, 1938), pp. 41–54, 360–92
4. J. Horton, *Edvard Grieg* (London, 1950)
5. J. Horton, *Grieg*, The Master Musicians (London, 1974)
6. C. E. Abbot, 'Composers and Tuberculosis: The Effects on Creativity', *Journal of The Canadian Medical Association*, 126 (1982), pp. 534–44
7. A. D. Harries, R. Speare and J. Wirima, 'A Profile of Respiratory Diseases in an African Medical Ward', *Journal of the Royal College of Physicians of London*, 22/2 (1988), p. 109

[3] The account is obviously exaggerated regarding the width of Grieg's chest. His progressive chest deformity was probably caused by concurrent tuberculosis and rickets. The latter, a bone disease due to vitamin D deficiency, was common in the nineteenth century, particularly in Northern Europe.

Gustav Mahler
(1860–1911)

The rise in Gustav Mahler's popularity dates from the early 1960s. The music of his long, complex romantic symphonies, with their combination of simple folk tunes and yearning spiritual themes, reflects his multi-faceted musical and psychological personality.

Mahler was a cosmopolitan figure with a capacity for almost incessant work; this and his high-voltage personality were legendary throughout Vienna. As a renowned conductor he was something of a despot: he searched relentlessly for perfection in his own life and in the life of the musicians who were his charges, and could find no orchestra to please him. Bruno Walter, his assistant for many years, said that he was an abrasive man, lacking even a modicum of social graces, and would dismiss mediocre musicians without a word of apology. Inwardly he was almost certainly beset by self-doubt. Sigmund Freud, whom he consulted in Leiden in 1910, felt that he had helped Mahler greatly in his brief encounter with the distressed composer. He was impressed by Mahler's genius but admitted that he had not been able to delineate the cause of Mahler's troubles in the brief interview. 'No light fell at the time on the symptomatic façade of his obsessional neurosis. It was as if you would dig a single shaft through a mysterious building.'

Mahler's marriage to Alma Maria Schindler, the beautiful daughter of a famous landscape painter, and Alma's sexual proclivities, most notably her infidelity with the architect Walter Gropius, have been the subject of much discussion since her death in 1964. Alma's memoir of her life with Mahler reveals her as a seductive and earthy woman who lived life to the hilt; throughout her life she was surrounded by distinguished suitors. Mahler, on the other hand, was a reserved man who probably sublimated his sexual instincts to a great degree in his work. Alma had a near pathological jealousy of any female that he came into even casual contact with. Their complex relationship was marked by Mahler's insecurities and anxiety and Alma's deep love and possessiveness of him, tinged with the desire for freedom on her part.

Mahler's exploration of the metaphysical, of the precepts which form the basis of Judeo-Christian theology, and of other religious philosophies, form programmes for his monumental symphonies. Like his great contemporary symphonist, Sibelius, he touched upon 'the great musical question of life and death', exploring this theme to an unprecedented degree.

Mahler was born in Kalischt, Bohemia, on 7 July 1860, the second of fourteen children. He showed early musical aptitude and studied harmony and composition at the Vienna Conservatory. After leaving he taught music for some years before embarking on his career as a conductor, beginning in small provincial opera houses and moving on through a steady series of increasingly important conducting appointments at numerous opera houses which culminated in his becoming musical director at the Vienna Court Opera. Brahms, Von Bülow and Bruno Walter were eloquent in their praise of his tremendous proficiency, and he soon became the most famous conductor in Europe.

Mahler conducted in the romantic tradition and did not refrain from reorchestrating a work if he thought it needed it. His conducting was idiosyncratic and highly emotive and often created a furore among his audiences. He was regarded as a conductor without peer until the advent of Toscanini – though for many Mahler still held the palm even after the arrival of the great Italian. His subjective and romantic style was in direct contrast to the classical and literal style of the Italian. Both men achieved their differing aims by a similar means – an almost despotic control of the orchestra enforced by their gigantic personalities – making of the orchestra a single instrument and a vehicle for their interpretations.

In 1907 Mahler journeyed to the USA to conduct the Metropolitan Opera in New York. Although initially a success in America, his later experiences were unhappy. There was much friction between him and the management of the Metropolitan Opera; artistic differences contributed to this friction, but it is also true to say that Mahler, with his authoritarian attitude, was not used to the less hierarchical organization of American musical institutions.

Mahler's principal compositions are the nine symphonies (a tenth was unfinished), *Das Lied von der Erde*, and the song cycles *Lieder eines fahrenden Gesellen, Des Knaben Wunderhorn* and *Kindertotenlieder*. His authentic voice is found in the First Symphony and continues to expand and advance in complexity throughout the series of symphonies. The programme of *Das Lied von der Erde*, which is based upon ancient Chinese poetic texts, is that of the earth's continual cycle of rebirth and renewal in contrast to the mortality and transient existence of man. Sketches for the work were begun shortly after the death of Mahler's elder daughter, Maria, from scarlet fever and tonsillitis at the age of four and a half. Perhaps her death intensified Mahler's search for immortality in his art.

MAHLER'S FATAL ENDOCARDITIS

Mahler was a remarkably healthy young man who enjoyed many outdoor activities, including climbing, swimming and cycling. Until the age of forty-seven, when his elder daughter died, Mahler had suffered from relatively minor problems. He had recurrent sore throats, and in 1901 he had a very large haemorrhage from his haemorrhoids. The first indications of the heart condition which was to kill him were found by his general practitioner, Dr Bluemthal. On listening to Mahler's chest with a stethoscope the doctor detected signs of mixed mitral valve disease,[1] which was then asymptomatic. This opinion was confirmed by a Viennese physician named Frederick Kovacs, who attempted to restrict Mahler's régime of physical exercise. Mahler rebelled against this, but the doctor's orders evidently caused him a great deal of anguish. Certainly he did not seem to have the frail constitution which many of his biographers have credited him with. He had a tremendous capacity for hard work and also frequently enjoyed fairly rigorous physical activity. Walks in the country and appreciation of the rural beauty of Europe stimulated his imagination and increased his urge to compose and set down his impressions in music.

Mahler's final illness dates from about 1911. He was suffering from a febrile illness which was at first related to his tonsillitis by his physicians. His illness was noted to be a fluctuating illness with intermittent fever. This, to the New York physician Dr Fraenkel, suggested endocarditis – a likely diagnosis in view of the knowledge that Mahler had a heart valve lesion of many years' standing. Fraenkel was an up-to-date physician who had reviewed the latest medical literature in which this

---

[1] symptomatic of cardiac valve damage due to past rheumatic fever

182

disease was described by William Osler and Emanuel Libman, both eminent Johns Hopkins physicians.

THE PATHOLOGY OF ENDOCARDITIS

Infective endocarditis is a disease whereby bacterial organisms, usually of low pathogenicity,[2] infect damaged heart valves – typically valves damaged by rheumatic fever, an inflammatory disease of childhood. The organisms, surrounded by inflammatory exudate (the body's natural defence against them), form masses on the heart valves called vegetations. The infection of the heart valves has many serious consequences. For one thing, the valves do not function properly and the vegetations themselves cause progressive damage to the heart valves. If the damage is severe enough, the patient may die of heart failure, with consequent pulmonary congestion or 'pulmonary oedema'. Another consequence of the disease is that emboli, or showers of bacteria, are spread through the bloodstream. They produce skin lesions and rashes as well as damage to the kidneys which may in itself be fatal. The disease is often characterized by swelling of the spleen and the lymph nodes. In untreated endocarditis the patient frequently dies in an emaciated and debilitated state after months of this disease, which affects many of the body's organ systems causing their failure. Thus it was with Mahler.

Infective endocarditis is still a very serious and dangerous disease. There is some evidence that it is rarer today than in Mahler's day, although this may not be the case. The diagnosis is often extremely difficult to make. Endocarditis is now treated with antibiotic therapy. Antibiotics are given intravenously for long periods in an attempt to kill the bacteria which adhere to the avascular heart valves beneath their covering of fibrinous protein. Despite antibiotic treatment, damage to the heart valves is often relentless and progressive: the antibiotics may be insufficient to kill all the bacteria on the valves and progressive valvular damage may occur. Sometimes the valve or its supporting muscles rupture, tipping the patient into catastrophic heart failure.

If damage to the heart valves has progressed to such an extent that the patient's life is threatened, surgeons are called in to operate on and replace the damaged valve with a mechanical one. If the operation takes place in the face of the acute illness the risk of complications

[2] low infectivity

is high because the surgeon is operating in an infected and non-sterile field.

The bacteria which infect the heart valves often arise in the mouth and are associated with dental disease, but they may be present in an apparently healthy mouth. Patients with known heart valve lesions therefore have antibiotic cover when dental procedures are undertaken, to prevent bacteria from growing on the damaged valves. The bacteria can enter the bloodstream during dental manipulation and spread via the bloodstream to the heart valves.

MAHLER'S DEATH

Mahler's final illness lasted about four months, from February to May 1911; slow deterioration is characteristic of the sub-acute course of the disease. As has been noted, modern treatment of the disease was still decades away: if Mahler contracted the disease today he would still have a significant risk of death, and there is still a considerable long-term morbidity associated with the disease. Mahler's physicians were reluctant to try any new treatment on their celebrated patient; the treatment available would not have afforded the composer any hope of cure but might have provided some symptomatic relief. The clinical armamentarium available to the physicians of 1911 included blood transfusion, anti-streptococcal vaccination and mild stimulants including caffeine – light ammunition indeed in the face of the relentless and aggressive disease.

Fraenkel suspected the presence of endocarditis and referred the patient to Emanuel Libman, who was an expert on the disease. Libman was a protégé of Sir William Osler, a former professor of medicine at Johns Hopkins, who did much of the initial work concerning this disease. Libman confirmed the diagnosis clinically by finding a loud systolic and presystolic murmur over the mitral valve which he concluded was characteristic of a heart previously damaged by rheumatic heart disease. He noted the history of low-grade fever, a palpable spleen and a characteristic rash on the conjunctiva and skin. All that remained was laboratory confirmation of the diagnosis by a blood culture. This was undertaken by the surgeon, George Baehr. The blood was taken with difficulty and a heavy growth of streptococci was noted. The streptococci were noted to be the 'attenuated' or non-pyogenic streptococci which are characteristically associated with the disease. These bacteria are now referred to as the 'viridans' group of streptococci. (The result of Mahler's blood culture has recently been published (6).)

Libman informed the composer of the diagnosis and of its inevitable outcome. Mahler decided to return to Europe. He, his wife and the composer Busoni set sail for Europe together. Mahler quelled his anxiety watching the ocean waves for long periods on the voyage home. He became ominously more emaciated, and lost his appetite. He suffered from intermittent fevers and was often delirious in his last months.

In Paris, the Mahlers consulted the eminent bacteriologist André Chantemesse.[3] Alma tells of the tactless way the diagnosis was broken to her: 'Now, Madame Mahler, come and look. Even I, myself, have never seen streptococci in such a marvellous state of development. Just look at these threads, it's like seaweed!' Alma was 'struck dumb with horror' at the scientist's remark. She was later to be equally appalled by the insensitive talk of the eminent Viennese physician Franz Chvostek at the dying composer's bedside and felt a marked antipathy to most of Mahler's physicians. It seems likely that she was experiencing guilt and remorse because of her relationship with Gropius.

Mahler rallied for his final trip to Vienna and spent his last days at the Löwe Sanatorium, intermittently delirious and very much emaciated by this stage. He was attended by Chvostek. He died at 12.00 a.m. on 18 May 1911, having been comatose for many hours, as Alma recounts in her memoirs:

He lay there groaning. A large swelling came up on his knee, then on his leg. Radium was applied and the swelling immediately went down. On the evening after, he was washed and his bed made. Two attendants lifted his naked emaciated body. It was a taking down from the cross. This was the thought that came to all of us.

He had difficulty in breathing and was given oxygen. Then uraemia – and the end. Chvostek was summoned. Mahler lay with dazed eyes; one finger was conducting on the quilt. There was a smile on his lips and twice he said: 'Mozart!' His eyes were very big. I begged Chvostek to give him a large dose of morphia so that he might feel nothing more. He replied in a loud voice. I seized his hands: 'Talk softly, he might hear you.' – 'He hears nothing now.' How terrible the callousness of doctors is at such moments. And how did he know that he could not hear? Perhaps he was only incapable of movement? The death-agony began. I was sent into the next room. The death-rattle lasted several hours.

That ghastly sound ceased suddenly at midnight on 18th May during

[3] André Chantemesse (1851–1919), pioneer of typhoid serology

a tremendous thunderstorm. With that last breath his beloved and beautiful soul had fled, and the silence was more deathly than all else. As long as he breathed he was there still. But now all was over.

The terminal complications of Mahler's condition were pulmonary oedema, pneumonia, renal failure and debility. The death certificate records endocarditis as the underlying illness. Mahler's physicians related his endocarditis to the chronic bouts of tonsillitis which he had had for many years. We now know that this was unlikely to be true. The attacks of 'quinsy' were due to a pyogenic strain of streptococcus, which differs from the streptococci which cause endocarditis. The attenuated or 'viridans' streptococci are commonly part of the complement of bacteria which live in the mouth. Dental disease and plaque are associated with overgrowth of these bacteria. Chronic streptococcal disease of the throat was, however, more prevalent in the last century and earlier when antibiotics were unknown. The crowded living conditions which prevailed in earlier times also favoured the development of streptococcal disease. Mozart is known to have suffered from chronic streptococcal tonsillitis, and George Washington is said to have died of 'quinsy', the most severe form of the disease (if not from the frequent bleedings and heavy doses of mercury which were part of its treatment).

REFERENCES

1. W. Osler, 'Gulstonian Lectures on Malignant Endocarditis', *British Medical Journal* (1885), pp. 467–70, 522–6, 577–9
2. A. Mahler, *Gustav Mahler: Memories and Letters* (London, 1946, trans. B. Creighton rev. 3rd edn, 1975)
3. E. Libman, *Subacute Bacterial Endocarditis* (London, 1948)
4. K. Martner, *Selected Letters of Gustav Mahler* (London, 1979)
5. D. Sickerson, *Mahler: His Life and Times* (New York, 1982)
6. K. Monson, *Alma Mahler, Muse to Genius* (London, 1984)
7. D. Levy, 'Gustav Mahler and Emanuel Libman: Bacterial Endocarditis in 1911', *British Medical Journal*, 243 (1986), pp. 1628–31

Frederick Delius
(1862–1934)
&
Scott Joplin
(1868–1917)

It is hard to imagine two contemporary musicians with such widely differing styles and backgrounds as Frederick Delius and Scott Joplin, although both composers lived and worked in the southern USA at about the same time. Delius, who was born in Bradford in 1862, was Joplin's senior by just six years. Both composers were affected by tertiary neurosyphilis which caused their deaths and blighted their lives for many years. The years in which they lived were marked by great progress in the diagnosis and treatment of syphilis.

SYPHILIS IN THE PRE-ANTIBIOTIC ERA

Syphilis is a venereally acquired infectious disease caused by a delicate, spiral-shaped organism called treponema pallidum. In the early part of the twentieth century, although ostensibly treatable, it was incurable. It is a slowly progressing disease which is protean in its manifestations and is still often difficult to diagnose. It may affect any organ system in the body. The causation and epidemiology of the disease, as well as its diverse clinical manifestations, were only slowly delineated by the medical profession – indeed, one of the best-known epigrams of the brilliant Canadian-born physician Sir William Osler was that 'he who understands syphilis understands medicine'.

It was not until 1905 that the causative organism was isolated by Fritz Schaudin. In 1907 August von Wassermann devised a blood test which relied not on direct demonstration of the treponema pallidum but on the demonstration of antibodies to syphilis, and which was of enormous help in determining whether patients were infected by the disease or were asymptomatic carriers. Many of the blood tests for syphilis which are available today are refinements of Wassermann's complement fixation test.

Studies of the European and North American population at the turn of the century indicated that 10–15% of the population had some evidence of syphilitic infection. The disease was commoner among the socio-economically deprived. One American study showed that 20% of poorer people had evidence of the disease while only 0.5% of the wealthiest socio-economic group were affected (4). Prostitution was a commoner vector than today because there was no effective treatment for prostitutes who would transmit the disease to their clients (15).

European medical literature of the mid-sixteenth century provides many accounts of the disease. Girolamo Fracastoro wrote a poem about a shepherd called Syphilis which describes a trip to the island of Haiti where the natives are beset by a repugnant disease. Syphilis was named after the shepherd who, in Fracastoro's poem, contracted the illness. Shortly afterwards an essay entitled 'On the Accursed Buboes' linked a genital ulcer with the disease. Many sixteenth-century writers felt that the illness originated in the New World and was brought to Europe by the Spanish explorers of the Americas. The geographical origin of syphilis is still controversial. Exploration and migration increased enormously in the fifteenth century and the disease may have been brought to Europe by a more circuitous route. It is endemic in Asia Minor, and many authors now believe it to be of Asiatic origin. Thus the island of Haiti may have been an epidemiologic 'staging post' for syphilis, as it was in more recent years for the acquired immune deficiency syndrome (AIDS), and not its ultimate place of origin. There is some evidence that linking syphilis with the New World was a literary device to extirpate some of the guilt occasioned by the destruction of the great pre-Columbian civilizations by European soldiers of fortune. Many of these civilizations were destroyed by the introduction of transatlantic diseases, of which syphilis may have been one.

Sixteenth-century Europeans lived in great fear of the illness, which was said to be virulent and rapidly fatal. We now know that syphilis is a slowly multiplying organism and is seldom fatal in the early stages. The explanation of the virulence of syphilis described by the Renaissance physicians is likely to be found in disease synergy. The population of Europe in those days was often malnourished. Armies were affected by multiple chronic disease including malaria, typhoid, scurvy, epidemic pyoderma (a skin infection) and many others. In the presence of chronic illness and nutritional disease syphilis often progresses more rapidly. The disease may have actually been more virulent: infectious disease achieves its maximum virulence during the exponential phase of an epidemic for reasons little understood. The medical profession still uses the Latin word 'lues' (plague) as a synonym for syphilis (often in front of sensitive patients to disguise the diagnosis).

Eighteenth- and nineteenth-century writers on medicine provided more comprehensive descriptions of syphilis, and there is little reason to believe that the disease as described by John Hunter (1) has changed greatly in its clinical manifestations.

Syphilis as we now know it develops in three stages. In the primary stage, a small ulcer, called a chancre, is found on the genital region. The local lymph glands are concomitantly enlarged. The chancre disappears in six to twelve weeks. The secondary stage is characterized by a rash accompanied by a moderate fever; occasionally, more severe symptoms such as meningitis or renal disease appear. After a variable period of time, the disease enters a latent period when no obvious stigmata are present. The disease often progresses to a tertiary stage characterized by destructive lesions occasioned by chronic inflammatory reactions to the syphilitic organism; also present at this stage may be tertiary neurosyphilis, a disease which causes gross destruction of the central and peripheral nervous systems. (Before the advent of penicillin the majority of beds in public mental institutions in Europe and the USA were occupied by sufferers from this condition.)

Two common types of neurosyphilis are general paralysis of the insane and tabes dorsalis. In general paralysis the cortex and substance of the brain become involved. There is often paralysis and a profound dementing illness. This manifestation of syphilis appears between fifteen and twenty years after primary infection, and death usually occurs within three or four years. Tabes dorsalis affects the spinal cord and the eyes. It is accompanied by shooting pains and progressive paralysis. Before the advent of antibiotics it was said to occur in 10% of cases of syphilis.

Mercury was used to treat syphilis for over four hundred years. In early times it was thought that the efficacy of mercury lay in 'salivation'. Mercury increases expectoration and its salts have diuretic properties. It was thought that the 'syphilitic parasite' was excreted in the process.

Salivation is actually a manifestation of mercury poisoning. Mercury is a highly toxic substance and its administration has been severely criticized – indeed, Goldwater calls it 'a hoax' (5). More careful review of the literature shows that mercury could actually damp down many of the manifestations of the disease. Many of the complications of syphilis resemble those of mercury poisoning, so that it was not until the causative organism was isolated (1905) and an effective blood test devised (1907) that physicians could study precisely the evolution of syphilis and ascribe symptoms to the illness or to its treatment. The 'Oslo Study of Untreated Syphilis' (1910–51) accurately prognosticated syphilis and showed that mercurial treatment was of little efficacy and had only a mild palliative effect.

Bismuth was introduced in the 1880s. It was more effective and certainly less toxic than mercury or iodine and became the mainstay of heavy metal treatment for syphilis after the First World War. Salvarsan, an arsenical developed by Paul Ehrlich in 1908, was even more effective than bismuth although it, too, could not always guarantee a cure.

Penicillin was used to treat syphilis by John Mahoney of New York in 1940. It was found that the causative organism was very sensitive to this antibiotic, which is still the drug of first choice; it will not, however, reverse the destructive lesions of tertiary syphilis. Mercury was still used in the earlier part of the twentieth century though in much smaller doses than previously; it finally became obsolete in the 1950s. During the era in which Joplin and Delius lived many specialist journals were devoted solely to the diagnosis and treatment of syphilis. The disease continues to be a serious problem in under-developed countries. Effective medical treatment has dramatically reduced the numbers of advanced cases seen in Western societies and made early syphilis a rarer and now curable condition.

FREDERICK DELIUS

Delius was born on 29 January 1862, in Bradford, Yorkshire. He was the fourth child of Julius and Elise Delius, who were of German birth. Delius was christened Fritz and was fluent in German from an early age. He spent much of his life travelling – on the Continent and in the southern United States. He lived his last years in Grez-sur-Loing in northern France.

The picture we have of Delius, drawn by Fenby in his moving book *Delius as I knew him*, is of a humourless, irascible invalid; it is an accurate portrait of the composer's later years. In his youth, however, Delius was a witty, lusty bon vivant and bohemian. He was a strong character who disavowed religion and was determined to succeed as a musician – a career choice disliked by his wealthy father. Delius's music reflects a broad, international musical culture; as the years passed it was deeply influenced, as was his character, by his chronic illness, due to the encroaching effect of tertiary syphilis: its style changes dramatically with the relentless approach of paralysis and blindness. But it is indicative of his rugged strength of character that his spirit remained unbroken despite his illness.

It has been said that Delius contracted syphilis in Florida in the 1880s, but the composer believed that he acquired the disease in 1895 from a prostitute in Paris, where he frequently attended brothels during his youth and where the disease was rife. Gauguin contracted it at about the same time.

Delius met the painter Jelka Rosen on his thirty-fourth birthday; the couple lived together for some years and were married in Grez on 28 September 1903. Their relationship caused Delius considerable personal difficulties. He knew well that syphilis was a sexually transmitted disease, but his fear was considerably alleviated when a doctor told him that his syphilitic skin lesions had 'scarred' and could not be communicated to his wife. In later years he told a friend that when they were young Jelka had wanted children, but he was against the idea because of the possibility of a child being born with syphilis. He was an aloof and demanding husband but we know that he loved his wife deeply. Clare Delius relates these characteristics also to their father in her biography of her brother (2).

Delius did not have faith in the conventional medical treatment of the time for syphilis. Like his friend Percy Grainger, he had a keen interest in homeopathy and preferred homeopathic remedies. He also took a course of iodides and saltpetre without cure, and as late as 1930 even consulted a hypnotist named Erskine to treat his condition.

In December 1910 Delius had a serious relapse of syphilis. He entered a sanatorium in Dresden where he was treated by Dr W.Bothe, who noted that Delius had had three relapses of syphilis since 1895 and had recurrent 'gastric crises'. He performed a physical examination and observed a substantial loss of strength in the proximal muscle groups of the limbs. He also noted a nodular tertiary syphilitic lesion on the composer's thigh. There was loss of deep tendon reflexes and the pupils were asymmetrical and did not react to light. The physician performed a Wassermann test and noted a strongly positive reaction. Delius refused a course of salvarsan, an arsenical compound efficacious in the treatment of syphilis. He preferred homeopathic remedies, which proved ineffective, and the disease progressed relentlessly (10). Later the skin lesion healed leaving a characteristic papery scar. (12, 18)

Delius's disease progressed. He had further 'gastric crises' – episodes of severe abdominal pain characteristic of tabetic syphilis – and episodes of leg pain which, although initially thought to be due to sciatica, were actually a manifestation of syphilis. He experienced eye pain and declining vision.

In 1921 Delius began to lose the use of his hands and by the end of the year was paralysed in both of them. He was still able to walk using two sticks but by the end of the year was confined to a wheelchair. He became irascible and difficult to live with because the mind within the diseased body was unimpaired. In 1922 he took a cure at Bad Oeynhausen near Hanover. His sister Clare actually failed to recognize him because he had become so shrunken and lifeless. The paralysis and wasting were due to syphilitic amyotrophy, involvement of the motor routes of the spinal cord – further evidence of syphilis involving the spine. (The muscles waste away when the nerves supplying them are destroyed.)

Delius was examined by the British physician Sir John Conybeare, whose notes on his patients were destroyed on his death. Before he died he communicated the contents of his report to his colleagues. Dr Philip Jones later wrote of the encounter between Sir John and Delius in *The Times* (13). Conybeare did not believe that Delius had syphilis. He examined the composer thoroughly and could not detect any evidence of dorsal column loss. He performed a Wassermann test, which this time was negative. Jones questioned the diagnosis of syphilis in Delius's case and proposed that he had all along been suffering from another neurological disease – hereditary spinocerebellar degeneration (13, 16).

This is incorrect. In one third of patients with late syphilis the non-specific Wassermann test returns to negative (17); moreover, it is difficult to assess dorsal column damage in patients with such advanced neurological disease. (Delius may have developed more pronounced dorsal column loss later in his illness.) The skin lesion, positive serology, and the well-documented history of early syphilis make the diagnosis of syphilis the correct one. Philip Jones, assisted by J.R.Heron, a neurologist, revised his earlier conclusions in their paper 'A Fever Diluted by Time' (18).

Delius's optic neuritis progressed with alarming rapidity. By 1922 he was blind, but he could still distinguish light. Because bright light produced severe eye pain he wore dark glasses out of doors.

DELIUS AND ERIC FENBY

Despite such profound neurological disease, Delius's intellect was largely unimpaired and he had lost none of his facility as a composer. He was now blind and paralysed and could not write music. Jelka did not have sufficient musical knowledge to transcribe his music, and Percy Grainger was occupied with his own projects and tactfully declined to help him.

Delius received the necessary help from Eric Fenby, a twenty-two-year-old Yorkshireman who turned out to be an ideal amanuensis. Fenby was patient, sensitive and altruistic. Sometimes the results of Delius's dictation were not to the composer's liking and he would ask Fenby to destroy days of work; the sessions often left both men exhausted. The principal compositions committed to paper by Delius and Fenby were *A Song of Summer*, the *Irmelin Prelude, Idyll* and *Songs of Farewell*. Fenby stayed with the composer from 1928 until his death in 1934.

Catherine Barjansky has left a vivid description of Delius in old age (6):

> Delius was a ghost, emaciated, bloodless, his long body stiff as a corpse. There was great spiritual beauty in his face, the forehead high and noble, the eyes unusually deep set, the eyelids half-closed, the nose thin and aquiline, the mouth fine and beautiful in shape. His narrow pale hands lay helpless on his knees. His grey hair was long, so long that it fell over the open collar of his white silk sports shirt ... Everything in his appearance reflected the great and thoughtful care his wife had given it. And despite his helplessness he looked extremely elegant.

The last photographs of Delius vividly substantiate Mrs Barjansky's eloquent description of the ailing composer. Despite advanced disease his face has a serene and other-worldly appearance. This appearance results from paralysis and wasting of the facial muscles. Drooping of the eyelids (ptosis) similarly results from paralysis of the muscles of facial expression. Severe muscle wasting, due to syphilitic amyotrophy, adds to the composer's frail and debilitated appearance.

THE DEATH OF DELIUS

The health of both Delius and his wife underwent a precipitous decline in 1934. Fenby describes their desperate situation touchingly in his monograph *Delius as I knew him*. He recalls that in April 1934 he began to hear disconcerting rumours about a decline in Delius's health. He wrote immediately to Jelka who allayed the worst of his fears. Delius's shooting pains, a legacy of tabetic syphilis, were worse than ever:

8.4.34

> My Dear Eric, – No, Fred is not seriously ill, but we must be most careful ... The worst is that he is troubled with the most dreadful shooting-pains that return every day at the same hour (5 p.m.) and persist through the whole night if he does not take a calming medicine, which he generally does. But, of course, all that makes him feel weak and fatigued in the morning.

Jelka also asked Fenby to come to Grez because she herself was in poor health and if Fenby could help with Delius's care she could attend more fully to her own problems.

Fenby arrived at Grez in May. He was shocked by the deterioration in Delius's condition. Delius was even more emaciated, no doubt because of the progression of his syphilitic muscle disease. His doctors had put him on a low-salt, low-protein diet, probably to treat heart failure which often supervenes in late syphilis owing to disease of the arteries and the aortic valve of the heart.

Delius was now in almost constant pain. Worse still, Jelka's illness turned out to be an incurable malignancy. Delius's doctors estimated that the composer would live only a few months, so news of his wife's condition was kept from him. Delius was still mentally alert. Fenby read to him to calm him and to keep his mind from the pain:

> With the days my difficulties increased. Backwards and forwards I went, keeping his condition from her, and hers from him, until at the end of a fortnight, the worry, suspense and responsibility became more than flesh and blood could bear. The pyrethane which they gave Delius to ease the pain upset him so that he could not retain his food, and he was gradually growing weaker and weaker and could not sleep, even during the reading. I was now reading nine hours a day and the greater part of the night. Unless one read to occupy his mind he seemed to be in constant pain. Nor could he rest in any one position for long without my having to move him, or lift him up to take the folds out of his pyjama-

jacket, which continually hurt his back. One could have done with an army of nurses, except that he would have dismissed the lot. He would now only tolerate his nurse at the more necessary times.

Fenby was obviously under deep personal strain. Fortunately, the situation was relieved by the careful ministrations of Delius's doctors, who were able to induce a remission of the pain. The composer Balfour Gardiner visited Delius in July. When he left Grez he noticed an obvious decline in Delius's health. On 8 June Jelka was brought back from hospital to visit the composer. Fenby was reading aloud as usual when he noticed that Delius was gradually drifting into a coma. He tells of the agony he experienced while awaiting the doctor and of Delius's last moments:

I noticed that, as I continued, he became less and less interested, and appeared to be sinking slowly into a coma. I summoned the doctor immediately. (One of the precautions that Delius had taken to preserve his privacy – his refusal to install a telephone – now became a serious handicap . . .)

The doctor came with his morphia syringe and soon there was calm, but when the effects of the drug had worn off, Delius became restless again and asked me to read. This I did until eight o'clock the following morning, when the doctor returned. There yet remained one chance of reviving him, said he. He would bring Mrs Delius back from the hospital that morning. By mid-day she was sitting by him, in a wheeled chair, and I left them alone. It was obvious that Delius was sinking rapidly; that he had not the strength to talk. All he wanted was the soothing drone of a voice to which he need make no response ... Each time he came to, Delius was in agony. The doctor was now coming every four hours. Towards evening on that day, Friday, June 8th, he was easier, and his wife was brought in to see him. 'Jelka, I'm glad!' he muttered when told she was there, and smiled faintly. Later that day his suffering was so intense that his features became distorted, and it was as much as his nurse and I could do to prevent him from falling out of bed. Finally, after a night the unspeakable horror of which I shall never forget, the doctor paid his second visit in the early hours of the morning with his morphia syringe, and from six o'clock that Saturday morning Delius was as if in a sound and noisy sleep . . .

They had persuaded me to take some rest ... At four o'clock that Sunday morning they roused me ... the nurse said that it would soon be over. The others said, 'Speak to him.' I knew it was hopeless, but I bent over him and called, 'Delius, Delius, this is Eric!'

I had not seen Death before, and it had always been linked in my

195

mind with doctor, priest, and tears, but when it came none of these attendants was present. Within five minutes he was as if dead, but when I undid his pyjama-jacket the heart was still flickering. I took his cold hand and felt it grow colder in mine. It was the end.

A death mask was taken and afterwards Delius's body lay in state in his home. The composer was buried in a temporary grave at Grez and in May 1935 the body was exhumed and taken to England. Delius is now buried at Limpsfield, Surrey. Jelka Delius spent her last months in a nursing home and when she died on 28 May 1935 she was interred next to her husband.

SCOTT JOPLIN

Scott Joplin was born on 24 November 1868, in Texarkana, Texas. His birth is not recorded in any official document and he is buried in a common grave. External circumstances, poverty, illness and the prejudice of society conspired to thwart the full realization of his talent, but what he did achieve is remarkable. In the last five years of his life, Joplin was affected by a profound dementing illness due to neurosyphilis.

Joplin was among the first black composers to have his works published. He is best known for his piano rags, which are of considerable harmonic sophistication. 'Ragtime', a corruption of 'ragged time' (a reference to the syncopations of this music), found in him its greatest exponent. He wrote two ragtime operas, the first of which is lost; the surviving one, *Treemonisha*, shows in its subject matter Joplin's keen perception of the contemporary racial situation in America. It deals with such issues as education, prejudice, superstition and self-determination and their effects on the black community.

In later life Joplin showed a sharp intellect, although he had received only a fragmentary education as a child. His considerable musical gifts attracted the attention of the music teachers in the black community, who taught him for little or no fee. He received training in Western musical forms as well as being familiar with traditional black music, and became a skilled composer and a gifted improviser. At a time when a white-dominated society suppressed much of black culture, he felt that the music of the American negro community should receive greater attention from the public at large. He had a persistence and dedication which, backed up by a streak of ambition, helped substantiate much of his dream.

When Joplin left home in the mid-1880s he became an itinerant pianist, traversing the Midwest by rail and river and earning a living by playing in saloons or at social functions. In the red-light districts of the major towns there was a minimum of segregation, and a talented musician who could uplift and entertain the customers was a considerable asset to any establishment. Joplin was a popular performer. He was a smallish man, 1.7 metres in height, though of a powerful build. His manner is described as quiet, considerate and thoughtful; he is said to have played his music more slowly and expressively than his rival pianists, seeing it as a mode of self-expression rather than of bravura display.

When *Maple Leaf Rag* was published in 1899, Joplin became something of a celebrity among the black community – the white publishing houses were usually reluctant to handle the works of a black musician – but even the wide commercial sale the piece achieved did little to enhance his prestige among the white population. (It also did little to alter his financial situation – his royalties amounted to only one cent a copy!)

When Joplin did earn money, he hired halls and arranged concerts in an effort to popularize his music more widely, but he remained generally appreciated only by the negro community and a few white connoisseurs. Alfred Ernst, the director of the St Louis Symphony Society, thought most highly of the young pianist composer and endeavoured to arrange a European tour for him, but nothing came of the venture or of the brief spate of publicity which accompanied it.

Joplin's last years were marked by chronic ill-health due to encroaching neurosyphilis. He had contracted syphilis during the 1890s; the disease was directly responsible for his decline, and its effects were manifest in his piano playing. In neurosyphilis the dorsal column of the spinal cord is often affected, with the result that the sufferer loses position sense and, in consequence, balance and motor control. Joplin's playing became unpredictable, amateurish. His associates found it disheartening and astonishing to see the once proficient pianist flail away wildly at the piano. As the paralysis progressed, his playing became expressionless and almost inaudible. A clinical diagnosis of syphilis was confirmed by syphilis serology (blood test); Joplin's doctors could do little to halt the progress of his disease.

Joplin's memory and intellectual functioning progressively declined. He became coarse and irritable, and his students left him. By 1916 his paralysis and weakness were so profound that it was necessary for him to be institutionalized. He was diagnosed suffering from 'general paralysis of the insane', a type of neurosyphilis which affects the cerebral cortex causing severe dementia. By the time he was admitted to Manhattan State Hospital, in autumn 1916, he could no longer recognize the few friends who came to visit him. He died on 1 April 1917, and was buried in a common grave.

SUMMARY

From the medical standpoint, the contrasting cases of Delius and Joplin (Joplin's career was rapidly abbreviated by disease, while Delius's affliction did not trouble him until later in life), illustrate the extent of morbidity and mortality due to syphilis before the discovery of penicillin. This disease, once a feared scourge of mankind, has been brought under control to a considerable extent, at least in the Western world.

Other aspects of the attitude to illness of early twentieth-century society, and the social and economic factors then affecting those with chronic disease, are revealed in the contrasting circumstances of the two composers' lives. Delius was successful in his career and fortunate in the considerable support of his wife and of close friends like Eric Fenby and Percy Grainger (who helped to carry Delius through the Norwegian mountains during a holiday in 1928). Delius had clearly acquired the means to preserve some of the quality of his life until the discomfort of his last days supervened. Joplin, by contrast, was a poor, itinerant pianist who drifted rapidly into obscurity when the disease destroyed his livelihood. Many of the urban poor who suffered from neurosyphilis ended their days in the obscurity of mental institutions.

TABLE 1

CHRONOLOGY OF FREDERICK DELIUS'S ILLNESSES

1895–1910
Secondary syphilis; takes iodine, saltpetre, homeopathic remedies; three relapses of secondary disease

1910
Collapse prompts admission to Dresden sanatorium. Has 'gastric crises' and evidence of neurological and muscle disease; skin lesion consistent with tertiary syphilis.

1921–1923
Onset of paralysis, beginning in hands; soon all limbs are affected; becomes blind and is confined to a wheelchair; 'gastric crises' become more painful and frequent.

1928–1934
Dictates last music to Eric Fenby

10 June 1934
Death? due to cardiovascular syphilis

28 May 1935
Body re-interred in Britain at Limpsfield, Surrey

REFERENCES

1. J. Hunter, *A Treatise on the Venereal Diseases* (London, 1818)
2. C. Delius, *Frederick Delius: Memories of my Brother* (London, 1935)
3. E. Fenby, *Delius as I knew him* (London, 1936) pp. 215–34
4. W. J. Brown, *Syphilis and Other Venereal Diseases* (Cambridge, Mass., 1970), pp. 1–142
5. L. J. Goldwater, *Mercury: A History of Quicksilver* (Baltimore, 1972)
6. A. Jefferson, *Delius* (London, 1972)
7. L. Carley, *Delius: The Paris Years* (London, 1975)
8. M. Evans, *Scott Joplin and the Ragtime Years* (New York, 1976)
9. L. Carley and R. Threlfall, *Delius: A Life in Pictures* (London, 1977)
10. J. Haskins and K. Benson, *Scott Joplin: The Man who Made Ragtime* (Garden City, N.Y., 1978)

11. E. Braunewald, R. G. Petersdorf, R. D. Adams *et al.* (eds), *Harrison's Principles of Internal Medicine* (New York, 1978), pp. 29, 716–25
12. S. F. Wainapel, 'Frederick Delius: A Medical Assessment', *New York State Journal of Medicine*, 80 (1980), p. 1886
13. T. Stuttaford, Medical Briefing, *The Times* (18 March 1983); response by J. R. Heron, 'Unsullied Delius', *ibid.* (13 April 1983)
14. C. Redwood, [Letter], *Delius Society Journal*, 80 (1983), pp. 46–7
15. K. K. Holmes (ed.), *Sexually Transmitted Diseases* (New York, 1984), pp. 288–330
16. P. Jones, [Letter], *Delius Society Journal*, 84 (1984), pp. 22–3
17. G. Hart, 'Syphilis Tests in Therapeutic Decision Making', *Annals of Internal Medicine*, 104 (1986), p. 368
18. P. Jones and J. R. Heron, 'A Fever Diluted by Time', *Delius Society Journal*, 98 (1988), pp. 3–8

Maurice Ravel
(1875–1937)

ASPECTS OF MUSICAL PERCEPTION

Investigation of the perception of music by medical scientists is in its infancy, and the information so far uncovered is fascinating. The 'higher neural functions' – those that involve symbolism and intellection – are located within the cerebral cortex, a layer of grey matter which covers the surface of the brain. On its outer surface it is fissured irregularly and its surface has been likened to that of a walnut. The cerebral cortex is divided by a central fissure into right and left hemispheres. The functions of the two hemispheres differ markedly and to a certain extent it is true that we have 'two minds'. A layer of nervous tissue, the corpus callosum, connects the two hemispheres. In operations such as those to treat intractable epileptic seizures, the corpus callosum was at one time cut, albeit reluctantly, by neurosurgeons. The patients who had this procedure done initially showed little difference in their day-to-day behaviour and, indeed, the operation benefited them greatly. When more accurate observation was made, however, it was seen that severing the two hemispheres made them act independently, and the right hand literally did not know what the left hand was doing when the patients could not use visual perception to co-ordinate their movements.

In a right-handed individual, the left hemisphere is usually the dominant one, and conscious activity and speech are based in it. The right hemisphere, while not primarily involved in verbal activity, has numerous important activities, calculation and aspects of musical perception being two of them. The area associated with musical perception is located in the posterior portion of the right temporal lobe.

The perception of music has a wide variety of emotional and visceral effects on the human body. The response of the autonomic nervous system, which acts to change the heart rate and increase the blood pressure as music is heard, is allied to the emotional response to the music. This has been demonstrated by experiments in which a professional conductor was connected to a machine which recorded heart rate and blood pressure. He was conducting Beethoven's Fifth Symphony; at a horn entry which particularly excited him, his pulse rate and blood pressure rose. When he listened to a recording of the symphony a similar response occurred, at precisely the same point. The ability of music to alter the electrical activity of the brain as observed by electroencephalography has also been noted.

As with all human traits, there is a wide range of ability with regard to musical talent. Musicianship is related to pitch discrimination and memory, playing to fine motor co-ordination. The indefinable quality of creativity also features prominently in all aspects of musicianship. There are three types of musical memory: visual, aural and a 'muscle memory'. 'Muscle memory' functions at the subcortical level and is independent of the language area of the left hemisphere: the basal ganglia are involved in the learning and repetition of complex motor skills.

Although musical ability resides primarily in the right hemisphere, the lateralization of music is not strictly segregated. There is evidence in experienced musicians that the left cerebral cortex also comes into function. Ear preference differs between trained musicians and members of the general public. Non-musicians show a left-ear preference and nerve fibres from the left ear are largely distributed to the right cerebral cortex. In professional musicians, ear preference is less marked, indicative of decreased lateralization of musical function.

Musical prodigies have heightened ability in the aforementioned musical skills. Mozart's memory was said to be so prodigious that he could write down Allegri's *Miserere* in toto after a single hearing. The pianist Josef Hofmann was able to name and discriminate notes differing by only a few cycles per second. Franz Liszt sight-read a violin sonata of Grieg's, incorporating the violin part into the piano part spontaneously. Beethoven's 'inner hearing' was so acute that he composed many complex late works in total deafness. Such levels of proficiency are rare phenomena indeed.

MAURICE RAVEL

In Maurice Ravel's illness we have an unusual case of a neurological disease which, from the time he was fifty-four, followed a progressive yet apparently episodic course, interrupting his language functions and ability to communicate while leaving his musical abilities intact until later in the course of the disease. Ravel was unable to transfer his music to paper as a consequence of his illness. At a later stage he became so profoundly demented that he made no attempt at musical or creative activity and could barely speak.

Ravel's music is distinguished by the precision and clarity which underlined his work. He was dubbed 'the Swiss Watchmaker' by his colleagues and his music is indeed less overtly emotional than that of many of his contemporaries. He himself stated, 'My object is technical perfection. I strive increasingly to this end. The important thing is to get nearer to it all the time.' His precision is seen in such works as *Gaspard de la nuit*, a complex piece of post-Lisztian virtuosity, and the works for piano and orchestra where piano and orchestral parts are skilfully integrated and the orchestration most adept. Ravel admitted that he found such intricate music extremely difficult to compose.

Ravel was a natty, combative, enigmatic man. He is not known to have developed a close personal relationship with anyone, and his dealings with, for example, Debussy and Diaghilev were marked by friction and competitiveness. He studied for some time at the Paris Conservatoire, where his failure to win the famous Prix de Rome was something of a national scandal. He first competed for the prize in 1901 when he was asked to submit a cantata. The text was not to his liking, and he submitted a waltz instead. The jurors were affronted and awarded their most brilliant student second prize. In 1902 and 1903 he again failed to win the prize. In 1905 he was disqualified from the competition on the grounds that he was already over thirty. Ravel consoled himself with the publicity he received from these attempts: on graduation he was already famous as a result of newspaper coverage of the scandal.

RAVEL'S ILLNESS

Ravel was a small man, approximately 150 cm tall. He was right-handed. He had a handsome face with a prominent, aquiline nose. His physique was thin and wiry. There is nothing in his physical appearance to suggest the development of neurological illness. In 1916 Ravel was rejected by the army because of an enlarged heart. This is the first record of anything amiss in his medical history. Enlargement of the heart may be caused by systemic hypertension (high blood pressure) or by cardiac valve lesions or by many other causes. We know that the composer smoked and drank alcohol, but there is no evidence that he indulged in these practices to excess.[1] Nor is there any evidence that he had syphilis: when his illness became apparent a Wassermann test was performed, with negative results. While the test does not definitively exclude neurosyphilis it makes the condition unlikely. (9, 10)

In 1927 Ravel became disorientated during a performance of his music at a concert. He made numerous blunders while writing music, and suffered from what was described as a 'nervous complaint'. Nevertheless, he made a successful tour of the United States in 1928 after a complete recovery from what was said to be a temporary indisposition. In October 1932 Ravel had what was described as a 'nervous breakdown' following an automobile accident in which he sustained a chest injury and broke one of his teeth. His lassitude and apathy were noted by many of his circle. In 1933 matters grew steadily worse. Ravel found writing difficult: it took him eight days to write a fifty-six-word letter consoling a friend on the death of his mother. He complained of a profound memory loss, and spoke of a 'fog setting in'.

Ravel's co-ordination became poor – he could scarcely direct an orchestra, and gait and fine motor co-ordination were noticeably disturbed. In November 1933 he attempted to conduct the G major Piano Concerto but was unable to do so and the orchestra proceeded on its own. Ravel's three songs *Don Quichotte à Dulcinée*, completed in 1933, represent the end of his distinguished creative output.

'APHASIA AND ARTISTIC REALISATION'

Ravel first consulted the famous French neurologist Théophile Alajouanine in 1933. His decision to consult the physician was probably prompted by his friends, and Ravel's pre-eminent worry was obviously his inability to express himself musically. He repeatedly said that he could hear music in his head but could not write it down. The inability to communicate speech, writing or music when the peripheral nervous system is largely undamaged is called an aphasia; Alajouanine wrote that for the creative artist 'to conceive is nothing – to express is all', highlighting the tragedy of Ravel's situation.

Alajouanine published the results of his observation and examination of Ravel in a paper entitled 'Aphasia and Artistic Realisation', which appeared in *Brain* in September 1948. Alajouanine does not tell us when

[1] Alcoholism is associated with pre-senile dementia and hypertension; smoking with cerebrovascular disease (strokes).

he made his observations, but it is fairly clear that it was late in the course of Ravel's progressive illness.

At the peak of his artistic achievement, rich through an abundant and varied work, already classic, which expresses a delicate climate, Maurice Ravel is struck down by an aphasia. His aphasia is more complex than the writer's: it is a Wernicke aphasia of moderate intensity, without any trace of paralysis, without hemianopia, but with an ideomotor apractic component.[2] The cause, though indefinite, belongs to the group of cerebral atrophies, there being a bilateral ventricular enlargement; but it is quite different from Pick's disease. Oral and written language are diffusely impaired, but moderately so, without any noticeable intellectual weakening. Memory judgment, affectivity, aesthetic taste do not show any impairment to repeated tests. Understanding of language remains much better than oral or written abilities. Writing, especially, is very faulty, mainly due to apraxia. Musical language is still more impaired, but not in a uniform manner. There is chiefly a quite remarkable discrepancy between a loss of musical expression (written or instrumental), and musical thinking, which is comparatively well preserved. With the help of two musicians, a favourite pupil of the master and a neurologist with great musical ability we could study as precisely as possible musical tune recognition, note recognition (musical dictation), note reading and solfeggio piano playing, and dictated musical writing (copied or spontaneous). I apologise for giving such an analysis, but it seems to me essential in respect of the value of such a case-history.

Recognition of tunes played before our musician is generally good and prompt. He recognizes immediately most of the works he knew, and anyway he recognizes perfectly his own works. That recognition is not a vague one, for he is able to evaluate exactly rhythm and style as shown by the following facts. He immediately notices the slightest mistake in the playing; several parts of the 'Tombeau de Couperin' were first correctly played, and then with minor errors (either as to notes or rhythm). He immediately protested and demanded a perfect accuracy. When playing the beginning of 'La pavane de Ma Mère l'Oye' which contains two exactly similar bars, one was omitted. The patient immediately stopped the pianist. He succeeded in explaining, in his halting speech, that the first bar was to link with the preceding part. The same is true for rhythm: if played too fast, he protests and has the music played again with its exact rhythm. Another remark: during these studies on musical interference of aphasia, my piano – because of the dampness of the winter – had become somewhat out of tune. The patient noticed

---

[2] the inability to perform certain patterns of movement (e.g. lighting a cigarette) despite the preservation of muscle power, sensibility and co-ordination

it and demonstrated the dissonance by playing two notes one octave apart, thus showing again the preservation of sound recognition and valuation.

On the contrary analytic recognition of notes, and musical dictation, are quite faulty, or seemingly so, since he could name only some notes hesitatingly and with difficulty. His numerous mistakes are due, very likely, to aphasia itself, and to the difficulty of finding the name of a note, a trouble exactly similar to name designation for common objects. The fact that reproduction of notes played on the piano, without giving their name, is quite good, seems to confirm this opinion.

Note reading is extremely difficult. From time to time a note is read exactly. Most often reading is impossible. The same is true for solfeggio. The trouble of name-finding may partly explain the failure. But there is something more, since piano playing is almost impossible after reading. A component due to apraxia supervenes therein. Anyway a quite definite discrepancy is noted between deciphering musical signs, and their visual recognition. If an analytic deciphering is almost impossible, on the contrary the patient is able to recognize at first glance whatever piece he has to find, and that without any error.

Piano playing is very difficult, since in addition to difficulty in reading, our aphasic patient has to search for the location of notes on the keyboard. He sometimes misplaces notes without being aware of it. For instance, he plays the mi-mi instead of the do-do arpeggio, and plays it again and again, until his fingers are placed on the proper keys. He plays scales quite well, both major and minor ones. Diesis and flats are well marked. There is just a praxic difficulty. He can play with only one hand (the right one) the beginning of 'Ma Mère l'Oye'. With both hands, he cannot decipher. He needs many exercises to play in that way. In spite of numerous exercises during a whole week he cannot succeed in playing the beginning of the 'Pavane', even with separate hands. On the contrary he has a greater performance ability when he plays by heart pieces of his own composition. He suddenly gives a right idea of the beginning of 'Le Tombeau de Couperin' which is, however, too difficult to finish. Seven or eight bars are played almost perfectly, and he plays them, transposing to the lower tierce, without any error. When attempting an unknown piece he finds a much greater difficulty: he cannot play more than two or three notes of a piece by Scarlatti, which he did not previously know.

Musical writing is very difficult, although better preserved than plain writing. He writes dictated notes slowly and with numerous errors, but copying is almost impossible and requires from the patient enormous effort. On the contrary, writing by heart a portion of his 'Entretiens de la belle et la bête', though difficult and slow, is better performed than the other tests. Notes are better and more quickly placed, and he

206

seems mainly disturbed by writing apraxia. Singing by heart is correctly performed for some of his works, but only if the first note or notes are given. He says that tunes come back quite easily, and that he can hear them singing 'in his head'. Musical thinking seems comparatively better preserved than musical language itself.

Though all artistic realisation is forbidden to our musician, he can still listen to music, attend a concert, and express criticism on it or describe the musical pleasure he felt. His artistic sensibility does not seem to be in the least altered, nor his judgment, as his admiration for the romantic composer Weber shows, which he told me several times. He can also judge contemporary musical works.

Thus, in our musician, because of aphasia, and as already mentioned, because of a simultaneous apraxia, musical reading, piano playing, use of musical signs are much more impaired than expression and recognition of musical themes. Severe disturbance of realisation, and difficulty of expressing a relatively preserved musical thinking, while affectivity and aesthetic sensibility are almost intact, are the main features of our composer's case-history. They explain why his work has been completely arrested by his cerebral affection.

Alajouanine felt that Ravel was suffering from a degenerative disease of the cerebral cortex. He confirmed his diagnosis by performing a ventriculogram which showed enlargement of the ventricular system[3] and presumed atrophy (loss) of the cerebral cortex. By 1937 Ravel could scarcely speak and was looked after by medical attendants. It is unclear whether his aphasia was due to global dementia or to more focal neurological disease which several medical authors have felt was responsible for his illness (6, 12).[4] Precise diagnosis is not possible at present. Others have suggested that Ravel suffered from Alzheimer's disease, which the ventriculogram and the later operation would seem to confirm (8).

RAVEL'S DEATH

Ravel's death was due to a poorly planned neurosurgical procedure. His friend Ida Rubenstein sought the opinions of several neurosurgeons, most of whom declined to operate. Rubenstein was of the opinion that Ravel was actually suffering from a brain tumour which was undetected by his physicians. The Paris neurosurgeon Clovis Vincent was of the

[3] The cerebral ventricles are the fluid-filled spaces within the brain.
[4] Henson argues for a left-hemispheric lesion (12).

opinion that Ravel was suffering from a tumour and obtained the consent of the composer's brother Édouard for an operation. He felt the tumour was obstructing the flow of cerebrospinal fluid and was causing progressive hydrocephalus. R A. Henson recently outlined the procedure adopted by Vincent in the *British Medical Journal* (12). He states that on Wednesday, 17 December Vincent operated on Ravel to assess the cause of ventricular dilatation. He opened the skull by the right frontal bone.[5] The brain was found to be 'slack' though not visibly abnormal. Pressure within the lateral ventricles was low. Puncture of the right lateral ventricle produced no spontaneous flow of cerebrospinal fluid. Vincent injected water into the ventricle to raise the pressure. He closed the skull prudently after the procedure was unsuccessful. The operation thus confirmed advanced cortical atrophy by excluding a frontal tumour and demonstrating abnormalities of the ventricular system. Henson's argument that the condition was focal rather than global is based in part on the normal appearance to the naked eye of the frontal cortex. He notes that focal conditions causing aphasia are described by M. Mesulam in *Annals of Neurology*, 11 (1982), pp. 592–8. Returning to Alajouanine's paper, it seems open to question whether the French neurologist is describing an isolated aphasia or a slowly progressive dementing illness.

Ravel lapsed into a coma and died on 28 December 1937. The relatives refused permission for an autopsy and the immediate cause of death is unknown. Henson suggests that death was due to a subdural haematoma (a blood clot formed as a consequence of the operation). Alajouanine, who was holidaying in the country when the operation took place, was said to be deeply distressed by the operation and its consequences.

Ravel's illness robbed him of his artistic gifts at the height of his powers and the pinnacle of his career. In the last four years of his life he composed only three songs. Because he could no longer transfer the symbols of music from his mind to the printed page, the music remained forever imprisoned within his mind.

REFERENCES

1. T. Alajouanine, 'Aphasia and Artistic Realisation', *Brain*, 71 (1948), pp. 232–4
2. V. Seroff, *Maurice Ravel* (New York, 1953)

[5] Vincent obviously operated over the non-dominant hemisphere in order to minimize the psychological effects of the operation.

3. R. H. Myers, *Ravel: Life and Works* (London, 1960)
4. C. R. Noback and R. Demcrest, *The Human Nervous System*, 2nd edn (Tokyo, 1975)
5. A. Orenstein, *Ravel: Man and Musician* (New York, 1975)
6. R. E. Cytowic, 'Aphasia in Maurice Ravel', *Los Angeles Neurological Society Bulletin*, 41 (1976), pp. 109–14
7. M. J. Steedman, 'The Perception of Musical Rhythm and Metre', *Perception*, 6 (1977), pp. 555–9
8. D. J. Dalessio, 'Maurice Ravel and Alzheimer's Disease', *Journal of the American Medical Association*, 252 (1984), p. 3412
9. S. T. Brown et al., 'Serological Response to Syphilis Treatment', *Journal of the American Medical Association*, 253 (1985), p. 1296
10. G. Hart, 'Syphilis Tests in Diagnostic and Therapeutic Decision Making', *Annals of Internal Medicine*, 104 (1986), p. 368
11. M. Marnat, *Maurice Ravel* (Paris, 1986)
12. R. A. Henson, 'Maurice Ravel's Illness: A Tragedy of Lost Creativity', *British Medical Journal*, 296 (1988), pp. 1585–8

Percy Grainger
(1882–1961)

Grainger, who was born on 8 July 1882 in Melbourne, used his artistic stature and genius to lead a life that was at times diametrically opposed to the conventions of the day. A highly extroverted eccentric, he was the first Australian musician to receive international renown, both as an instrumentalist and as a composer. He mingled with the most import-ant artistic figures of his day and numbered among his friends Frederick Delius, Ferruccio Busoni, Edvard Grieg, Ralph Vaughan Williams and Benjamin Britten. Grainger was also an inveterate diarist and letter writer. In his letters he has left an important first-hand account of the development of the arts in his lifetime, from the 1890s until the 1960s. Possessed with an acute sense of posterity, he founded his own museum at the University of Melbourne and decreed in his will that his skeleton be publicly displayed there.

Grainger was a keen athlete and had a penchant for physical activity. He excelled in cricket and football and was an avid jogger long before the activity became fashionable. He would often put his knapsack on his back and jog or walk briskly between concert engagements in differ-ent towns. On one concert trip in New Zealand he covered a ninety-kilometre stretch between concerts in sixteen hours (between 2.00 p.m. and 6.00 a.m. the next day), resting for only thirty minutes en route. He continued these feats until well into his sixties.

Grainger stood 170 cm tall but actually looked taller because of his lean, well-proportioned figure. His impressive appearance was an important factor in his sensational success as a virtuoso pianist. With his finely chiselled features and passion for physical activity, he exuded a healthy vitality which was reflected in his musical style and which he communicated vividly to his audience. He was a man of both brilliant ideas and bizarre eccentricities, although his originality was often dis-guised by banal display and a compulsion to obtain publicity. In many ways he was a man of extraordinary vision, and the more profound products of his intense creative drive have justly accorded him a place in posterity.

GRAINGER THE MUSICIAN

From early childhood, Grainger showed exceptional talent in the arts. In addition to being a musical child prodigy, he was also a gifted draughtsman, and the choice between a career in music or one in painting was difficult to make. Grainger's earliest musical training was provided by his mother, Rose. Later he studied with Louis Pabst, whose brother was an opera composer in Dresden; his training culminated in the master classes of Ferruccio Busoni.

In addition, Grainger was influenced greatly by the surgeon John Hamilton Russell, himself a gifted pianist, who introduced the young musician to the works of Robert Schumann. Grainger was so entranced by the surgeon's playing that when Sir Charles Hallé visited Melbourne, Grainger told Hamilton Russell that he found Hallé's playing dull and pedantic in comparison with the surgeon's more vivid interpretations of the classics (6). Grainger quickly became something of a matinée idol and a favourite of London society when he arrived there in 1901. His calm and confident outward appearance belied the fact that he was an extremely self-critical man who strove constantly towards perfection in his music. He was undoubtedly one of the most gifted pianists of this century (5). He also became a pioneer in the field of musicology, and was one of the first classically trained musicians to make field record-ings of folk songs, in Britain and the South Pacific, at the time when Bartók and Kodály were advancing the understanding of the origins and evolution of Hungarian music (6).

Grainger continued to be a musical pioneer throughout his life. As an elderly man in the 1950s he began to experiment with what he called 'free music', an electronic music in which the usual constraints of rhythm, melody and harmony were abandoned. Together with Burnett Cross, he devised and designed electronic musical instruments which predate today's more sophisticated synthesizers. Some of these machines have colourful names such as 'The Inflated Frog Blower' and 'The Cross-Grainger Double Decker Kangaroo Pouch Flying Disc Paper-graph for Synchronizing and Playing Eight Oscillators'.

THE GRAINGER FAMILY

Grainger's early childhood was spent in troubled times. The 1890s were years of recession after the speculation boom of the 1880s. In May 1895 Grainger left for Europe with his mother; he had in his pocket £50 that had been raised at a benefit concert. He was among sixty thousand of his fellow countrymen who left Australia for the more favourable economic climate of Europe during the 1890s (8). These national economic troubles were compounded by more immediate family problems. Grainger's father, John, had been a talented architect, and in his prime an important man in the colony of Victoria. He was a close friend of the Mitchell family, who were builders. (Their daughter, Helen, was to become the opera singer Dame Nellie Melba.) However, John Grainger's career was ruined through alcoholism and the contraction of syphilis in a spree of alcohol-induced promiscuity shortly after Percy's birth. This was the final indignity which destroyed any hope of reconciliation with his wife. John Grainger was later to die, impoverished and intestate, of tabes dorsalis.[1] He was buried in Box Hill cemetery in a pauper's grave. His death certificate gives the cause of death as 'chronic rheumatoid arthritis', often a medical euphemism for syphilis at the time (6).

Percy Grainger was not himself affected by syphilis: serological testing was performed many times with negative results. However, the disease had important indirect ramifications on the young man because it disorganized the family nucleus. When Rose Grainger contracted the disease from her husband she was shocked and disgusted by the knowledge that she had syphilis. From then on she never touched her baby, but entrusted his intimate care to a series of servants. She supervised his care and education closely, but at a physical distance. Fearing that Percy would follow her husband's moral decline, she kept a horsewhip in the parlour of her house with which she reportedly beat her young son when she considered his piano practice to be inadequate. She also used it to chastise her husband, to keep him away from her physically and to control his drunken philandering. It is not difficult to perceive in these conditions the origins of Grainger's later sado-masochistic behaviour (8).

Rose was Grainger's mentor and support during his formative years and even throughout the years of his greatest success she organized

[1] a type of neurosyphilis which affects the spinal cord and the eyes

his concert tours and supervised his life, to the extent of determining with which women he should form relationships. The two had a highly unusual relationship which was characterized by love, mutual dependency and shared ambitions. Its nature caused speculation that it was incestuous, but it is known that this was not the case – although, as John Bird described it, 'the umbilical cord was never completely severed' (6). The relationship between the pair was more symbiotic, as Percy provided Rose with an opportunity to forge a new life away from the shambles of marital discord and, with Rose's careful ministrations, he became an artist of international stature. The myriad existing letters point to a relationship of enormous complexity. Rose wrote in one of her last letters to her son, 'In spite of everything that has been said, I have never for one moment loved you wrongly ... you and I have loved one another purely and rightly' (6).

At this point a few words should perhaps be said about Grainger's sexual life. Grainger, a sado-masochist, discovered flagellation during his teenage years in Frankfurt, his experiments with it coinciding with the onset of puberty (8). Although Rose was horrified to discover this, Percy continued to practise both self-flagellation and flagellation with his sexual partners. These sessions became so violent that he left a letter stating that if either he or his wife, Ella, were to be found dead after such activity, it should be noted that to him flagellation was the highest manifestation of his love. He also left ample documentation in the form of photographs, letters and diaries which he instructed his solicitor to release to the Grainger Museum ten years after his death. When these were released they created a furore. This facet of Grainger's life is well documented in John Bird's biography (6).

Rose, as did her husband, developed neurosyphilis, manifested initially by neuralgia and leg pain. It was her illness which led Grainger to become an itinerant concert pianist and to deviate from his preferred path of composer. Rose Grainger was aware of the slow encroachment of neurosyphilis on her health. She perceived the progressive decline of her mental faculties and the insidious advance of paralysis. The associated dementia and the rumours of an incestuous relationship between Rose and Percy, circulated allegedly by one of Percy's mistresses, may have led to her suicide by leaping from the eighth floor of the Aeolian building in New York on 30 April 1922. She died of a fractured skull and multiple internal injuries (6). After her death Grainger was beset by guilt and remorse for many years. Ella Ström, a Swedish artist whom he married in 1928 was to take on the burden

213

of Rose's mantle and to bear the brunt of her husband's sexuality and his demanding nature. She was often an unhappy woman: she wrote of her relationship with Grainger that 'it was hell to be with him and hell to be without him' (6). However, the pair were ostensibly a glamorous couple; their marriage took place before an audience of twenty thousand at the Hollywood Bowl.

GRAINGER'S LAST YEARS

Grainger developed carcinoma of the prostate, and suffered from the disease for nearly eight years before his death at seventy-eight. The disease was diagnosed after Grainger consulted Dr Cai Holten, the brother of his mistress, Karen Holten, with regard to a long history of difficult urination and bladder pain. X-ray examination indicated metastatic spread of the tumour to the pelvis, and Holten performed a suprapubic prostatectomy after making a clinical diagnosis of cancer. A histological examination of the prostatic tissue confirmed the diagnosis. The operation was performed in June 1953 in the Aarhus Municipal Hospital, Denmark (2, 6, 8).

Grainger spent much of his eight remaining years productively. There were concerts and a never-ending round of public engagements, and he also continued his experiments with free music. In his letters to Elsie Bristow, Grainger indicated that he was well aware of the implications of the diagnosis. However, he soldiered on regardless.

The most disturbing immediate complications of his illness were the painful pelvic metastases.[2] These were treated initially with stilboestrol and local radiotherapy. As a result the symptoms improved considerably. However, Grainger also experienced frequent episodes of acute urinary retention, which necessitated a transurethral dilatation of the urethra and prostatic bed. This series of operations was performed by Kaare Nygaard at the White Plains Hospital in New York between 1953 and 1954. A bilateral orchidectomy (castration)[3] was performed to provide relief when the pain (due to the bony metastases) became refractory to stilboestrol therapy. This operation was performed in February 1960, and was 'eminently successful', according to Grainger. However, the pain recurred late that year and he was readmitted to hospital in late November with a pathological fracture of the left hip. In spite of his

[2] spread of the tumour to the bones of the pelvis
[3] Grainger had his testicles preserved in formalin and sent them to the Grainger museum.

evident suffering, Grainger's last letters have an optimistic quality about them.

Nygaard had noted a progressive decline in Grainger's mental faculties late in 1960 and the frequent episodes of mental confusion. Consequently, he suspected metastatic disease of the brain. Grainger's terminal admission to hospital lasted six days. Three days after his admission he lapsed into a coma, and never recovered consciousness. His death occurred on 20 February 1961.

An autopsy was performed on the morning of his death by Dr J. Lester. It confirmed extensive metastatic disease to the brain and skull. Large haemorrhagic masses of tumour had protruded into the cranial cavity from the dura, and the venous sinuses of the dura were also filled with tumour. A large, recent cerebral haemorrhage had destroyed the basal ganglia and internal capsule and much of the parietal temporal lobes of the left cerebral cortex. The tumour had also spread into the skeletal system. Its spread into the bone marrow accounted for extra-medullary haematopoiesis[4] in the spleen and liver (4). Grainger was buried in the Aldridge (his mother's) family vault in Adelaide's West Terrace cemetery.

During his illness Grainger had formed a close friendship with his surgeon Kaare Nygaard, who had been an admirer of Grainger since attending a recital by the pianist in 1912 in Lillehammer, in his native Norway. Nygaard has written and lectured on Grainger since the composer's death. He now lives in New York and is also a sculptor of some renown: his bronze sculptures of Grainger have pride of place in the Grainger Museum.

Grainger left an immense musical legacy that includes a series of unique and interesting compositions and a considerable number of piano recordings, both acoustic and on piano rolls. A recording of his last performance of the Grieg A minor Piano Concerto in 1957, when beset with advanced illness, forms an eloquent testimony to Grainger's charisma as a pianist. It is not technically a perfect performance, but it is one of immense power and musicianship which belies the composer's frail and debilitated condition. Benjamin Britten commented that it was the most noble performance of the work ever recorded (6). It is evocative of the romantic generation of concert pianists, and of the era to which Grainger belonged.

---

[4] production of blood by these organs

REFERENCES

1. P. Grainger, 'The Aldridge–Grainger–Ström Saga', 1933 (Melbourne, Archives of Grainger Museum; unpublished)
2. The Medical Records of Percy Grainger during his Admissions to the White Plains Hospital, New York' (Melbourne, Archives of Grainger Museum; unpublished)
3. 'Letters of Percy Grainger to Elsie Bristow dated July 7, 1960 and August 8, 1960' (Melbourne, Archives of Grainger Museum; unpublished)
4. J. Lester, 'Autopsy Report of Percy Grainger' (Melbourne, Archives of Grainger Museum; unpublished)
5. H. C. Schonberg, *The Great Pianists from Mozart to the Present* (London and New York, 1963), pp. 76–82, 327, 345–54
6. J. Bird, *Percy Grainger: The Man and the Music* (London, 1976, 2nd edn 1982), pp. 19, 43–51, 107, 116–17, 158, 173–5, 200, 246–7
7. K. Dreyfus, *The Farthest North of Humanness: The Letters of Percy Grainger* (London and Melbourne, 1985), pp. 193, 201, 229, 301–3, 329, 330
8. K. Nygaard, 'The Percy Grainger Lecture 1985: Percy Grainger's Psyche: His Surgeon's View' (Melbourne, Archives of Grainger Museum; unpublished)
9. J. G. O'Shea, 'Percy Grainger', *Medical Journal of Australia*, 147 (1987), p. 578

George Gershwin
(1898–1937)

Gershwin was in many ways the personification of the American immigrant dream. His fame was the product of hard work and determination combined with innate talent. He was a handsome, vigorous individual of unbounded energy and enthusiasm, and his natural charm and personality led to his being surrounded by brilliant and glamorous people. Tragically, his life was short. Gershwin died at only thirty-eight of an illness diagnosed too late for effective treatment.

George Gershwin was born Jacob Gershvin, the son of a moderately wealthy Russian Jewish businessman, on 26 September 1898. Energy and restlessness, accompanied by boundless enthusiasm and joy for living, distinguished young George from his peers. There was no record of musical talent in the family and George's parents were extremely surprised at the results when they bought the twelve-year-old boy a piano. Within a few months their son was playing Sousa marches and soon he produced his first attempts at composition. His first job when he was sixteen years old was accompanying a local choir.

Young George grew into a fine physical specimen. He was tall and athletic and exceptionally proficient at sports, his extraordinary co-ordination leading to quick mastery of any sporting challenge. He excelled at horse riding, tennis and swimming. Gershwin was a fine dancer, could do a passable imitation of Astaire and actually made choreographic suggestions to the dancer when working with him on screen musicals.

From his mid-twenties Gershwin was a successful song composer, and his New York apartment had the atmosphere of a railway terminus as the cream of society gathered to meet there. He would try out his compositions on his Steinway with the prominent artists of the day. Irving Berlin, Fred Astaire and Jerome Kern were frequent guests. The first synchronized sound film was *The Jazz Singer* of 1927 and soon Hollywood producers beckoned Gershwin to write for them. *Delicious*, his first film musical, appeared in 1931, and the opera *Porgy and Bess* in 1935. He had already won the Pulitzer Prize for drama in 1932 with *Of Thee I Sing*. Film was emerging as the foremost medium for popular artists and so he moved to Hollywood. Again his personality and vigour drew an entourage of brilliant people; a series of love affairs followed, as he was immensely attractive to women despite a basically shy nature. Gershwin was always eager to escape marriage and offered many excuses to stave off permanent attachment; the real reason was probably his deep commitment to his work. Even at his most vibrant and frivolous, music was the prime motivator in his life and he was always ready to accept new challenges to his creativity. He once said it would take him 'one hundred years to write down all the music in [his] head'.

ILLNESS

Until 1936, Gershwin had been an immensely successful extrovert, freely exploiting his huge talent. The year began well with the scoring of two musicals, *Shall We Dance* with Ginger Rogers and Fred Astaire and *A Damsel in Distress* with Astaire and Joan Fontaine. He was still leading an active social life but gradually it began to pall for him. He told one of his closer friends, 'I am thirty-eight years old, wealthy and famous but I am deeply unhappy.' He began to think marriage might solve his problems and wrote to his old girlfriends from the East coast, hoping to persuade them to come to California. He became severely depressed when none came. He also began to worry about baldness. He bought an apparatus advertised as a cure for baldness which consisted of a suction cap fitted to the scalp and driven by a motorized pump. He sat beneath this device for half an hour each day hoping to improve the growth of hair on his head.

At a Hollywood gala, Gershwin met Paulette Goddard and felt an immediate deep attraction to her. But she was married to Charlie Chaplin at the time and refused to leave him. Stunned by this rejection, Gershwin's depression worsened. He became irritated by things which previously would not have bothered him. He began to consult doctors who, despite repeated medical examinations, could find nothing wrong with him. Outwardly, he was the picture of physical good health – tall,

lean and tanned – but his interest in parties and gaiety was waning and he complained vociferously to his friends, 'Nobody believes me when I say I'm sick.' Soon he was to develop positive signs of physical illness.

On 11 February 1937, while playing his Concerto in F with the Los Angeles Symphony Orchestra, Gershwin suffered a blackout lasting between ten and twenty seconds; he remained upright but missed the music altogether. Oscar Levant, who had been in the audience, went backstage and said, 'Did I make you nervous or did you think Horowitz was in the audience?' Gershwin complained that immediately prior to the fit he had a revolting sensation of smelling burnt rubber. (The same sensation occurred two months later when he had another epileptic seizure.) He mentioned this symptom to his doctors, but with only one exception they thought his illness psychogenic in origin.

Gershwin also spoke of a severe headache which was worse in the mornings. This is the typical pattern of a headache produced by an intracranial lesion such as a brain tumour. He complained of the condition to his doctors and friends who failed to grasp its significance. He was listless and muddle-headed, drained of his usual energy and vitality. Gershwin was now working on his fourth motion picture, *The Goldwyn Follies*. He failed to attend the sound-stage and was found sitting up in his bed staring vaguely into space; he did not appear to remember how long he had been sitting there. By now he was displaying the symptoms of both cerebral irritation and raised intracranial pressure. The headache was dismissed as being psychogenic in origin. Gershwin did not exhibit any discernible signs of focal neurological lesion, but a keen observer would have noticed a generalized bradyphrenia,[1] atypical of the composer's normally vigorous disposition. The diagnosis of his condition was maintained to be 'Hysteria – brought on by the pressures and artificiality of Hollywood life'.

In April 1937, as previously mentioned, Gershwin had another epileptiform manifestation of his disease. He blacked out while sitting in a barber's chair in Beverly Hills. His consciousness became clouded and he nearly collapsed. Once more the episode was preceded by the smell of burnt rubber. He told his doctors but again they did not connect the symptom with epilepsy or organic disease.

In June Gershwin's condition improved briefly after a holiday in Colorado, and for a short while he appeared once more to be his normal self. At a party given by Irving Berlin on 20 June, he complained of

[1] slowing of body movements and responses due in Gershwin's case to an enlarging brain tumour

an intolerable headache and appeared slow-witted and withdrawn. When he drove his car, he wove unsteadily through the traffic, and his friends became alarmed. Arrangements were made to admit him to hospital. The physical examination revealed a diminished sense of smell on the right side but there was no papilloedema (congestion of the optic disc) at this stage. The Wassermann reaction (a test for syphilis) was negative. Gershwin's physicians planned a lumbar puncture but the composer refused to undergo the procedure because he considered it too painful. He was discharged from the hospital and arrangements were made for domiciliary nursing and follow-up psychoanalytical treatment. Shortly afterwards Gershwin developed papilloedema and photophobia (painful vision on perceiving light). Nothing was done to relieve these symptoms.

Gershwin's deterioration progressed alarmingly. After a party, he sat down at the edge of a street, put his head in his hands and complained bitterly of headaches and the repulsive smell of burnt rubber which was now with him all the time. On another occasion when given chocolates he crushed them into a sticky residue and rubbed them into his skin as an ointment. He spilled his meals and played the piano irregularly and erratically. He recovered briefly when admitted to a nursing home.

On 9 July Gershwin's condition took an alarming turn for the worse. His brother Ira visited him in the morning, but he was not awake. Ira decided to return later in the day. George did not wake until 5.00 p.m. and was so feeble that he had to call his nurse. He collapsed suddenly and lost consciousness. He was taken immediately to Cedars of Lebanon Hospital. On arrival he was deeply comatose and had a left-sided paralysis, and there was severe papilloedema. It was now apparent after all these delays that Gershwin had in fact been suffering from a progressive organic disease due to a malignant brain tumour and that his symptoms were not due simply to stress and fatigue. How Gershwin was to be treated remained to be decided. Everything was done to mobilize the country's foremost specialists.

The most famous neurosurgeon of the day was Harvey Cushing, who practised at Johns Hopkins Medical School in Baltimore. He was contacted by telephone. He declined to operate himself because he had recently retired from surgery and he recommended his successor, Walter E. Dandy. It was found that Dandy was at sea, taking a holiday on a yacht on Chesapeake Bay. He was contacted by the coastguard destroyers and escorted to Cumberland, Maryland, by police where an American Airlines plane waited ready to fly him to Cedars of Lebanon Hospital in Los Angeles. Meanwhile, Gershwin's condition had deteriorated further and it was thought that immediate surgery was necessary. Dandy called off his trip. He discussed the case with Howard Nafziger, a respected neurosurgeon who practised in California. At Dandy's suggestion a ventriculogram, a procedure which he himself had pioneered, was performed to locate the tumour more precisely.

The ventriculogram indicated displacement of both lateral ventricles towards the left-hand side. The right ventricle was flattened and the right temporal horn had not filled at all. The intracranial pressure was immensely high. The result suggested a right temporal tumour with brain herniation. This was confirmed by surgery. The operation began on the evening of 10 July, immediately after the ventriculogram. The cranium was opened and it was noted that the dura, the membrane which covers the brain, was under severe tension, ostensibly from the pressure of an underlying tumour. In the right temporal lobe the tumour was found. The surgeons noted a malignant cyst which, on aspiration, yielded an ounce of dark yellowish fluid. The tumour was found to extend deep into the substance of the brain. It was partially resected and the skull was closed. The operation took over five hours to conclude. The pathologist reported the mass as a 'spongioblastoma multiforme' which equates with a high-grade malignant astrocytoma in today's terminology (2). Astrocytomas, derived from the brain's supporting cells, are a common form of brain malignancy in adults.[2]

Gershwin did not live long after the operation. He died at 10.30 the next morning without regaining consciousness. His pulse and temperature rose rapidly before he died. Ira was at his bedside. The immediate cause of death was brain herniation, that is, a shift in the brain from its normal position due to the bulky tumour. The nation was plunged into mourning by the unexpected death of its most famous and still youthful composer. Gershwin had suffered all along from an organic neurological disease caused by a brain tumour. Its first signs were subtle – personality change caused by cerebral irritation. The psycho-motor fits which are characteristic of a rapidly growing temporal astrocytoma were dismissed by Gershwin's physicians as neurotic or paranoid behaviour. By the time the condition was diagnosed he had irreversible brain damage due to brain herniation.

Walter E. Dandy requested the details from his attending physician, Gabriel Segall, of Gershwin's condition together with details of the

---

[2] Cushing calls the tumour a 'spongioblastoma' because of the resemblance of the anaplastic cells to embryonal tissue.

surgery employed and the pathology reports. He must have been upset by the delay in the diagnosis but in his response was most understanding. In a letter to Segall four weeks later he took the view that earlier diagnosis would not necessarily have improved the outlook for the composer. He concluded:

> I do not see what more you could have done for Mr Gershwin. It was just one of those fulminating tumours that have uncinate attacks [seizures that begin with olfactory hallucinations such as the foul odour experienced by Gershwin] that are removable, and it would be my impression that although the tumour in a large part might have been extirpated and he would have recovered for a little while, it would have recurred very quickly since the whole thing fulminated so suddenly at the onset. I think the outcome is much the best for himself; for a man as brilliant as he with a recurring tumour it would have been terrible. It would have been a slow death.

Dandy was obviously being diplomatic in his summary. However, in the 1930s a few medical centres would have embarked on invasive diagnostic procedures much earlier when operation and radiotherapy might have afforded a chance of long-term remission.

The tumour followed a slower and more progressive course than was suggested by Dandy in his letter. 'Fulmination' in the end was probably due to acute swelling of the brain. Gershwin himself was extremely unwilling to undergo invasive procedures and refused a lumbar puncture, which might have revealed raised intracranial pressure and would have pointed to the presence of a tumour. Gershwin's fame may have intimidated his physicians who seemed very indecisive in their approach to his illness. All in all, as Dandy suggests, there was little prospect of Gershwin's life being saved.

GERSHWIN AND NEUROSURGERY

Gershwin's illness brought him into indirect contact with two men who are among the most respected pioneers in medicine, Harvey Cushing and Walter E. Dandy. Ironically, they were early proponents of procedures which might conceivably have saved Gershwin's life; certainly the composer would have benefited from their wide experience and knowledge if they had been consulted earlier.

Harvey Cushing (1869–1939) graduated from Harvard Medical School in 1895. He is accredited as the founder of contemporary

222

neurosurgery and an outstanding clinical surgeon; he also collected medical books and was a noted medical historian. His biography of the physician William Osler won a Pulitzer prize. Cushing was a distinguished neuropathologist and wrote, with P.Bailey, an outstanding book on the classification of tumours of the central nervous system. The book, entitled *Tumours of the Glioma Group*, appeared in 1926 (2). Cushing and Bailey used histopathological techniques developed by Ramon Y.Cajal and Rio Hortega to study neoplastic disease of the brain. They invented a classification of brain tumours which, in its essentials, survives today. They also described the response of the various tumours they encountered to radiotherapy. Cushing's name is generally associated with cortisol-producing tumours. He described cortisol overproduction associated with basophil adenomas of the pituitary (Cushing's disease) in 1929. In the same paper he also wrote that the syndrome could be caused *inter alia* by hyperplasia of the adrenal gland itself (Cushing's Syndrome).

Walter E.Dandy (1886–1946) pioneered pneumoencephalography, the method used to determine the location of Gershwin's tumour. He experimented with the injection of air into the spinal canal to outline the cerebral ventricles (the fluid-filled cavities within the brain) between 1918 and 1923 (1). He wrote that the method disclosed the location of 95% of clinically diagnosed brain tumours whereas simple clinical determination of the whereabouts of a tumour was accurate in only about 50% of cases. Cerebral angiography was pioneered by Moniz of Portugal who discussed the procedure at the International Neurological Conference of 1931. Today computerized tomography provides accurate and non-invasive determination of the position of tumours of the brain and spinal cord and has made the location of brain tumours far easier.

REFERENCES

1. W. E. Dandy, 'Localization of Brain Tumours by Cerebral-Angiography', AMJ Roentgenology, 10 (1923), pp. 610–16
2. H. Cushing and P. Bailey, *Tumours of the Glioma Group* (Philadelphia, 1926)
3. H. Cushing, 'The Basophil Adenomas of the Pituitary Body and their Clinical Manifestations', *Bulletin of the Johns Hopkins Hospital*, 50 (1932), pp. 137–95

4. M. Armitage (ed.), *George Gershwin, the Man and Legend* (New York, 1938)
5. N. Fabricant, *Thirteen Famous Patients* (Philadelphia, 1960)
6. J. G. Greenfield, *Neuropathology*, 3rd edn (Baltimore, 1976)
7. L. Carp, 'George Gershwin, the Illustrious American Composer: His Fatal Glioblastoma', AMJ Surg. Pathol. (1979), pp. 473–8
8. W. L. Fox, *Dandy of Johns Hopkins* (Baltimore, 1984)

Béla Bartók
(1881–1945)

Béla Bartók arrived in New York with his third wife Ditta in the spring of 1940. He had contemplated leaving Hungary as early as 1938 due to the deteriorating political situation in Europe but his deep attachment to his family and homeland had kept him there. The Atlantic crossing did not go well; he lost his baggage and he wrote regretfully to his son Peter:

> Everything that linked us to the past is broken ... all we possess is scattered ... it is as if we are driven here by a storm with no more than the clothes on our backs.

The Bartóks told their friends that they would stay for a few months but they actually made plans for a far longer stay and must have had grave doubts about even seeing their homeland again. They were domiciled in a tiny apartment on Queens Boulevard, Forest Hills. Concert engagements were few – Bartók was not well known as a composer or performer and when he and his wife appeared on the stage critics objected to the couple playing from the music – American performers played by heart, not from the score! To make matters worse they were evicted from their apartment; neighbours objected both to the sound of constant piano music and to Bartók's wife pounding wiener schnitzel for the couple's evening meal. He in turn was not initially impressed by the Americans:

> Human beings ruminating like cows ... every second person chewing gum ...

The Hungarian community found the distinguished emigré both a suitable house and job. He was to transcribe Serbo-Croatian folksongs at the University of Columbia. He was immensely impressed with the quality of the recorded sound and the number of folksongs that constituted the Parry Collection. Once engaged in his work he seemed as if transported to those distant villages in Serbia. The job was only a temporary one, however, and soon he was reduced to performing and living off the royalties of his records.

In 1942 Bartók had what was initially thought to be a bout of "influenza". He never fully recovered and was noted for intermittent spike fevers. He lost weight and was found to be anaemic. He consulted four prominent New York physicians who, after performing blood and bone marrow examinations, avoided directly telling him about his condition. He was told only that he was a 'baffling case' and that he perhaps had a recurrence of the 'tubercular lesion' that he had suffered from as a young man. The true nature of his terminal illness was kept from him.

The antibiotic Streptomycin was used to treat tuberculosis and when an indignant friend asked Bartók's chief physician Dr Rappaport why he was not on this medication he was told the truth. Bartók was actually suffering from chronic leukaemia for which there was nothing but symptomatic treatment available. He was therefore treated with intermittent hospitalisation and blood transfusions (2,6).

Bartók suffered from chronic myeloid leukaemia, the commonest form in the middle-aged population. Chronic leukaemia usually begins insidiously but ends with an abrupt transformation, an aggressive and terminal phase (blast cell crisis). Thus it was with Bartók, who was aware of the diagnosis towards the end of his illness and may indeed have suspected it earlier. Certainly the onset of his illness and may indeed have suspected it earlier. Certainly the onset of his illness corresponded to a productive phase of composition. That year he was in a depressed and melancholy state of mind. He looked unwell and emaciated; he was introverted and his skin had an unhealthy translucent appearance. He wrote that he had lost 'all confidence in people, countries ... and in everything' (6).

To add to his miseries the Baldwin Piano Company repossessed a piano they had loaned to him and in turn threatened to sue the Columbia Record Company over lost royalties.

Bartók's melancholy abated somewhat when he stayed with his friend Agatha Fassett, who lived in the country at Roberta, Vermont. The rural scenery drew him to profound contemplation – in his correspondence he used the analogy of a tree being eaten by omnipresent insects as a metaphor for the destruction of European civilization by Nazism. Bartók often used insects to represent the obscurity and transience of human existence:

> While the tree was standing tall and upright, it was already being eaten by millions of little bugs buzzing under its layers ... by soft worms and hard bugs, yellow, brown and black ... millions in the body of one upright tree. The tree comes down and the bugs take over completely (6).

He also longed for rural Hungary.

> How well I understand those people whose lives are lived in close proximity to nature far away from so-called civilization and the questionable benefits of doctors and hospitals (6).

Bartók's resented his dependency on doctors, nurses and medical care to maintain his life and disliked the blood transfusions and the inactivity imposed by his convalescence.

LAST WORKS

Bartók's American publisher, Ralph Fox, wrote to him and urged him to compose. But he wrote back that he had nothing left of the 'joy, strength and high-spiritedness' needed to create.

However, the Boston conductor Serge Koussevitsky was able to persuade him to begin work anew. He visited Bartók in hospital and offered him $1,000 for a new work. The work was commissioned for the Koussevitsky Foundation and to honour the memory of the conductor's recently deceased wife. Bartók initially refused the commission on the grounds of ill-health but Koussevitsky showed such persistence, enthusiasm and faith in Bartók that he indirectly inspired three of the composer's major works – a trio of compositions which represent the end of his creative output and show-case his diverse musical skills.

Bartók began work on the 'Concerto for Orchestra' in rural North Carolina in the summer of 1944. He composed this complex work with astonishing rapidity and intensity and Koussevitsky premiered it with the Boston Symphony Orchestra later that year. After some initial reservations Bartók was happy with Koussevitsky's interpretation. Bartók's happy experience with this work triggered a further outburst of creative activity and so in 1944 he completed the 'Sonata for Solo Violin' which was commissioned by Yehudi Menuhin. It is an aggressive, introspective and intense masterpiece which reflects his turbulent state of mind during the period.

Subliminally aware of impending death he contemplated the relationship between death and life as he saw it in those cool, North American forests.

> Now the dead trunk is decorated once again. Life begins here in its slow way – encroaching imperceptibly as did death before. The eternal cycle ... a layer of death – a layer of life ... layer upon layer to the core of the earth.
>
> Life invades these dead bodies (the tree trunks) claiming them entirely for its own and will cover every inch of them with glittery fresh green as the dead bodies sink away under the living weight, their existence fulfilled and completed (6).

The composer's last work is his Third Piano Concerto (1945). He completed all but the last seventeen bars before his untimely death. The concerto is the third major work inspired by the approach of death and perhaps in this case by a brief moment of joy when his son Peter arrived from Hungary. Bartók had always been interested in the songs of birds and insects and transcribed the song of one of the birds he had heard in the North Carolina forests – the Rufus Sided Tohee – into the middle of the second movement. The inspiration for the second movement is the beauty and grandeur of the American wilderness. It is a slow and reflective andante religioso evocative of tranquil woodlands and the play of the small creatures which inhabit them. Bartók found a peace in rural America that he could not find in its cities. In North Carolina the Bartóks had rented a secluded cottage and Bartók had even convinced himself that he was rid of his illness. However, in August the bouts of temperature and malaise returned and he began to be ill and precipitately lose weight – 5'1" tall, he weighed approximately eighty pounds before his death.

The family returned to New York in 1945 to a small three-bedroom apartment on 57th Street. Initially febrile, his temperature abated and he was admitted to hospital. Bartók was reluctant to go because he was still working on his third piano concerto (7). His deterioration was inexorable and progressive; he died in September 1945. His rapid deterioration was due to abrupt transformation of leukaemia to the more malignant form of the disease (blast cell crisis). Mostly musicians and members of the Hungarian community attended the funeral.

228

In 1988 Bartók's body was exhumed and returned to Hungary. It was found that the cheap coffin had rotted away and his remains were scattered in disarray. They were placed in a new coffin which left New York on 23rd June 1988 on a journey through six countries that would bring it finally back to Hungary where it was reinterred at Budapest – the national capital. Along the way there were performances of Bartók's music and the unhappy but productive exile was metaphorically ended.

CHRONIC LEUKAEMIA

Leukaemia is a malignancy of the bone marrow. Mature cells of the blood and immune system derive from stem cells of the marrow of the flat bones, the spine and the skull. In chronic myeloid leukaemia the peripheral blood contains cells resembling cells from the bone marrow because of the abnormal proliferation of these cells which spill over from the bone marrow to the blood.

Rudolph Virchow (1821–1902) gave a famous description of chronic leukaemia in his case study *Weisses Blut* (White Blood) of 1845. Virchow, who was born in Pomerania, studied medicine at the Kaiser Wilhelm Academie, a training institution for army surgeons. He received his medical degree in Berlin. Virchow showed such aptitude for scientific medicine that in 1848 after his brilliant work concerning an epidemic of typhus in Silesia he was appointed Professor of Pathology in Wurzberg. In 1858 after the untimely death of Professor Hemsbach he was given the chair in pathology in Berlin. His book, *Cellular Pathologie* (1858) in which he gave his famous dictum *'Omnis Cellula a Cellula'* was the most influential book on pathology since Morgangnis' *De Sedibus et Causis Morborum* of 1761. Virchow served in opposition to Bismarck for thirteen years as the leader of the Radical Party and when he died in 1902 delegates from all over the world assembled to do him honour.

Virchow's case study reveals many features of chronic leukaemia; the patient Marie Straide, a fifty-year-old cook, was unwell for one year before her death. She lost weight insidiously and noticed swelling of her lower limbs and abdomen. She experienced severe pains and altered bowel habit. She began to bleed easily and had several nosebleeds. She developed multiple superficial skin infections before she died of 'rapid loss of strength'. Virchow conducted a post mortem and noticed a 'yellowish white coagula' in the arteries and veins in place of normal red blood. He noticed enlargement of the heart, and an enormously enlarged spleen 'nearly a foot long, very heavy, homogenous and waxy like a large ague cake'. When he examined the blood he noted that the greater part was composed of white with irregular nucleii and that the normal rule that the blood is composed predominantly of red cells seemed reversed. (Surprisingly he does not mention the state of the bone marrow.) An Englishman, John Hughes Bennet (1812–1875), also penned a comprehensive description of leukaemia in the same year and yet another contemporary report is found in Rokitansy's archive in the Vienna General Hospital. Virchow modestly disclaimed to tender the first description of leukaemia but claimed the honour of noticing that leukaemia was a proliferative disorder of the blood cells. Bennet mistook the abnormal lymphocytes for pus cells. Today therapeutic modalities such as chemotherapy and bone marrow transplantation have dramatically improved survival in many types of leukaemia.

REFERENCES

1. John Hughes Bennet, 'Two Cases of Disease and Englargement of the Spleen in which death took place from the presence of purulent matter in the blood', *Edinburgh Medical and Surgical Journal*, 64 (1845), pp. 412–3.
2. Rudolph Virchow, "Weiss Blut", in Neue Notizen aus dem gebreit der Natur und Heilkunde, 34 (Weimar 1845), p. 151.
3. Anderson J. R. (ed.), *Muirs Textbook of Pathology*, 10th edn, London Edward Arnold (1976), pp. 488–495.
4. Kerner, D., *Bartók's Tod in New York*, Munchener Medizinische Wochenschrift, 123 (1981), pp. 525–9.
5. Harditsy, R. M. and Weatherall, D. J. (eds), *Blood and its Disorders*, 2nd edn, London, Blackwell Scientific (1982).
6. Sturrock, Donald (director), 'After the Storm – The American Exile of Béla Bartók, BBC Television, 1989.
7. Serly T., 'A Belated Account of the Reconstruction of a Lost 20th Century Masterpiece', *College Music Symposium* 12 (1975), pp. 7–25. A detailed account of the orchestration of the third piano concerto.

APPENDIX A

Other composers and their illnesses

GEORGES BIZET (1838–75) died at 36 years of age after a lifetime of ill-health: he was troubled by chronic streptococcal throat infections and complained of dyspnoea and palpitations on exertion, suggesting rheumatic valvular heart disease. At his death he had a massive retropharyngeal abscess and an exacerbation of his chronic rheumatic fever.

ALEXANDER BORODIN (1833–87) died of a myocardial infarct (heart attack) at a fancy-dress ball in St Petersburg. He was 53 years old. Borodin was also qualified as a physician and was well known as a research chemist.
D. O'Neill, 'Alexander Borodin, MD', *Journal of the Royal Society of Medicine*, 81 (1988), pp. 591–3.

JOHANNES BRAHMS (1833–97) is reported to have died of cancer of the liver. It is not clear whether this was a primary or secondary tumour. Brahms's close friend was the great surgeon Theodor Billroth.
D. Kerner, 'How Johannes Brahms Died', *Münchener medizinische Wochenschrift*, 121 (1979), pp. 565–8.

BENJAMIN BRITTEN (1913–76) suffered a stroke following cardiac valvular surgery. He had difficulty in speaking for some time after the stroke but gradually recovered the power of speech. Britten had difficulty notating music because of pain and weakness in the right arm and shoulder. This problem was the only persistent complication of the stroke. Britten's activities were extremely limited by angina pectoris and by the severe heart failure which precipitated his death in 1976.

CLAUDE DEBUSSY (1862–1918) is said to have died of a rectal carcinoma diagnosed in 1909.

MODEST MUSORGSKY (1839–81) was a Russian army officer and civil servant whose career was interrupted by alcoholism. He died of delirium tremens.

SERGEY RAKHMANINOV (1873–1943) was plagued by bouts of severe depressive illness that threatened his career. He was so grateful to his psychiatrist that he dedicated his Third Piano Concerto to him. Rakhmaninov died in Beverly Hills, California. He suffered malignant melanoma (skin cancer) which had spread widely, to his liver, lung and brain.

There has been recent speculation as to whether the composer possessed a Marfanoid bodily habitus. Marfan's syndrome is a connective tissue disorder and its sufferers have, inter alia, enormous hyperextensible hands. Rakhmaninov was 180 cm tall and could easily span a twelfth at the keyboard with both hands. Some of his works (notably the opening of the Third Piano Concerto) require enormous stretches. Sufferers of Marfan's syndrome are also prone to shortsightedness and back pain. Young has made a convincing argument for these symptoms in Rakhmaninov's case and his hypothesis is an intriguing one but requires further study to be validated.

D. A. B. Young, 'Rachmaninov and Marfan's Syndrome', *British Medical Journal*, 293 (1986), pp. 1625–6.

DIMITRY SHOSTAKOVICH (1906–75) died of motor neurone disease (amyotrophic lateral sclerosis).

ALEXANDER SKRYABIN (1872–1915), Rakhmaninov's great contemporary (they attended the Moscow Conservatory together in 1888), had a problem with alcohol which dated from his student years. He died of the consequences of an infected carbuncle on his lip – probably from a cavernous sinus thrombosis or septicaemia.

APPENDIX B

Hector Berlioz's experiences as a medical student in Paris

Hector Berlioz arrived in Paris with his friend Alphonse Robert in 1822 to take up medical studies at the instigation of his father, a physician. Berlioz lodged at 104 rue St-Jacques in the Latin quarter. He received a considerable allowance from his father which he spent on his musical pursuits. He soon abandoned medicine. Medical historians will note that formalin was not used to preserve the cadavers for dissection, which was therefore of necessity a hasty process:

On arriving in Paris in 1822 with my fellow-student Alphonse Robert, I gave myself up wholly to studying for the career which had been thrust upon me, and loyally kept the promise I had given my father on leaving. It was soon put to a somewhat severe test when Robert, having announced one morning that he had bought a 'subject' (a corpse), took me for the first time to the dissecting-room at the Hospice de la Pitié. At the sight of that terrible charnel-house – the fragments of limbs, the grinning faces and gaping skulls, the bloody quagmire underfoot and the atrocious smell it gave off, the swarms of sparrows wrangling over scraps of lung, the rats in their corner gnawing the bleeding vertebrae – such a feeling of revulsion possessed me that I leapt through the window of the dissecting-room and fled for home as though Death and all his hideous train were at my heels. The shock of that first impression lasted for twenty-four hours. I did not want to hear another word about anatomy, dissection or medicine, and I meditated a hundred mad schemes of escape from the future that hung over me.

Robert lavished his eloquence in a vain attempt to argue away my disgust and demonstrate the absurdity of my plans. In the end he got me to agree to make another effort. For the second time I accompanied

233

him to the hospital and we entered the house of the dead. How strange! The objects which before had filled me with extreme horror had absolutely no effect upon me now. I felt nothing but a cold distaste; I was already as hardened to the scene as any seasoned medical student. The crisis was past. I found I actually enjoyed groping about in a poor fellow's chest and feeding the winged inhabitants of that delightful place their ration of lung. 'Hallo!' Robert cried, laughing, 'you're getting civilized. "Thou giv'st the little birds their daily bread".' 'And o'er all nature's realm my bounty spread,' I retorted, tossing a shoulder-blade to a great rat staring at me with famished eyes.

So I went on with my anatomy course, feeling no enthusiasm, but stoically resigned. An instinctive affinity drew me to my teacher, Professor Amussat, who showed a passion for this science as great as I felt for music. Here was an artist in anatomy. Today his name is known throughout Europe as that of a daring innovator in surgery, and his discoveries arouse the admiration and hostility of the academic world. A twenty-four hour working day is hardly long enough to satisfy him, and although the strain of such an existence tells, nothing can weaken the determination of this melancholy dreamer to pursue his hazardous researches to the end. Everything about him suggests a man of genius. I see him often, and am devoted to him.

Other powerful compensations were soon added. The lecturers given by Thénard and Gay-Lussac at the Jardin des Plantes, the one in chemistry and the other in physics, and the literature course in which Andrieux's sly humour could hold a class enthralled, all delighted me; I followed them with increasing interest. I was on my way to becoming just another student, destined to add one more obscure name to the lamentable catalogue of bad doctors, when one evening I went to the Opéra. They were giving *The Danaïds*, by Salieri. The pomp and brilliance of the spectacle, the sheer weight and richness of sound produced by the combined chorus and orchestra ... excited and disturbed me to an extent which I will not attempt to describe ... I hardly slept that night, and the anatomy lesson next morning suffered accordingly. I sang Danaüs' aria 'The kindly strokes of destiny' as I sawed my 'subject's' skull; and when Robert, impatient at my humming 'Descend into the sea-nymph's breast' when I should have been looking up the chapter in Bichat on nerve tissue, exclaimed, 'Oh do come on, we're not getting anywhere, and in three days our subject will be spoiled – eighteen francs down the drain. You really must be sensible,' I replied with the hymn to Nemesis, 'Goddess insatiable for blood', and the scalpel fell from his hands ...

Notwithstanding all these distractions and the hours I spent every evening brooding over the melancholy discrepancy between my studies and my inclinations, I persisted in this double life for some time longer, without much benefit to my medical career and without being able to extend my meagre knowledge of music. I had given my word, and I was holding to it. But when I learnt that the library of the Conservatoire with its wealth of scores was open to the public, the desire to go there and study the works of Gluck, for which I already had an instinctive passion but which were not then being performed at the Opéra, was too strong for me. Once admitted to that sanctuary, I never left it. It was the death-blow to my medical career. The dissecting-room was abandoned for good.

From H. Berlioz, *The Memoirs of Berlioz*, trans. D. Cairns (London, 1969, 2nd edn 1977), pp. 46–9

Index